PROGRESS IN EDUCATION

VOLUME 26

PROGRESS IN EDUCATION

Additional books in this series can be found on Nova's website under the Series tab.

Additional E-books in this series can be found on Nova's website under the E-books tab.

PROGRESS IN EDUCATION

VOLUME 26

ROBERT V. NATA
EDITOR

Nova Science Publishers, Inc.

New York

Library of Congress Cataloging-in-Publication Data

ISSN: 1535-4806

ISBN 978-1-61324-321-3

Published by Nova Science Publishers, Inc. †*New York*

CONTENTS

PREFACE

This series presents substantial results from around the globe in selected areas of educational research. The field of education is consistently on the top of priority lists of every country in the world, yet few educators are aware of the progress elsewhere. Topics discussed include undergraduate public health education; evaluation and accreditation in higher education; reading goals and text relevance for assigned course readings; globalized classrooms; the effects of students performance and family backgrounds towards motivation in the classroom and reforms in technology integration.

Chapter 1 - The national initiative, *The Educated Citizen and Public Health,* promotes that an understanding of public health issues is a central component of an educated public and is necessary to develop social responsibility. This initiative supports the Institute of Medicine's recommendation that "all undergraduates should have access to education in public health." Both of these movements are well-aligned with the philosophy of liberal education which recommends that baccalaureate students receive a wide breadth of knowledge, adaptable skills, principled values and a sense of societal responsibility. This chapter explores this new application of liberal education and its implications for key stakeholders in the learning community as it pertains to curriculum and pedagogy. First, the author defines and examines an integrative learning methodology for a course in the public health science of epidemiology. The author illustrates that an epidemiology course can serve as a conduit for creating a population of undergraduates who possess "life tools" based in a liberal education viewpoint that enables them to effectively respond to the challenges of their learning community. The professional skills obtained through such a course will not only result in an educated population but one who can think broadly, make informed decisions, and participate in community health issues. This integrative and relative course framework can serve as a model for other liberal arts institutions that are attempting to heed this call for an educated public via a theory and practice approach. Second, the value associated with community-based learning is well documented. Learning by doing is an effective teaching and learning pedagogy that is well established in the health sciences. To attract new fields and disciplines to the public health community learning movement, the author identifies and addresses issues associated with faculty and program development. The chapter presents four specific challenges related to community-based learning: a). faculty development, b.) program development, c.) assessing student learning and awarding academic credit, and d.) the recruitment of (new) fields and disciplines to public health and community-based pedagogies. The author proposes specific recommendations related to using service and experiential learning approaches in higher education to realize the goals of *The Educated Citizen and Public Health* initiative. The chapter concludes with a summary of how expanding public health literacy and community-based learning into undergraduate liberal education can accomplish the following: encourage life-long learning and a commitment to social responsibility; allow for new course/major/minor development in public health in two-year and four-year colleges; promote collaboration with the public health community; and enable faculty to expand their expertise.

Chapter 2 – In this chapter the authors focus on discursive practices of research higher degree supervision as crucial elements in constructs of international student subjectivities when undertaking studies in Australian universities. The authors position our discussion within an Australian context, but the authors would argue that the issues they raise regarding the supervision of such students are applicable to other western English-speaking countries that attract international Higher Degree Research students. In doing so, the authors focus on discursive fields emerging within domains of internationalization, globalization, and resistance. The authors examine processes and protocols in a number of Australian universities postgraduate divisions' practices in the conduct of research higher degree supervision—in the context of increasing pressures towards internationalization within frameworks of globalizing influences. The authors take issue with western custom and tradition as privileged within the field of supervision of research higher degree students. The authors suggest variations of supervision of International candidates as intentional and systematic interventions, based on literature deriving from existing research of supervision which acknowledges the problematic natures of cultural relationships in relation to teaching, learning, and knowledge production, and student resistance within these fields. The authors examine issues of discursive practices and the problematic natures of power relationships in supervisor/supervisee protocols and possibilities suggested by alternative models of higher degree by research supervision of international students.

Chapter 3 – The effectiveness of behavioral intervention programs for children with Autistic Spectrum Disorders has been the subject of several studies. However, most of the studied programs were usually from UK and USA, although these types of programs exist in many more countries. Additionally, there is lack of cross-cultural studies, which could indicate to what extent the findings from the studied programs can be generalized and the impact of cultural environment to the effectiveness of intervention programs. The study in this chapter constitutes one of the first cross-cultural studies on the effectiveness of intervention programs for children with Autistic Spectrum Disorders. It compares the effectiveness of both behavioral and eclectic intervention programs for 6.5-to 14- year old children with Autistic Spectrum Disorders, from Greece and UK/Republic of Ireland, in a period of nine months. Some of the developmental factors that were assessed were the non-verbal IQ, language understanding, adaptive behavior, repetitive and stereotypic behaviors and other developmental difficulties of the children. The findings of the study indicate, that (a) the ABA and eclectic programs in English speaking countries were equally effective, (b) the Greek ABA programs were almost equally effective as the programs in the English speaking countries and superior to the eclectic Greek programs, (c) the Greek eclectic programs were less effective than all the other programs both in Greece and UK/Republic of Ireland.

Chapter 4 – The main focus of this article is evaluation, its relevance, complexity and potential, in the perspective of higher education accreditation. Accreditation, institutional and at program level, has a history of twenty years in Chile, through sequential stages. In parallel, the Universidad de Santiago de Chile-USACH has been involved in self-study and systemic evaluation since 1997. The senior authors of this article, in different roles, have participated in this experience, which is the basis of the studies and results here reported. As highlighted in the recent Annual Meeting of the Middle States Commission on Higher Education in the U.S., evaluation is a key factor for fostering quality, accountability, and institutional learning. Two main subjects of evaluation are considered critical: institutional effectiveness and student learning. The USACH experience, as much as the national one, has shown the authors a concern for academic goals and their usually qualitative and subjective nature, since the absence of measurement implies seldom certainty that the goals have been really met. The Chilean National Accreditation Commission (CNA) is at present revising its institutional accreditation criteria in order to pass from a "declarative" stage to a "demonstrative" one. In this, to demonstrate means to show evaluated results. Evaluating is often compounded by a lack of clear purposes of evaluation subject or object, by use of inappropriate instruments, by mismanagement of political variables, and by a lack of the necessary means for recording and storing relevant information. Here the authors present, in a systematized way, the results of exploring several areas of evaluation within the perspective of quality assurance. These areas include learning outcomes, accreditation's impact on institutions, and graduates' follow-up, among others. This experience has led to the development of a general evaluation model, which considers political, technical, financial and operational variables. The model is the outcome of a varied experience on evaluation that includes different subjects, such as public program's performance, learning outcomes, undergraduate programs, graduate programs, higher education institutions, and alumni and employers' assessment of professional education relevance. In this article some conclusions are drawn that intend to show and stress the big relevance and complexities of systemic institutional evaluation as a unique tool for quality assurance and, particularly, for strengthening institutional integrity. Integrity means, among other things, the capacity of stating goals and verifying results in a consistent way. Practice has led these authors to believe that the former implies developing institutional capacities of which many universities seem to be unaware of.

Chapter 5 – The purpose of this study was to investigate how students determined text relevance for their assigned course readings. *Text relevance* refers to the instrumental value of text information for enabling a reader to meet a reading goal (McCrudden, Magliano, and Schraw, 2010). Undergraduates (n = 38) enrolled in introductory educational psychology course were asked to provide written responses to several open-ended prompts about their goals for the assigned readings, what they focused on while they reading, the strategies they used while reading, and how they evaluated whether they had understood what they read. Readers' responses were analyzed and emergent themes were identified. Readers described an array of different goals, they described using various contextual cues to identify text relevance, described using surface and transformational strategies while reading, and held various beliefs about what constitutes good comprehension. Results are interpreted within the goal-focusing model of relevance. Future directions and educational implications are provided.

Chapter 6 – Workers exposed to ionizing radiation must be insured by a high quality radiation dosimetry. The dosimetric process requires the use of a dosimeter, which is a device used to measure the cumulative amount of radiation that a person is exposed. To evaluate that, each kind of dosimeter has its specific reading mechanism, using a specific physical property.

Whole-body dosimeters for individual monitoring are calibrated to measure the operational quantity personal dose equivalent at a depth of 10.00 mm in soft tissue, Hp(10) (deep dose), as a best estimate for the effective dose, E. Dosimeters designed to measure the dose to the skin and to the eye lens should measure personal dose equivalent at a depth of 3.00 mm and 0.07 mm respectively, Hp(3) (shallow dose) and Hp(0.07) (lens dose) (NCRP-116, 1993), (ISO-14146, 1999), (ISO-12794, 2000) and (ISO-4037, 1994)). The main requirement of a personal dosimeter for the monitoring of gamma radiation doses is the capability of measuring the ICRU (ICRU-46, 1992) quantity of Hp (10) with satisfactory accuracy, independently of the radiation incident angle and the gamma radiation energy.

Chapter 7 – School is one of the main arenas of violence among children and youths. Findings indicate that home-school cooperation is a key component for the success of combating school violence. Using qualitative interview data, this paper analyzes 48 teachers and school staff's perceptions of self-efficacy in dealing with parents concerning school violence. Three indicators were used to examine teachers' self-efficacy: personal teaching efficacy (PTE), teachers' efficacy in school as an organization (TESO), and teachers' outcome efficacy (TOE). Findings revealed that PTE was found to be high and complicated: most teachers' believe in their capabilities to collaborate with parents, but have low expectations from this cooperation. The majority of teachers described TESO as high: the interpersonal relationships among the team are supportive in dealing with parents. Likewise, teachers' experience and gender is considerably correlated with TOE.

Chapter 8 – Since the advent of Audiolingual method as the first scientific, psychometric-based method (Richards and Rodgers, 2003) till the emergence of Communicative Language Teaching Approaches in 1970s, the language teaching pendulum has been swinging from one perspective to another (from empiricist to rationalist), appreciating one method over another (Task-based approaches over functional notional method) and accepting one method at the expense of rejecting another.

With the advent of communicative approaches to language teaching, the history of language teaching has witnessed many changes in quality of methods till the emergence of new paradigm to appropriate the teaching practice to meet the students' attainment prosperity.

Chapter 9 – In this study the authors introduce the concepts of *egomorphism* to the field of environmental education. Egomorphism determines that humans understand their environment through their own personal experience with the environment, and that the speaker's *self* or *ego* is the focus point for such understanding. Using concepts of discourse analysis and cultural historical activity theory as theoretical framework, the authors conclude by asserting that in the field of environmental education, egomorphism mediates learning by constructing a hybrid language (scientific and non-scientific) that is appropriate to the environmental education context in which participants may find themselves.

Chapter 10 – A classroom conditions is essential to meet the students' educational needs. These conditions include cordial classroom atmospheres where the lecturers and the students openly discuss instructional matter and explore learning activity. It is often argued that students whose learning environment is perceived to be conclusive for studies unfold the tendency to achieve more then those with fundamental requisites of instruction such as physical facilities and equipment, among others are inadequately provided.

Chapter 11 – This chapter aims to provide current status of technology integration and practical policies for technology integration to reform Turkish educational system (TES). With the new technological developments, it is necessary to embed these new technological devices into the educational system to increase students' achievement. Based on the theoretical framework and previous academic researches, this chapter provides different options of reforms to be done in education systems in order to use technology effectively. The chapter specifically uses TES as a case, describes the current development, and discusses how these new reforms could be effective for students' learning.

Chapter 12 – Part-time nursing students who are seeking for academic qualification besides their everyday working life are confronted with manifold strains: Finding a balance between work, study and family commitments, high work load and the "foreignness" of academic demands are often reported to be stressful (Evans, Brown, Timmins, and Nicholl, 2007). In order to ensure a motivating and healthy learning environment universities have to consider the students' needs. Universities have been identified as an important setting for health promotion (Whitehead, 2004). In the case of nurse education health promotion plays a crucial role focussing two perspectives: The authors have to care for the students' health and health promotion is an integral part of the curricula. Following these considerations a course for health promotion for part-time nursing students at the Carinthia University of Applied Sciences (Austria) was designed. Besides lectures regarding theories and concepts of health promotion different methods for assessing strains and resources were presented. Health circles (Meggeneder, and Sochert, 1999) and a standardized questionnaire for work strains (Prümper, Hartmannsgruber, and Frese, 1995) were not only discussed theoretically. Students actively took part in health circles (2 circles with 8 and 10 participants) which were dedicated to explore strains and resources at the university. They also completed a questionnaire (N = 17) which helped to identify stressors at their workplace. Balancing work, study and family, time pressure as well as the organizational structure of the study programme were found to be the major stressors. The students also reported a lack of variety of tasks and task identity in their workplace. The results indicate a need for action in the university, but also at the workplace. A concept integrating "Health Promoting University" and "Health Promoting Workplace" is required. Furthermore, the students had the possibility to become acquainted with health promotion from a practical point of view using introspection which promotes active learning.

Chapter 13 - Wetland science emerged as a distinct discipline in the 1980s. In response, courses addressing various aspects of wetland science and management were developed by universities, government agencies, and private firms. Professional certification of wetland scientists began in the mid-1990s to provide confirmation of the quality of education and experience of persons involved in regulatory, management, restoration/construction, and research involving wetland resources. The education requirements for certification and the need for persons with specific wetland training to fill an increasing number of wetland-related positions identified a critical need to develop curriculum guidelines for an undergraduate wetland science and management major for potential accreditation by the Society of Wetland Scientists. That proposed major contains options directed toward either wetland science or management. Both options include required basic courses to meet the general education requirements of many universities, required upper-level specialized courses that address critical aspects of physical and biological sciences applicable to wetlands, and a minimum of four additional upper-level specialized courses that can be used to tailor a degree to students' interests. The program would be administered by an independent review board that would develop guidelines and evaluate university applications for accreditation. Students that complete the required coursework will fulfill the education requirements for professional wetland scientist certification and possess qualifications that make them attractive candidates for graduate school or entry-level positions in wetland science or management. Universities that offer this degree program could gain an advantage in recruiting highly qualified students with an interest in natural resources. Alternative means of educating established wetland scientists are likewise important, especially to provide specialized knowledge and experience or updates related to new management discoveries, policies, and regulations.

In: Progress in Education. Volume 26
Editor: Robert V. Nata, pp. 1-30

ISBN 978-1-61324-321-3
© 2011 Nova Science Publishers, Inc.

Chapter 1

PUBLIC HEALTH LITERACY AND COMMUNITY-BASED LEARNING: KEYS TO EXPANDING UNDERGRADUATE PUBLIC HEALTH EDUCATION

Rosemary M. Caron [*]

University of New Hampshire, College of Health and Human Services
Department of Health Management and Policy
Durham, NH 03824, USA

ABSTRACT

The national initiative, *The Educated Citizen and Public Health,* promotes that an understanding of public health issues is a central component of an educated public and is necessary to develop social responsibility. This initiative supports the Institute of Medicine's recommendation that "all undergraduates should have access to education in public health." Both of these movements are well-aligned with the philosophy of liberal education which recommends that baccalaureate students receive a wide breadth of knowledge, adaptable skills, principled values and a sense of societal responsibility. This chapter explores this new application of liberal education and its implications for key stakeholders in the learning community as it pertains to curriculum and pedagogy. First, the author defines and examines an integrative learning methodology for a course in the public health science of epidemiology. The author illustrates that an epidemiology course can serve as a conduit for creating a population of undergraduates who possess "life tools" based in a liberal education viewpoint that enables them to effectively respond to the challenges of their learning community. The professional skills obtained through such a course will not only result in an educated population but one who can think broadly, make informed decisions, and participate in community health issues. This integrative and relative course framework can serve as a model for other liberal arts institutions that are attempting to heed this call for an educated public via a theory and practice approach. Second, the value associated with community-based learning is well documented.

[*] E-mail: Rosemary.Caron@unh.edu; Phone – 603-862-3653; Fax – 603-862-3461.

Learning by doing is an effective teaching and learning pedagogy that is well established in the health sciences. To attract new fields and disciplines to the public health community learning movement, the author identifies and addresses issues associated with faculty and program development. The chapter presents four specific challenges related to community-based learning: a). faculty development, b.) program development, c.) assessing student learning and awarding academic credit, and d.) the recruitment of (new) fields and disciplines to public health and community-based pedagogies. The author proposes specific recommendations related to using service and experiential learning approaches in higher education to realize the goals of *The Educated Citizen and Public Health* initiative. The chapter concludes with a summary of how expanding public health literacy and community-based learning into undergraduate liberal education can accomplish the following: encourage life-long learning and a commitment to social responsibility; allow for new course/major/minor development in public health in two-year and four-year colleges; promote collaboration with the public health community; and enable faculty to expand their expertise.

"Public health is an essential part of the training of citizens"

- Institute of Medicine, 2003

CALL FOR CHANGE IN LIBERAL EDUCATION

Liberal education is a "…philosophy of education that empowers individuals with core knowledge and transferable skills and cultivates social responsibility and a strong sense of ethics and values" (AAC&U, 2010a). General education is "the part of a liberal education curriculum shared by all students. It provides broad exposure to multiple disciplines and forms the basis for developing important intellectual and civic capacities" (AAC&U, 2010a). Liberal education incorporates a wide breadth of knowledge into the teaching and learning process. The Association of American Colleges and Universities' (AAC&U) *Greater Expectations* initiative for liberal education was designed to identify principles and promote strategies that enable the undergraduate learner to become a knowledgeable, empowered, informed, and responsible citizen in the new millennium (AAC&U, 2002). To prepare educated citizens in this century, a liberal education must also be a practical education that develops the skills or "life tools" required of every adult, i.e., "analytical skills, effective communication, practical intelligence, ethical judgment, and social responsibility" (AAC&U, 2002). Hence, liberal education requires an integrative approach that is not limited to general education or major discipline of study. AAC&U's *Liberal Education and America's Promise (LEAP)* report proposes a joint approach

"…that advocates for integrative, interdisciplinary, and applied knowledge and practice, for community outreach and civic responsibility across all undergraduate programs, for global awareness and responsibility, and for open pathways among the arts and sciences and professional schools and between the campus and the wider world. The campaign underscores the importance of learning for a free society and development of human talent" (AAC&U, 2007).

LEAP describes a framework that is comprised of essential learning outcomes to be attained by the undergraduate student in the educational environment and utilized in the student's working environment. These essential learning outcomes are complemented by a set of effective educational practices that allow for the integration of knowledge with real-world application (AAC&U, 2007). The objective of this framework is to provide the undergraduate student with the following:

> "...an education that intentionally fosters, across multiple fields of study, wide-ranging knowledge of science, cultures, and society; high-level intellectual and practical skills; an active commitment to personal and social responsibility; and the demonstrated ability to apply learning to complex problems and challenges" (AAC&U, 2007).

To this end, it would seem a liberal education curriculum that connects theory with practice would contribute to the goal of meeting such challenges.

PUBLIC HEALTH RESPONDS TO THE CALL

This chapter proposes that the discipline of public health can serve as a vision for the direction of liberal education. Public health can contribute to the call to change liberal education to produce an educated citizenry. Winslow (1920) defined public health, often referred to as population health, as

> "...the science and art of preventing disease, prolonging life and promoting physical health and efficacy through organized community efforts for the sanitation of the environment, the control of community infections, the education of the individual in principles of personal hygiene, the organization of medical and nursing services for the early diagnosis and preventive treatment of disease, and the development of the social machinery which will ensure every individual in the community a standard of living adequate for the maintenance of health...to enable every citizen to realize his or her birthright and longevity."

The Institute of Medicine (IOM) (IOM, 1988) of the United States' National Academy of Sciences defines public health as "fulfilling society's interest in assuring conditions in which people can be healthy." Thus, public health's primary mission is to promote health and prevent disease in human populations. In order to achieve this mission, public health operates at various levels of government, private and non-profit sectors to implement the core functions of public health: assessment, policy development and assurance. Assessment involves the systematic collection, analysis and reporting on the health status of a community; policy development utilizes scientific knowledge and a shared process to develop and implement policies that are protective of the public's health; and assurance confirms that agreed upon health services are provided and effective (IOM, 1988). However, no one health agency, whether in the public or private sector, can provide these core functions of public health, hence a public health system comprised of a complex network of organizations such as emergency medical personnel, physicians, faith-based community, volunteer organizations, parks and recreation facilities, hospitals and local health clinics, politicians, public health agencies, etc. are relied upon to carry out the public health mission. The results of public health are often measured as a public good, such as a functional sanitation system, as opposed to a private good, such as individual treatment, as seen with medicine (Hemenway, 2010).

In 2003, the IOM concluded that a well-educated public health workforce was essential to keeping the public healthy. As a result, the IOM (2003) recommended that "all undergraduates should have access to education in public health." The IOM (2003) further challenged that undergraduate public health be viewed as part of the process of educating citizens and not solely as a professional credential.

Previous research also affirms the appropriateness of using the discipline of public health as an incubator for liberal arts courses that foster professional skill development. Riegelman et al. (2007) suggest that studying the discipline of public health has both educational and intellectual importance, due to its interdisciplinary foundation. The study of public health involves critical thinking; provides a methodology for understanding populations and their health; and requires contemplating health issues on a population-scale.

Baccalaureate education in the arts and sciences, specifically public health, the *Greater Expectations* initiative and the *LEAP* framework are all intended to create an educated population capable of not only appreciating the art in science but who possess professional skills in inquiry, analysis and evaluation. Furthermore, the interdisciplinary learning goals of *LEAP* support the "integration of public health education into general and liberal education with an aim to produce an educated citizenry" (Albertine, 2008). For example, knowledge of human cultures and the physical and natural worlds; intellectual and practical skills; personal and social responsibility; and integrative learning and complex problem solving are *LEAP* learning outcomes that are aligned with the public health outcomes of recognizing and integrating the arts and science disciplines into public health; using the public health science of epidemiology to develop critical thinking and quantitative skills; incorporating experiential learning; and providing a global perspective on learning, respectively (Albertine, 2008).

The need and value for creating a liberal arts curriculum to educate citizenry about key public health principles is succinctly summarized by Albertine et al. (2007) in the following statement:

> "We need citizens who can help as individuals to change social behavior and who are aware of the need for systemic health care, good nutrition, decent housing, and sustainable urban centers. We need to rely on leaders who are able to consider benefits and harms to groups, minority as well as majority, and to engage in systems thinking, understanding how multiple factors interact. These are abilities essential to citizenship for the health of the world."

AN EDUCATED CITIZENRY

Based on the public health challenges facing the world today, for example, bioterrorism, globalization, demographic transitions, environmental degradation, health disparity, food insecurity, etc., it is imperative that we educate our students for citizenship to think and act in a way that is protective of the health of their community. The IOM (2003) stated that an educated citizenry is essential to a healthy society. Albertine et al. (2007) further declared "We need citizens who possess an ability to think about the big picture, beyond the individual or the constituency."

The AAC&U, the Association for Prevention Teaching and Research (APTR) and the Council on Colleges of Arts and Sciences' response to fulfill the IOM's challenge that "all undergraduates should have access to education in public health" (IOM, 2003) is recognized through their *Educated Citizen and Public Health* initiative. This initiative supports that an understanding of public health issues is a core component of an educated public and is necessary to develop one's social responsibility. Public health is an interdisciplinary branch of learning that combines the social sciences, sciences, humanities and the arts and also develops skills in examining and developing evidence-based methods, comprehensive analysis, critical evaluation, effective oral and written communication and serves as the basis for lifelong learning (AAC&U 2010b).

The IOM's recommendation that "all undergraduates should have access to education in public health" (IOM, 2003) was not solely focused on educating citizens at traditional four-year colleges and universities but has also expanded its reach to two-year or community colleges. The *LEAP* framework is appropriate for various types of undergraduate programs since the ultimate goal is to educate a citizenry who can utilize the knowledge and experience attained from an interdisciplinary experience offered by the field of public health to see the issues on a broad scale and be able to address them to assure a healthy population. In addition, community colleges can provide public-health related associate degrees and certificate programs that contribute to the public health workforce (Fulcher et al., 2010).

ONE UNIVERSITY'S RESPONSE TO THE CALL FOR CHANGE IN LIBERAL EDUCATION: A PUBLIC HEALTH COURSE GROUNDED IN SOCIAL JUSTICE

"Epidemiology is fundamentally engaged in the broader quest for social justice and equality"
- John C. Cassell (University of North Carolina at Chapel Hill)

A general liberal education, such as the one offered at the University of New Hampshire, is designed to emphasize the "major modes of thought necessary to understanding oneself, others, and the environment. It seeks to develop a critical appreciation of both the value and the limitations of significant methods of inquiry and analysis" (UNH, 2009). Lifelong learning and its associated competencies are an essential skill set of the educated citizen.

An undergraduate course in the public health science of epidemiology is appropriate to illustrate the dual benefit of being a liberal art and a professional skill. Epidemiology is defined as "the study of the distribution and determinants of health-related states or events in specified populations, and the application of this study to the control of health problems" (Last, 2001). Merrill and Timmreck (2006) characterize epidemiology as an integrative discipline which utilizes knowledge from many scientific disciplines to assist in preventing injury, disease, and death; promoting health education efforts; and developing, implementing, and evaluating public policy. Fraser (1987) proposes that epidemiology should be an undergraduate-level liberal art course since it is a "low-technology" science and may be utilized to approach an issue and generate "the kinds of thinking that a liberal education should cultivate: the scientific method, analogic thinking, deductive reasoning, problem solving within constraints, and concern for aesthetic values." Ibrahim (1983) evokes that epidemiology not only contributes to the scientific assessment of the health needs of a community, but also contributes to the management aspect of health administration, such as the planning for health care services, the development and implementation of public health policy, and evaluation of the effectiveness of those health care services offered at the community level. These examples of the utility of epidemiology emphasize its features that enable it to be considered both a liberal art and a professional skill.

Thus, a course in epidemiology teaches the importance of an integrated population approach to health promotion and disease prevention, as well as the relevance of the social, cultural, physical, and environmental determinants of health. This knowledge is utilized to introduce the practical competencies necessary to assess the health needs of a community, develop and implement policy, and evaluate interventions at the community, regional, national, or global level. Epidemiological principles also allow for information pertaining to broad outcomes from "across multiple fields of study" to be assessed. For example, epidemiology has utility in not only determining a population's housing, workforce, or infrastructure needs and the management and utilization of related community services but in illustrating the differences between those who "have" and those who "have not" in our society so our social responsibility will be called into action. The knowledge and proficiencies offered by such a course of study should be required of the general education curricula and disciplinary majors, in order that it can contribute to the process by which undergraduate students will become members of an educated public in today's society.

Epidemiology, as the basic science of public health, is a field of study that is well aligned with the *LEAP* framework and outcomes. For example, epidemiology prepares students to think critically, utilize quantitative skills, engage in ethical reasoning, effectively communicate and to use these skills to understand populations and to become civically responsible and engaged (Maranz, 2008).

PEDAGOGY OF A LIBERAL ART AND PROFESSIONAL SKILLS COURSE

The *Epidemiology and Community Medicine* course taught at the University of New Hampshire can serve as a case example of how this public health science contributes to a liberal education and an educated citizenry. This course is catalogued as a university-wide liberal art, biological science course and is open to all undergraduates. There is no prerequisite coursework. The course is a required part of the curriculum in the Health Management and Policy (HMP) major and is offered each academic year in the Fall and Spring semesters. The course enrollment of approximately 50-90 students is comprised of one-half baccalaureate students who are matriculated in the HMP major; one-third who are matriculated for the Nutrition and Wellness Option of the Nutrition major; and the remaining are non-HMP majors taking the course as a general science course.

This epidemiology course exposes students to indices of health, sources of health data, risk factor analysis, and the concept of multi-factorial causes of health-related events on a local, national and international scale, analysis of associations between a risk factor and health-related outcome, research study design, and screening for infectious and chronic disease. The course objectives (Table 1) are achieved through actively engaging students via discussion, inquiry, and experiential learning, as well as operating by the viewpoint of "quality over quantity" – that is, it is more important that the students understand a few important and relative concepts very well, as opposed to covering a broad scope of material and having them experience difficulty in recalling and correctly applying concepts and theories.

Table 1. *Epidemiology and Community Medicine* **course objectives**

A. Knowledge
At the conclusion of the course, students should be able to describe and generally assess the following:
1. The historical roots of epidemiology and its contribution to the scientific method
2. The role of epidemiology as a tool to study populations and health care systems
3. The practical applications of epidemiology and the ethical issues to be considered before conducting an epidemiological study
4. The distinctions between different epidemiological study designs (e.g., case control, cohort, cross-sectional, etc.)
5. The use, strengths and limitations of public health data sources
6. The concepts and implications of sampling error, bias and confounding in epidemiological studies and the strategies available to deal with them
B. Skills
After taking this course, students will be able to:
1. Use rates and proportions to numerically express the amount and distribution of health-related outcomes
2. Given the distribution of a health-related outcome, generate hypotheses that might explain that distribution
3. Utilize disease frequency measures (e.g., prevalence and incidence) and measures of effect (e.g., risk versus rate. crude, specific, and adjusted rates) to analyze the health of a population
4. Conceptualize and analyze the issues that need to be considered when determining whether there is a causal link between exposure and disease
C. Values
At the conclusion of this course, students will:
1. Appreciate the critical role epidemiology plays in securing and maintaining the public health of the world's populations and its significant impact on health management practices
2. Appreciate the complex task of generating hypotheses to explain the causal link between exposure and disease in human populations
3. Appreciate epidemiology's valuable role in addressing health disparity and social injustice

The course objectives reflect the expansive philosophy of liberal education through the utilization of didactic methods that incorporate the basis and theory of epidemiological principles, proficiency in determining measures of association and significance, applying the determinants of health to a community population, implementing the core functions of public health, and appreciating the role and value of epidemiology in maintaining the health of populations.

The course is organized into five main sections which detail the history, descriptive and analytical branches of epidemiology, association and causation aspects, and practical applications of epidemiology to the broader discipline of evidence-based public health.

Lecture - Epidemiologic concepts are taught through the utilization of two eighty-minute class sessions each week. The students are asked to read the assigned chapters from the required text and any supplemental journal articles following the class in which the epidemiological principles are scheduled to be discussed. The point of requiring the reading to be done following the class, as opposed to coming to class already having read the material, allows for the students to hear the epidemiological concepts and topics from the instructor first. Having the students read the assigned materials following the class aids in reinforcing the topics that were discussed. Each class is comprised of an interactive lecture given by the instructor who introduces new concepts by way of example. For instance, the students can discover the application, strengths and weaknesses of a case-control study by reviewing such a study design in a small group setting that allows for active discussion. The instructor can then reconvene the class and have the students answer questions about the epidemiological principle being taught. This technique creates the opportunity for the students to feel "ownership" of the epidemiological principle because they discover the important concepts for themselves. Teaching tools found to be most effective in facilitating student learning include the whiteboard, video documentaries, and presentations by practicing public health professionals (Table 2).

The limited use of PowerPoint slides and the primary use of the whiteboard proved to be effective as measured by the ensuing discussions. This technique also allows for the emphasis of major points and concepts, assists with the pace of the class, and provides for "active" learning. Another useful tool is the showing of documentaries that detail epidemiological principles and practices as they were implemented in infectious disease outbreaks, such as Avian Flu, Severe Acute Respiratory Syndrome, and the cholera epidemic in Haiti.

Table 2. Pedagogy utilized in the course *Epidemiology and Community Medicine*

1. Introduce basic principles and theory
   - Lecture
   - Use of literature and the arts
2. Explore and question basic principles and theory in depth
   - Discussion
3. Application of basic principles
   - Laboratory Exercises, Case Study Assignments, Individual and Group Exercises
4. Practical application of basic principles in a "real world" setting
   - Guest speakers and media
5. Reinforcement
   - Study guides
   - Review sessions
   - Office hours
6. Evaluation and assessment
   - Examinations, homework assignments, case studies

This tool catalyzes discussions that highlight the different aspects of culture and society and their epidemiological significance when considering the health of populations. Lastly, the real-world application of epidemiology is brought into the classroom through the invitation of public health practitioners who share the importance and utility of epidemiology in their every day projects, planning, accomplishments and challenges. This is a valuable component of the course as it provides a "face" to epidemiology and illustrates how the discussions, problem sets, and assignments are essential to the practice of this public health science in the real world. This format allows for a balance between theory and practice to be achieved throughout the duration of the course. The major course assignments are computer lab-based projects, homework, a mid-term and cumulative final examination, and a community health assessment or infectious disease case study.

Homework – In order to explore the epidemiologic theory and principles taught in class, ten focused homework assignments are distributed throughout the semester. The focused assignments are made available in class only and the student has one week to complete the assignment, unless otherwise noted. Representative homework assignments are illustrated in Table 3.

Table 3. Representative homework assignments[a] utilized in the course *Epidemiology and Community Medicine*

Assignment: Critical Review of Public Health Headlines

Consider the article titles below, which have recently appeared in a variety of popular media sources. Taking a critical epidemiological point of view, develop a list of questions you might have about the studies described in each article (Hint: Think about study design, measures, sampling, data collection, analysis, etc.)

a) Poorest People at Highest Heart Disease Risk: U.S. Data
b) Hmong-American Women Far Less Likely to Get Pap Test
c) US Dietary Supplements Not as Safe as Consumers Might Assume
d) Spray Cleaners Pose Poison Hazard to Babies, Toddlers
e) Teen Moms More Likely to Have Premature Babies, Study Finds

****

Assignment: Critique and Selection of Study Design

Read the article "Environmental Influences on Young Adult Weight Gain: Evidence From a Natural Experiment" by K. Kapinos and O. Yakusheva, in the *Journal of Adolescent Health*, 2011 48(1): 52-58 and respond to the questions below.

1. In your own words, provide rationale for the authors' claim that, "…we were able to get an unbiased estimate of the causal effect of physical environment on behaviors and weight without reverse causality bias."
2. What potential confounders may have been introduced in this study?
3. Since this study was conducted on only one campus, you are interested in conducting a follow-up study on additional campuses.
   a) What type of study design would you use?
   b) Describe the strengths and limitations of using your selected study design for this particular research study.

****

Table 3. (Continued)

Assignment: Critique of a Cross-Sectional Study

Read the article "Pre-migration Exposure to Political Violence and Perpetration of Intimate Partner Violence Among Immigrant Men in Boston" by Gupta, J., Acevedo-Garcia, D., Hemenway, D. Decker, M., Taj, A., and Silverman, J.G. which appears in the March 2009 issue of the *American Journal of Public Health*, 99(3): 462-469 and respond to the questions below.

1. What is the exposure of interest in this study?
2. What is the outcome of interest in this study?
3. Describe the attributes of the study which classify this as a "cross-sectional" study.
4. Imagine you are interested in conducting a case-control study to assess the relationship between the exposure and outcome of interest listed in questions 1 and 2 above. What would your eligibility criteria be for your cases? Controls?
5. Which study design (cross-sectional or case-control) do you feel is better suited to assess this relationship? Provide rationale for your response.

****

Assignment: Interpreting Data for Public Health Priorities

Imagine the scenario that you are an Epidemiologist employed in the Division of Public Health Services at the New Hampshire Department of Health and Human Services. The Commissioner has requested your assistance in prioritizing the state's public health needs, based on health indicator data published by the non-profit organization Trust for America's Health, available at: http://healthyamericans.org/states.

1. Identify your recommended top three public health priority areas based on this data. Provide rationale for your selections.

****

Assignment: A picture is worth 1,000 words

1. Review the breast cancer data and information below, from the Centers for Disease Control and Prevention, and create a visual representation intended to relay its importance to others.

Breast Cancer

7 million women still need to be screened for Breast Cancer.

Screening for breast cancer prevents cancer and saves lives.

- Breast cancer is the most common cancer among adult women in the United States and second leading cause of death from cancer among women.
- One of every eight adult women will get breast cancer in her lifetime. The risk of cancer increases with age.
- In 2006, more than 190,000 women were discovered to have breast cancer, and more than 41,000 died of the disease.
- Although white women are more likely to get breast cancer, African American women are the most likely to die of it. Minority women are most likely to have advanced breast cancer when the cancer is first discovered.
- If a close family member (mother, grandmother, sister, and father or brother) has had

> breast cancer, the risk for other family members getting breast cancer may be higher. If you think you may be at increased risk, ask your doctor if you should be tested earlier or more often than other women.
>
> *What test looks for breast cancer?*
> - The best way to find breast cancer is by having a mammogram. A mammogram is an X-ray of the breasts.
> - Mammograms can find breast cancer early, before it is big enough to feel or cause symptoms and when it is easier to treat.
>
> *Women are not getting screened for breast cancer as often as recommended*
> - In 2008, about one of five adult women between the ages of 50 and 74 never had a mammogram or were not up-to-date with getting screened.
> - Overall, mammography screening rates in the United States have not improved since 2002.
> - Getting a mammogram every 2 years should be a priority for women aged 50–74 years. Screening can find breast cancer at an early stage, when treatment is most effective.
> - From Centers for Disease Control and Prevention website: http://www.cdc.gov/vitalsigns/LatestFindingsBC.html. Accessed July 19, 2010.
>
> **********
> *Assignment: Public Health in Poetry*
> Read the poem titled, The Lungs, by Alice Jones and respond to the questions below:
>
> 1. Interpret and summarize the main theme of the poem, in your own words. Please limit your response to 50 words or less.
> 2. Briefly describe how epidemiology may be used to help create conditions in which lungs can be healthy

[a]The author acknowledges Brenda Kirkwood, MPH for her work in assisting with the development of these homework assignments as part of an instructional leadership doctoral program requirement at the George Washington University School of Public Health.

The homework assignments are collected on their respective due date in class and are graded upon the following criteria:

- Completeness of addressing the requirements for each assignment

- Breadth and depth of analysis of principles and their application

- Adherence to standards of writing style and grammar, when appropriate

- Quality of analysis and level of critique for each assignment

Laboratory Assignments - Students are required to attend one eighty-minute lab session on a weekly basis. The laboratory assignments are peer-reviewed case studies that mirror the epidemiological concepts covered in the course. The laboratory assignments are team-oriented, interactive and computer-based. These exercises allow for the hands-on application of epidemiological principles taught during lectures. For example, students apply descriptive and analytical epidemiological techniques, such as graphing data using Excel; generating hypotheses; role playing as an epidemiologist who must conduct a disease outbreak investigation in a community hospital; developing policy that explores the issues surrounding personal freedom and public health authority; and discussing ethical issues posed by historical human experimentation events. These laboratory assignments provide a vehicle for students to practically learn professional skills, such as data analysis, critical thinking, and evidence-based decision making, all of which are important "life tools."

Examinations - The purpose of the mid-term and cumulative final examinations are to not only determine that the student has been successful in comprehending and applying the concepts and principles discussed in class and the laboratory, but that the instructor taught the material in an effective manner. Both exams are comprised of multiple choice, short answer, fill-in-the blank and essay questions.

Community Needs Assessment – What Does a Healthy Community Look Like? This assignment is designed to allow students to explore course topics in further depth and encourage practical application of epidemiological principles to the area of public health and health management. A community health assessment is essential to understanding the health problems and priorities of a population. Conducting such an assessment involves obtaining and interpreting information to determine the health status of a community's population. Once the community's needs have been identified, public health interventions can be developed and their effectiveness can be evaluated. Table 4 provides further details for this assignment.

Table 4. Community Needs Assessment – *What Does a Healthy Community Look Like?*

> The following assignment is designed to allow students to explore course topics in further depth and encourage practical application of epidemiological principles to the area of public health and health management.
>
> A community health assessment is essential to understanding the health problems and priorities of a population. Conducting such an assessment involves obtaining and interpreting information to determine the health status of a community's population. Once the community's needs have been identified, public health interventions can be developed and their effectiveness can be evaluated.
>
> *Part I:* Each student will examine what a healthy community looks like by researching determinants that contribute to the overall health of the *assigned community, county, State of New Hampshire and the United States.* Specifically, each student will be assigned to one of the following five communities in which to research representative health indicators utilizing publicly available datasets (reviewed in class):
>
> *1. City of Manchester, Hillsborough County, New Hampshire*
>   Please cite the source for <u>each</u> indicator.
> • Demographics (age, gender, race, and median household income) for the year 2000 at the city, county, state, and national level
> • Birth rate for teens (ages 15-19) for the 2000-2006 time period at the city level
> • National teen birth rate (cite most recent data)
> • By age group and gender, injury prevention (e.g., seat belt use, firearm injuries) for the 2001-2004 time period at the state level
> *2. City of Portsmouth, Rockingham County, New Hampshire*
>   Please cite the source for <u>each</u> indicator.

- Demographics (age, gender, race, and median household income) for the year 2000 at the city, county, state and national level
- Top ten leading causes of death (rates) for New Hampshire residents for the 1999-2001 time period at the city level
- Prevalence of tobacco use by age group, gender, education and income for the 2001-2004 time period at the state level
- Prevalence of current smoking among adults (18 years of age and older) in the United States (cite most recent data)

3. Town of Durham, Strafford County, New Hampshire
  Please cite the source for each indicator.
- Demographics (age, gender, race, and median household income) for the year 2000 at the city, county, state and national level
- Colorectal and lung cancer incidence for New Hampshire residents, by gender, for 2005 at the county level
- National lung cancer incidence rate (cite most recent data)
- Emergency department visits for asthma among New Hampshire residents in 2005 at the county level

4. City of Berlin, Coos County, New Hampshire
  Please cite the source for each indicator.
- Demographics (age, gender, race, and median household income) for the year 2000 at the city, county, state and national level
- Proportion of women who have ever had a Pap test, by age, for the 2001-2004 time period at the state level
- Suicide death rates for New Hampshire residents for the 1999-2001 time period at the county, state and national level
- National suicide death rate (cite most recent data)

5. Town of Hanover, Grafton County, New Hampshire
  Please cite the source for each indicator.
- Demographics (age, gender, race, and median household income) for the year 2000 at the city, county, state and national level
- Proportion of New Hampshire adults with no health care coverage by age group, gender, education and income for the 2001-2004 time period at the state level
- Proportion of U.S. citizens who are uninsured (cite most recent data)
- Prevalence of obesity in male and female high school students in 2007 at a national level

Part II: Based on your research and analysis, please consider the following questions:
- Compared to national data, is there a health issue for the population of this community? Why or why not?
- Considering the multiple determinants of health (e.g., Evans and Stoddart Health Field Model) we have discussed in class, what else would you want to know about this community?
- List three (3) criteria you would use to allocate resources to either develop interventions to address these issues or prevent these indicators from becoming a health problem for the community. For example, prevalence and/or severity of health condition, etc.
- Based on the data you have researched, propose three (3) practical recommendations for how your particular community can improve their health status. (Consider the CDC Guide to Community Preventive Services; Guide to Clinical Preventive Services, etc.)

In general, this assignment has been constructed into three main parts: quantitative data collection, critical interpretation, and proposing feasible recommendations. The first part of the assignment requires students to examine what a healthy community looks like by researching determinants that contribute to the overall health of the assigned community, county, state and the United States. Specifically, each student is assigned to one of five communities in which to research health indicators utilizing publicly available datasets. Representative health indicators include the teen birth rate, unintentional injury rate, intentional injury rate, leading causes of death, tobacco use, cancer rates, emergency room visits for asthma, preventive screening, uninsured population, and obesity prevalence. Based on the student's research and analysis, he/she is asked to consider the following questions for the second part of the assignment:

- Compared to national data, is there a health issue for the population of this community? Why or why not?

- Considering the multiple determinants of health (e.g., Evans and Stoddart Health Field Model (1990), what else would you want to know about this community?

- List three criteria you would use to allocate resources to either develop interventions to address these issues or prevent these indicators from becoming a health problem for the community.

- Based on the data researched, propose three practical recommendations for how your particular community can improve their health status.

Infectious Disease Case Study – What's Bugging You? The infectious disease case study assignment is designed to allow students to explore course topics in further depth and to encourage practical application of epidemiological principles, such as frequency measures, demographics, disease distribution, social determinants of health and intervention development relative to an infectious disease that exists in the United States and/or is present internationally, or poses a global public health threat. Table 5 provides further details for this assignment. In general, the infectious disease case study assignment is constructed into three parts: quantitative data, epidemiology of the disease, and public health intervention measures.

The first part of the assignment requires the student to access readily available local, state, national, and international data sets pertinent to their selected infectious disease, in order to understand quantification measures used in population health, such as prevalence and incidence rates, age and sex distribution, morbidity, mortality, and geographic distribution over time. The student should be able to discuss the natural history of the disease, such as, who is getting the disease, when, where, and how often.

The second part of the assignment explores the epidemiology of the disease by requiring that the student inquire about the etiology of the disease; the impact of the disease not only on human health but what has been the impact of human activities on the disease; the concept of disease diffusion; role of the natural environment and climate change on the spread of the disease; and discuss if the disease is not already present in a specific locality, what is the probability of it occurring there, and the risk factors that would have to be present for it to occur in the United States.

The last part of the infectious disease case study assignment requires the student to explore intervention measures that are currently implemented and if intervention measures exist but are not implemented the student is asked to explore the barriers that may be present, from a social and political standpoint, in the affected population. Furthermore, the student is also asked about policies and/or legislation that may have been passed with respect to disease control measures, as well as the related economic and social costs to the community.

Table 5. Infectious Disease Case Study – *What's Bugging You?*

Part I – Quantitative Data: Choose an infectious disease of interest to you. Collect quantitative data for the disease you are researching, including pertinent epidemiological information (*e.g.*, rates for prevalence, incidence, morbidity, mortality, age distribution, sex distribution, *etc.*) and geographic distribution over a significant period of time. You should be able to discuss who is getting the disease, where, when, and how often. If your disease is global, select a particular region of the world for study.

As you begin your data collection, you may want to use the Internet to search statewide, national, and/or international sources for the most recent data available. Other sources of information include World Health Organization reports, health atlases, and peer-reviewed academic literature.

Part II – Epidemiology of the Disease: Explore the epidemiology of the disease you are studying and look for information that can help you answer the following questions:

- How did the disease get to its current location(s)? How long ago? What is the ecology of the disease?
- What explanations exist with respect to its occurrence and location?
- What has been the impact of humans on this disease?
- What is the risk of further infection within the already susceptible population?
- What is the risk of the disease spreading into new populations or areas? Explain how mobility plays a role in enabling the disease to establish itself in a new location?
- What prevention measures have individuals, public health officials, and government(s) taken to address the spread of the disease?
- Describe specific legislation that has been created and passed in response to the disease?
- What types of attention have the media given to the subject?
- What are people doing, or not doing, to protect themselves?
- What role does the natural environment and global change have in the spread of the disease, i.e., could it occur here? Why or why not?
- Describe health promotion, disease prevention and protection measures.

Part III – Public Health Interventions and Recommendations: In the last part of your research, you should explore intervention measures and responses. Consider the following questions as you conduct your research and prepare your case study:

- What public health intervention measures are there and which would you recommend? Why or why not?
- Toward whom would the intervention measures be directed? Explain your rationale.
- When would intervention measures be appropriate to implement?
- What is the cost of the intervention measures from an economical and social perspective?
- Describe why the world's populations still experience morbidity and mortality with infectious diseases that seem readily preventable.
- Propose a solution to the dilemma mentioned in the previous bullet.

Lastly, the student is required to assimilate this information and provide their own perspective on the epidemiology of the infectious disease they have chosen to study. They are asked if they agree with the methods by which the disease is controlled in its respective location and what are their recommendations to assure the health of those populations while considering the main determinants of health.

Both of these assignments are distributed towards the end of the course, in order to allow the students enough time to not only learn and discuss the necessary epidemiological principles and theories, but to allow them to practice and fully comprehend these concepts in an active laboratory environment prior to applying them to a real public health issue. In addition, these assignments highlight that multiple and complex determinants affect one's health and students are often surprised to learn that that an inequality of health exists in the world, e.g., where you live impacts your health in numerous ways.

Evaluation – The students are given the opportunity to evaluate the instructor's teaching methods at the end of each semester. The pedagogical methods described herein have been favorably received by the students as they report that it provides them with an appropriate balance between theory and practice via class lecture, discussions, and hands-on assignments. In addition, the students strongly agree that the teaching tools utilized throughout the course allow for the course objectives to be met (UNH, 2010).

PRACTICAL APPLICATION OF A LIBERAL ART AND PROFESSIONAL SKILLS COURSE

This course provides the knowledge necessary to not only understand the role of the social and environmental determinants of health in contributing to disease in populations, but it also builds upon this knowledge by introducing the skills necessary to engage in assessing a community's needs, develop appropriate health interventions, and how to evaluate if such efforts were successful in reducing the burden of disease in the community. A course in epidemiology is one way for an academic department, located in a professional college, to contribute to the university's mission in educating the general student in a liberal education environment (Gorsky, 1989).

Epidemiology can be considered an instrumental tool for many professional disciplines. For example, it represents an essential skill for health care management and planning professionals since it allows for the analysis of risk factors and their associated health-related events in a community, identification of resultant health care needs, and determining the feasibility in providing those health care services (Gorsky, 1989). In fact, a joint workshop between the Association for Undergraduate Programs in Health Administration and the United States' Centers for Disease Control and Prevention emphasized the theme of promoting interdisciplinary efforts between the fields of epidemiology and health administration (Malison, 1993). Similarly, it has been argued that a course in epidemiology for those pursuing a career in health administration is also necessary so that students with this interest will approach the health care environment with a population focus, as opposed to concentrating on the individual (Fos et al., 1998). Fos et al. (1998) further exemplify this point in the statement "In fact, epidemiology is a core discipline pertinent to all branches of health care, including management." In addition, Fos et al. (1998) outline the application of abilities acquired in an epidemiology course to the management sector. For example, epidemiological skills allow for the assessment of the quality of care that is delivered, planning and marketing of health care services, monitoring disease occurrence, distribution, impact and the evaluation of health care interventions and programs (Fos et al., 1998). This analytical approach offered by a course in epidemiology is unique when compared to health administration and general business administration curricula.

The above example of the utility of epidemiology in the field of health care management is but one application of this liberal art and professional skill. The social sciences, physical sciences, humanities, and business disciplines, to name a few, are all concerned, at some level, with the quality of care, quality of life, and the ability of individuals to function in a population-based setting. Thus, the analytical methods that epidemiology provides allows for information pertaining to broad outcomes from these varied fields to be assessed. Further support for the extensive application of epidemiology is in reference to policymakers who should understand the usefulness and implications of epidemiological data for making recommendations and establishing procedures that impact many aspects of the lives of populations (Malison, 1993). Epidemiology is a crucial tool that can be utilized to identify, highlight, and address social, economic, and health disparities in populations.

ROLE FOR EPIDEMIOLOGY IN DEVELOPING A CITIZENRY LITERATE IN PUBLIC HEALTH

Is a course in epidemiology the solution to educating undergraduate students to becoming educated citizens? Though a course in epidemiology, in and of itself, is not the answer to this question, it can be part of the solution. Lilienfeld (1979) states "…the time is not too far off when the frontiers of epidemiology will be expanded to include a pre-baccalaureate major in epidemiology…" This course taught at the University of New Hampshire can serve as a model course for similar academic institutions focused on liberal arts education that do not possess an established undergraduate public health program. This course facilitates the development of many skill sets or "life tools" necessary for an educated population, for example, intellectual adaptability, problem solving, and an understanding of risk and probability that could improve a population's capacity to make educated decisions based upon accurate interpretations.

If the call has been put forth for an educated population via a public health curriculum, who will carry forth this mission? The response to this call that has been described in this chapter is to utilize the well-developed science of epidemiology to connect liberal education with professional skills to educate our future citizens. This is an established model at the University of New Hampshire that supports the University's mission, yet, based on this call to action by AAC&U, the question is raised as to who could teach such a well serving course at other institutions without a baccalaureate curriculum in public health or health management and policy? Albertine et al. (2007) reply that the response to this call will require an interdisciplinary effort from multiple departments. Some departments, in several colleges and universities, have already responded to this call and have engaged in unique collaborative endeavors (APTR, 2008). This interdisciplinary effort may be the only means by which liberal education can heed this call without an established baccalaureate public health program. The development of one pertinent course at a time is better than no effort at all. Furthermore, it is possible that faculty with backgrounds in sociology, geography, anthropology, as well as the traditional sciences could either incorporate epidemiology into their course objectives or teach a course in epidemiology.

Courses in epidemiology tend to attract students who have a broad interest in health. Thus, a course in epidemiology is well-poised to serve as a general education course and contribute to the call for an interdisciplinary liberal education to develop an educated population. In an effort to further integrate public health into the liberal education curriculum, the University of New Hampshire recently implemented an integrative course in environmental health into the Public Health option of the HMP major. Similar to the current course in epidemiology, this course in environmental health can serve as an incubator for a future liberal arts class. The importance of such a course is significant since the role of the environment in today's society and the aptitude necessary to evaluate the impact of populations on the environment contributes to educating undergraduate students towards assuming their role, significance, and responsibility as members of an educated public.

COMMUNITY COLLEGES – A KEY TO EXPANDING UNDERGRADUATE PUBLIC HEALTH EDUCATION AND THE PUBLIC HEALTH WORKFORCE

Healthy People 2020, a national health promotion and disease prevention initiative led by the United States Department of Health and Human Services, recently included a goal to "Increase the quality, availability, and effectiveness of educational and community-based programs designed to prevent disease and injury, improve health, and enhance quality of life" (HP 2020). In order to achieve this goal, the offering of public health education at the undergraduate level will be important. Despite most of the growth in recent years in undergraduate public health education occurring at four-year academic institutions, there is a role for two-year community colleges. For example, the number of community colleges offering associate degrees or certificate programs in public health would not only impact the public health workforce, as previously mentioned, but could also contribute to achieving this *Healthy People 2020* goal. The number of community colleges offering associate degrees or certificate programs is growing but the precise number is not currently known (Fulcher et al., 2010).

In order to contribute to this call for a citizenry educated in public health, many four-year undergraduate programs are well-poised to: 1.) work with undergraduates to complement their liberal education with public health courses; 2.) work with students who are part of a Community College System to introduce a liberal education that includes the field of public health. The University of New Hampshire has experience collaborating with a local community college to broaden the target audience for public health education. For example, the Community College System in New Hampshire is comprised of seven Community Technical Colleges offering two-year associate degrees, professional training and certificates, and serving as conduits to four-year degrees which are part of the University System of New Hampshire. These colleges, located throughout the state, have recently experienced an increased enrollment due to their affordable tuition, so there is a large student audience who can be introduced to the importance and value of public health. Furthermore, many of these enrolled students transfer to four-year academic institutions that offer a liberal education (Community College System, 2010a).

APTR's publication titled, *Recommendations for Undergraduate Public Health Education* (Riegelman and Albertine, 2008), proposes three core public health courses: Public Health 101, Epidemiology 101, and Global Health 101 to support an institution's general education program. The UNH undergraduate HMP curriculum currently includes expertise in Public Health 101 and Epidemiology 101-type courses which fulfills the general liberal education program and core course requirements, respectively. The Public Health 101 course presents an overview of the structure, function, and organization of the public health system/services and how they operate, emphasizing core functions and major divisions. The course surveys contemporary problems facing society, e.g., workforce issues, epidemics, and lifestyle choices contributing to obesity, tobacco and alcohol use and challenges students to think critically about these issues. The course also introduces public health careers. The Epidemiology 101 course, as previously described, examines the distribution and determinants of disease, illness, and health in the community, measures of association, health status, and data sources. Development of hypotheses and study designs to reduce community health problems using epidemiological reasoning, methods, and analyses are skills that are practiced. The UNH HMP undergraduate program did not offer a course in Global Health 101 and applied for funding from APTR to develop such a course. Funding was awarded to design, teach and evaluate a Global Health course in the undergraduate curriculum of the UNH HMP Department and one Community Technical College in New Hampshire. The partnership between a four-year university and two-year community college has accomplished the following:

1. Supported AAC&U's (2007) *LEAP* framework which encourages life-long learning and a commitment to personal and social responsibility;

2. Allowed for this course in Global Health to be incorporated into the UNH Discovery Program, an interdisciplinary program for freshmen students that encourages inquiry (UNH, 2011). In addition, these students are introduced to public health principles early on in their academic career;

3. Encouraged the development of additional courses, new majors and/or minors in public health in a skills-based environment that is characteristic of two-year community colleges;

4. Encouraged mutually supportive collaboration with the surrounding public health community to engage in service-based learning experiences with diverse populations;

5. Attracted students to the public health field to pursue additional public health coursework and preparation to join the public health workforce;

6. Enabled faculty to expand their expertise (knowledge and skills) and teach a Global Health course

7. Broadened the attractiveness of the UNH HMP Department and its course offerings in public health to a varied undergraduate population in a liberal education environment;

8. Broadened the attractiveness of these two-year community colleges and introduced a vocation-based student population to the value of public health;

9. Promoted an awareness and increased appreciation of the benefits of and the threats to public health from a global perspective and facilitate an understanding of critical issues associated with the international health disparity as it exists around the world;

10. Supported the American Public Health Association's (2008) initiative titled, *Connecting with the Colleges* which is "…designed to encourage an increasing awareness of public health in undergraduate liberal art-oriented institutions lacking a formal public health curriculum. The aim is to support community-based service-learning in public health, in addition to engaging public health practitioners in classroom education."

In addition, this collaboration supports the strategic goals of the Community College System of New Hampshire (2010b) which include the following:

- Offer rigorous, accredited programs of career and technical education that prepare New Hampshire residents with skills to thrive in the modern-day economy
- Prepare students for successful college transfer and increase opportunities for transfer
- Develop in students a sense of service and a capacity for responsible citizenship
- Implement a statewide, collaborative workforce development system and significantly reduce the number of under-prepared workers in the New Hampshire workforce

Furthermore, it is estimated that 250,000 public health workers will be needed at the local, state, and federal levels by the year 2020 (ASPH, 2008). Community colleges can assist four-year academic institutions in reducing this deficit through the offering of public health-related associate degrees and certificates which will help to prepare college students to enter baccalaureate programs and eventually the public health workforce.

COMMUNITY-BASED PUBLIC HEALTH (SERVICE) LEARNING: PUBLIC HEALTH LITERACY IN ACTION

Public health is a theory and practice-driven profession that is focused on community health. The emphasis on "community" is evident in Winslow's (1920) definition of public health which states:

"…the science and art of preventing disease, prolonging life and promoting physical health and efficacy through organized community efforts for the sanitation of the environment, the control of community infections, the education of the individual in principles of personal hygiene, the organization of medical and nursing services for the early diagnosis and preventive treatment of disease, and the development of the social machinery which will ensure every individual in the community a standard of living adequate for the maintenance of health...to enable every citizen to realize his or her birthright and longevity."

Public health's primary mission is to promote health and prevent disease in human populations. To achieve this goal, the IOM (2003) recommended that "all undergraduates should have access to education in public health." The academic institution and community setting are both relevant learning environments for providing the undergraduate student with an opportunity to apply public health principles obtained through coursework to a community-based experience. A community-based public health learning experience, also known as service learning, can highlight the complexity of public health issues affecting segments of a community's population.

Cashman and Seifer (2008) state that "Service learning, a type of experiential learning, is an effective and appropriate vehicle for teaching public health and developing public health literacy." Specifically, Seifer (1998) defines service learning as the following:

> "...a structured learning experience that combines community service with preparation and reflection. Students engaged in service-learning provide community service in response to community-identified concerns and learn about the context in which service is provided, the connection between their service and their academic coursework, and their roles as citizens."

The benefit of a community-based service learning experience is two-fold: 1) the student applies public health principles to a real-life setting, reflects on the experience, develops skills necessary to work in a community environment and ultimately works to affect social change; 2) provides faculty with the opportunity to leave their "ivory tower" and forge collaborations with community partners, practice the public health principles taught in the classroom, and engage the community in a mutually beneficial relationship that produces social change and scholarship.

However, the development of a community-based service learning experience can be challenging. In some cases, the community is opposed to academicians leaving their "ivory tower" to assist with a local public health issue since the community, and not the academician, is most familiar with the problem (Serrell et al., 2009). In other instances, the academicians utilize an evidence-based approach to prioritize the community's public health issues, but the community wants a less significant public health issue addressed first, despite the data illustrating otherwise (Caron and Serrell, 2009). These examples represent the values and approach of community-based participatory research (CBPR), "a systematic effort to incorporate community participation and decision making, local theories of etiology and change, and community practices..." (Wallerstein and Duran, 2006). CBPR principles include open communication and mutual respect for the knowledge, expertise and resources of all partners (Metzler et al., 2003). The role of trust and the importance of recognizing that trust evolves in relationships over time is critical to effective CBPR (Wallerstein and Duran, 2006). In CBPR, the academic collaborator assumes the role of co-learner with the goal of translating findings into social action and change (O'Fallon et al., 2000; Wallerstein and Duran, 2006). Specifically, Serrell et al. (2009) propose that adaptability, consistency, shared authority and trust are values common to CBPR and community-based partnerships. Faculty need to consider that building campus-community partnerships can take time and that these relationships need to be in place prior to establishing community-based service learning experiences for the undergraduate student.

Ernest Boyer (1996), in describing the scholarship of engagement with the community, stated "…the academy must become a more vigorous partner in the search for answers to our most pressing social, civic, economic and moral problems…" A statement that is reminiscent of the goal of the *Educated Citizen and Public Health* initiative. However, "…not all community-based outreach constitutes engagement – not all is done with the community – and not all community engagement activities by faculty constitute scholarship" (Sandmann, 2006). Often, community-based service learning fulfills the service mission of academic institutions and is not considered engaged scholarship. As a result, for purposes of career advancement, faculty working in the community need to clarify how their campus-community partnership is categorized by their academic institution (Caron, 2010).

Another challenge presented by community-based service learning is assessing student learning and awarding academic credit. Approaches to this challenge may vary from one academic institution to another. For example, the University of North Carolina at Greensboro (2011) states that "Students should be required to differentiate clearly between learning and experience. College credit is not appropriate for experience alone." Another example from the University of New Hampshire is a community-based service learning experience offered in three undergraduate public health courses (Introduction to Public Health, Epidemiology and Community Medicine, and Global Public Health Issues) as an optional extra credit assignment. The reason this is a voluntary assignment is because the student enrollment in these courses ranges from twenty-five to eighty-seven students and poses a placement challenge for the surrounding community organizations. However, a university's Office of Community Service and Learning could be a good resource when one is considering to work with community agencies since many working relationships between the campus and community have already been established by this Office and they are aware of the agencies and organizations in the community that could use assistance provided from a community-based service learning opportunity. The assignment is structured so that the mission of public health to promote health and prevent disease in populations is described. Next, the many forms of promotion and prevention are outlined, all of which involve providing services to communities. The goal of the assignment is to have the student become an *active* participant in public health by working with a community agency to provide services to a population. During and following the completion of the community-based service learning assignment, the student addresses the following ten questions in a written essay:

1. What are the mission and goals of the organization/agency?

2. Why did you choose this community service activity?

3. What were your thoughts about the population being helped prior to engaging in the activity?

4. Describe what you did and the purpose of your activity.

5. Describe the perceived impact of your contribution.

6. What part of the experience meant the most to you? Why?

7. What are your recommendations on how this activity could be sustained throughout the year?

8. What were the other needs of the population that you observed?

9. Would you volunteer with the agency again? Why or why not?

10. Include the name and contact information for the point person you worked with on this activity.

Due to the short duration of the service activity, the student is typically integrated immediately into the community organization's work and the student becomes aware that they are one of the stakeholders in the work being conducted by the organization. The student quickly realizes the community's challenges, priorities, infrastructure and position with respect to the given public health issue. The student is often surprised by the complexity of the problem and the solution. The student learns to see many facets of public health and tests their skills in a short period of time.

Albertine (2008) describes, through experience, the value of integrating public health into the area of literary study. Albertine (2008) states that "Such an integrative program can enrich students' entire liberal education as well as their pre-professional and major programs of study." Faculty from different disciplines are encouraged to invest in developing interdisciplinary study by including the lens of public health in the practice and teaching of their discipline. Albertine (2008) reveals that her experience demonstrates how she "never left [her] discipline and expertise, but [she] began to practice [her] discipline and know [her] expertise in a new way." Furthermore, Albertine (2008) states the following:

> "The best we can know about learning tells us that we need integrative and experiential programs if we want deep and lasting knowledge, skills, and attitudes. There is an advantage to deep engagement of both faculty and students as they attempt through integrative inquiry to find answers to big questions."

Just as Albertine (2008) supports "the value of integrative public health education for undergraduates" and "benefits to faculty" from new fields and disciplines, we also need to broaden the campus-community partnership to include governmental public health departments which can offer community-based pedagogies for undergraduate students. "Governmental public health departments are responsible for creating and maintaining conditions that keep people healthy" (NACCHO, 2005). The governmental public health department at the local level is often referred to as a local health department which "may be locally governed, part of a region or district, be an office or an administrative unit of the state health department, or a hybrid of these" (NACCHO, 2005). "All local health departments, as governmental entities, derive their authority and responsibility from the state and local laws that govern them" (NACCHO, 2005). The National Association of County and City Health Officials (2005) developed the following standards as a guide to the basic responsibilities of a local health department:

1. Monitor health status and understand health issues facing the community
2. Protect people from health problems and health hazards
3. Give people information they need to make healthy choices
4. Engage the community to identify and solve health problems
5. Develop public health policies and plans
6. Enforce public health laws and regulations
7. Help people receive health services
8. Maintain a competent public health workforce
9. Evaluate and improve programs and interventions
10. Contribute to and apply the evidence base of public health

These standards are similar to the essential public health services which describe the public health activities that should be undertaken in all communities (Table 6) (CDC, 1994).

Table 6. Ten Essential Public Health Services[a]

1. Monitor health status to identify and solve community health problems
2. Diagnose and investigate health problems and health hazards in the community
3. Inform, educate, and empower people about health issues
4. Mobilize community partnerships and actions to identify and solve health problems
5. Develop policies and plans that support individual and community health efforts
6. Enforce laws and regulations that protect health and ensure safety
7. Link people to needed personal health services and assure provision of healthcare when otherwise unavailable
8. Assure a competent public health and personal healthcare workforce
9. Evaluate the effectiveness, accessibility, and quality of personal and population-based health services
10. Research for new insights and innovative solutions to health problems

[a]Source: Centers for Disease Control and Prevention. (1994). The Core Public Health Functions Steering Committee, National Public Health Performance Standards Program. http://www.cdc.gov/od/ocphp/nphpsp/EssentialPHServices.htm

A local public health department is considered part of the public health system, i.e., "the individuals, public and private entities that are engaged in activities that affect the public's health," (NACCHO, 2005) and can offer a rich community-based service learning opportunity to both faculty and students. However, the structure of the public health system may differ for each community.

For example, some communities in New Hampshire lack a local health department in each town and city, yet, there is a state health department and efforts are underway to establish a regional public health system (NHDHHS, 2011).

Thus, the opportunity exists for innovative and fruitful community-based learning and it may take on many forms, such as a local governmental public health department working to reduce adolescent pregnancy to a community organization whose goal is to feed the homeless – public health is at the root of the mission of each of these components of the public health system.

The significance of the academic and practice communities working together to strengthen public health was recognized to be of such importance that the Council on Linkages Between Academia and Public Health Practice was formed by the Public Health Foundation "to assure that public health education is relevant to practice and to encourage lifelong learning among public health workers" (PHF, 2010).

Thus, community-based learning in higher education supports that an understanding of public health issues is a core component of an educated public and is necessary to develop one's social responsibility. Community-based learning is a tool by which to realize the goals of the *Educated Citizen and Public Health* initiative".

The initiative intends to address public health not only by training more health professionals but also by educating future citizens" (Albertine, 2008).

PUBLIC HEALTH LITERACY ACHIEVED THROUGH HEEDING THE CALL FOR CHANGE IN LIBERAL EDUCATION

This chapter describes several approaches to answering the contemporary call for change in liberal education whereby a wide breadth of knowledge, adaptable skills, principled values and a sense of social responsibility is required to prepare educated citizens to effectively respond to the challenges of today's society. Public health is proposed as the discipline well-suited to serve as a vision for the direction of liberal education. Specifically, an integrative methodology for the social justice field of epidemiology is described for preparing a population of baccalaureate students who possess "life tools" based in a liberal education viewpoint that enables them to improve the health of their society as educated citizens. Public health literacy can lead to the baccalaureate student's ability to think broadly and engage in professional skill development. Expanding public health literacy and community-based learning into undergraduate liberal education can accomplish the following: encourage life-long learning and a commitment to social responsibility; allow for new course/major/minor development in public health in two-year and four-year colleges; promote collaboration with the public health community; and enable faculty to expand their expertise. This interdisciplinary approach, both academic and community-based, to a liberal education can serve as a model for other academic institutions that heed this same call. Table 7 lists resources for public health education, practice and professional for both the student and faculty member interested in learning more about this integrative discipline.

Table 7. Resources for public health education, practice and professional development

Textbooks
1. Friis RH., Sellers, TA. Epidemiology for Public Health Practice. Fourth Edition. Jones and Bartlett Publishers, Boston, MA. 2009.
2. Merrill, RM., Timmreck, TC. Introduction to Epidemiology. Fifth Edition. Jones and Bartlett Publishers, Boston, MA. 2010.
3. Aschengrau, A., Seage, G.R. III. Essentials of Epidemiology in Public Health. Second Edition. Jones and Bartlett Publishers, Boston, MA. 2008.
4. Friis, R.H. Epidemiology 101. First Edition. Jones and Bartlett Publishers, Boston, MA. 2010.
5. Centers for Disease Control and Prevention (CDC). Principles of Epidemiology in Public Health Practice: An Introduction to Applied Epidemiology and Biostatistics. Third Edition. U.S. Department of Health and Human Services, Atlanta, GA.

Classroom and Laboratory Assignments
1. Young Epidemiology Scholars (YES), Epidemiology Teaching Units, http://www.college board.com/yes/ft/iu/units.html
2. Centers for Disease Control and Prevention (CDC). Epidemiologic Case Studies, http://www2a.cdc.gov/epicasestudies/
3. Prevention Education Resource Center (PERC), http://www.teachprevention.org/
4. Merrill, R.M. Principles of Epidemiology Workbook: Exercises and Activities. First Edition. Jones and Bartlett Publishers, Boston, MA. 2010.

Practice
1. Community-Campus Partnerships for Health, http://www.ccph.info/
2. Commission on Community-Engaged Scholarship in the Health Professions, http://depts. washington.edu/ccph/kellogg3.html
3. CES4Health, Community Engaged Scholarship for Health, http://www.ces4health.info/
4. National Association of County and City Health Officials (NACCHO), http://www. naccho.org/
5. Pathways to Public Health, Association of Schools of Public Health (ASPH), http://www.asph.org/document.cfm?page=734

Professional Development
1. American Public Health Association (APHA), http://www.apha.org/
2. State Member Affiliate of APHA – for example, New Hampshire Public Health Association, http://www.nhpha.org/
3. Association for Prevention Teaching and Research (APTR), http://www.aptrweb. org/prof_dev/index.html
4. Association of American Colleges and Universities (AAC&U), http://www.aacu.org/ membership/index.cfm
5. TRAIN, Public Health Foundation, https://www.train.org/DesktopShell.aspx

Selected Websites
1. Association of Schools of Public Health (ASPH), http://www.asph.org/document. cfm?page=823
2. Centers for Disease Control and Prevention (CDC), http://www.cdc.gov/
3. National Institutes of Health (NIH), http://www.nih.gov/
4. Public Health Foundation (PHF), http://www.phf.org/Pages/default.aspx
5. World Health Organization (WHO), http://www.who.int/en/

In conclusion, the success of the *Educated Citizen and Public Health* initiative by AAC&U and APTR "will depend on population-based understandings of human sustainability and convergent thinking drawn from the best achievements of the arts and sciences" (Albertine et al., 2007). The integrative and relevant pedagogical framework presented here for a public health literacy course in epidemiology that connects theory with practice in a liberal education curriculum can serve as a model for other academic institutions heeding this challenge. This proposal is supported by Lilienfeld et al. (1978) who state that epidemiology "...has matured to the point where it can be considered as an independent scientific discipline." The future implications of this effort are that the professional skills obtained through such a model that incorporates public health coursework, community-based learning, and innovative collaborations with our academic partners will not only result in an educated population but one who can make informed decisions and participate on a personal level in activities that promote health not only for themselves, but their community, state, nation, and the world in which they live. This expectation is shared by Albertine et al. (2007) who state that "Integrative public health programs in the liberal arts and within a liberal education can produce an informed citizenry capable of living – and one hopes living well – in the world that is becoming."

ACKNOWLEDGMENTS

The author acknowledges the following colleagues for their mentorship, collegiality, and collaborative spirit: James B. Lewis, MBA, ScD 9for his critical review of the chapter); Lee F. Seidel, PhD; Marc D. Hiller, DrPH; Holly Tutko, MS; Thandi Tshabangu-Soko MPH, MS, MA; Brenda Kirkwood, MPH; Pamela Langley, LPD; and Karen Mercer, MPH.

REFERENCES

Albertine, S., Persily, N.A., and Riegelman, R. (2007) Back to the pump handle: Public health and the future. *Liberal Education* 93(4):32-39.

Albertine, S. (2008) Undergraduate public health: Preparing engaged citizens as future health professionals. *American Journal of Preventive Medicine* 35(3):253-257.

American Public Health Association. (2008) Issue Paper: *Connecting with the Colleges Initiative.*

Association for Prevention Teaching and Research (APTR). (2008) *Annual Meeting: Undergraduate Public Health Education Session.* Austin, Texas.

Association of American Colleges and Universities (AAC&U). (2002) *National Panel Report: Greater Expectations: A New Vision for Learning as a Nation Goes to College.*

Association of American Colleges and Universities (AAC&U). *What is Liberal Education?* http://www.aacu.org/press_room/media (accessed October 18, 2010a).

Association of American Colleges and Universities (AAC&U). (2007) *A Report from the National Leadership Council for Liberal Education and America's Promise (LEAP): College Learning for the New Global Century.*

Association of American Colleges and Universities (AAC&U). *The Educated Citizen and Public Health*. http://www.aacu.org/public_health (accessed October 18, 2010b).

Association of Schools of Public Health (ASPH). (2008) ASPH Policy Brief: Confronting the Public Health Workforce Crisis http://www.asph.org/UserFiles/Workforce%20Shortage%202010.pdf (accessed November 1, 2010).

Boyer, EL. (1996) The scholarship of engagement. *Journal of Public Outreach and Service* 1(1):11-20.

Caron, R.M. and Serrell, N. (2009) Community ecology and capacity: Keys to improving the environmental communication of wicked problems. *Applied Environmental Education and Communication: An International Journal* 8(3): 195-203.

Caron, RM. (2010) Community-campus partnerships for health listserve (cbpr@u.washington.edu) (accessed September 1, 2010).

Cashman, S.B. and Seifer, S.D. (2008) Service-learning: An integral part of undergraduate public health. *American Journal of Preventive Medicine* 35(3):273-278.

Cassel, J.C. (2010) American College of Epidemiology Workshop http://www.epiresearch.org/students/resources (accessed October 18, 2010).

Centers for Disease Control and Prevention (CDC), United States Department of Health and Human Services. (1994) The Core Public Health Functions Steering Committee, National Public Health Performance Standards Program, The Essential Public Health Services http://www.cdc.gov/od/ocphp/nphpsp/EssentialPHServices.htm (accessed December 1, 2010).

Community College System of New Hampshire. *Community Colleges Report Increased Enrollment.* http://www.ccsnh.edu/news/08enrollment.html (Accessed October 18, 2010a).

Community College System of New Hampshire. *Strategic Goals.* http://www.ccsnh.edu/mission (Accessed October 18, 2010b).

Evans, R.G. and Stoddart, G.L. (1990) Producing health, consuming health care. *Social Science and Medicine* 31(12):1347-1363.

Fos, P.J., Fine, D.J., and Zuniga, M.A. (1998) Managerial epidemiology in the health administration curriculum. *Journal of Health Administration Education* 16(1):1-12.

Fraser, D.W. (1987) Epidemiology as a liberal art. *New England Journal of Medicine* 316(6):309-14.

Fulcher, R., Honore, P., Kirkwood, B., and Riegelman, R. (2010) Ready for prime time: Ramping up public health education. *Community College Journal* April/May 2010.

Gorsky, R.D. (1989) Epidemiology: A liberal art and a professional skill. *Journal of Health Administration Education* 7(2):382-388.

Healthy People 2020 (HP 2020). Educational and Community-based Programs http://www.healthypeople.gov/2020/topicsobjectives2020/overview.aspx?topicid=11 (accessed December 15, 2010).

Hemenway, D. (2010) Why don't we spend enough on public health? *New England Journal of Medicine* 362(18):1657-1658.

Ibrahim, M.A. (1983) Epidemiology: Application to health services. *Journal of Health Administration Education* 1(1):37-69.

Institute of Medicine (IOM). (1988) *The Future of Public Health*. Washington, DC: National Academies Press.

Institute of Medicine (IOM). Gebbie, K., Rosenstock, L., and L.M. Hernandez, eds. (2003) *Who Will Keep the Public Healthy? Educating Public Health Professionals for the 21st Century.* Washington, DC: The National Academies Press.

Last, J.M. ed. (2001) *A Dictionary of Epidemiology.* Fourth Edition. Oxford: Oxford University Press.

Lilienfeld, A., Garagliano, F., and Lilienfeld, D.E. (1978) Teaching epidemiology 101: The new frontier. *International Journal of Epidemiology* 7(4):377-380.

Lilienfeld, D.E. (1979) Epidemiology 101: II. An undergraduate perspective. *International Journal of Epidemiology* 8(2):181-183.

Maranz, P.R. (2008) Epidemiology 101: Toward an educated citizenry. *American Journal of Preventive Medicine* 35(3):264-268.

Malison, M.D. (1993) Report on the joint AUPHA/CDC workshop on promoting linkages between epidemiology and health administration. *Journal of Health Administration Education* 11(4):617-619.

Merrill, R.M. and Timmreck, T.C. (2006) *Introduction to Epidemiology.* Fourth Edition. Sudbury, MA: Jones and Bartlett Publishers.

Metzler, M.M., Higgins, D.L., Beeker, C.G., Freudenberg, N., Lantz, P.M., Senturia, K.D., et al. (2003) Addressing urban health in Detroit, New York City, and Seattle through community-based participatory research partnerships. *American Journal of Public Health* 93(5):803-811.

National Association of County and City Health Officials (NACCHO). (2005). Brochure: Operational definition of a functional local health department.

New Hampshire Department of Health and Human Services (NH DHHS) (2011) Public Health Notes: All health hazard regions become public health network regions http://www.dhhs.nh.gov/dphs/documents/phnotesnovdec10.pdf (accessed January 3, 2011).

O'Fallon L.R., Tyson F., and Dearry, A. (2000) *Successful models of community-based participatory research - Final report.* National Institute of Environmental Health Sciences. March 29-31, 2000, Washington, DC.

Public Health Foundation (PHF). Council on Linkages Between Academia and Public Health Practice http://www.phf.org/programs/council/Pages/default.aspx (accessed December 1, 2010).

Riegelman, R.K., Albertine, S., and Persily, N.A. (2007) *The Educated Citizen and Public Health: A Consensus Report on Public Health and Undergraduate Education.* Council of Colleges of Arts and Sciences.

Riegelman, R. and Albertine, S. (2008) *Recommendations for Undergraduate Public Health.* Monograph published by the Association for Prevention Teaching and Research and the Association of American Colleges and Universities.

Sandmann, L.R. (2006) Scholarship as architecture: Framing and enhancing community engagement. *Journal of Physical Therapy Education* 20(3):80-84.

Seifer, S.D. (1998) Service-learning: Community-campus partnerships for health professions education. *Academic Medicine* 73:273-277.

Serrell, N., Caron, R.M., Fleishmann, B., and Robbins, E.D. (2009) An academic-community partnership: building relationships and capacity to address childhood lead poisoning. *Progress in Community Health Partnerships: Research, Education, and Action* 3(1):53-59.

University of New Hampshire. 2008-2009 *Undergraduate Catalog*.

University of New Hampshire. (2010) *Epidemiology and Community Medicine, Course Evaluations*.

University of New Hampshire. Discovery Program http://www.unh.edu/discovery/ (accessed January 3, 2011).

University of North Carolina at Greensboro. Assessing Experiential Learning. http://csc.dept.uncg.edu/internships/faculty/assessing/ (accessed January 3, 2011).

Wallerstein, N.B. and Duran, B. (2006) Using the community-based participatory research to address health disparities. *Health Promotion Practice* 7(3):312-323.

Winslow, C.E.A. (1920) The untilled field of public health. *Modern Medicine* 2:183-191.

In: Progress in Education. Volume 26
Editor: Robert V. Nata, pp. 31-52

ISBN 978-1-61324-321-3
© 2011 Nova Science Publishers, Inc.

Chapter 2

HOW DO I FAULT THEE? DISCURSIVE PRACTICES IN WESTERN HIGHER EDUCATION STUDIES AND THE CONSTRUCTION OF INTERNATIONAL STUDENT SUBJECTIVITIES

Margaret Zeegers[1] and Deirdre Barron[2]
[1]University of Ballarat, Ballarat, Australia
[2]Swinburne University of Technology, Victoria, Australia

INTRODUCTION

In this chapter we focus on discursive practices of research higher degree supervision as crucial elements in constructs of international student subjectivities when undertaking studies in Australian universities. We position our discussion within an Australian context, but we would argue that the issues we raise regarding the supervision of such students are applicable to other western English-speaking countries that attract international Higher Degree Research students. In doing so, we focus on discursive fields emerging within domains of internationalization, globalization, and resistance. We examine processes and protocols in a number of Australian universities postgraduate divisions' practices in the conduct of research higher degree supervision—in the context of increasing pressures towards internationalization within frameworks of globalizing influences. We take issue with western custom and tradition as privileged within the field of supervision of research higher degree students. We suggest variations of supervision of International candidates as intentional and systematic interventions, based on literature deriving from existing research of supervision which acknowledges the problematic natures of cultural relationships in relation to teaching, learning, and knowledge production, and student resistance within these fields. We examine issues of discursive practices and the problematic natures of power relationships in supervisor/supervisee protocols and possibilities suggested by alternative models of higher degree by research supervision of international students.

POSTGRADUATE TEACHING AND SUPERVISION OF INTERNATIONAL STUDENTS

Our argument is premised on the notion that the discourses that shape the ways we view supervision of international students only partially draw on discourses of globalization. Current thinking in the social sciences is consistent in its attitude to globalization as contributing to the shaping the contemporary world. In most accounts of globalization there is an emphasis on economic imperatives, while those such as Lash and Urry (1994) and Harloe, Pickvance and Urry (1990) highlight the effects of globalization on cultural practices. The following, from Australia's Education Minister, was reported in early 2009 in a respected national daily broadsheet newspaper, *The Australian*:

> Julia Gillard has seized on record overseas student enrolment figures to highlight the strength of Australia's third-largest export market. Enrolments by overseas students in Australian educational institutions rose a record 20.7 per cent to 543,898 in 2008 - the largest increase since 2002 - according to the latest Australian Education International figures. ``This is the first time international enrolments have exceeded 500,000 in a calendar year," federal Education Minister Ms Gillard said. The rise in student enrolments from Asia - up 21.5 per cent - was recognition of Australia's ongoing relationship with its Asian neighbours and the strong awareness of Australia as a quality education destination, she said (Healy, 2009a).

It is the sort of press release that is issued with some regularity by that department and whatever its incumbent minister. This sort of confidence in the country's popularity with international students received a blow with a spate of attacks specifically aimed at Indian students in Australia in that same year, causing very real alarm in the department and universities across Australia. The estimated cost to Australia in terms of international students has been estimated at $78 million Australian dollars by the highly respected Australian Broadcasting Commission (2009), pointing to a major drop in the sorts of numbers published in 2003 and beyond. So prominent was this development, even Wikipedia (2010) has a section on it:

In May and June 2009, Indian media reported what it saw to be racially motivated attacks against Indians, especially students. Rallies were organised in Melbourne and Sydney, and intense coverage of the perceived hate crimes commenced in India, being especially critical of Australia and Australian police services.

The result has been a delegation of politicians and tertiary educators to convene a mission to India to try to neutralise, or at least limit or manage, the harm that the attacks have done to international students and their potential enrolments in tertiary institutions in Australia. So effective was the high level government intervention, by September the same year the same newspaper's reporter was able to publish a very optimistic article on the same subject:

> The reputation-battered Australian tertiary education industry may have defied a barrage of negative global publicity over the treatment of foreign students after posting a record high in overseas students enrolments. Months after shrugging off predictions that the Australian industry would suffer adverse effects from the global financial crisis, overseas student enrolments numbered 547,663 in July, up from the previous record of 543,898 last December. The record enrolments represent a more than 20 per cent increase on this time last year, driven

by continued strong growth in vocational education's key Asian markets, and backed by stronger growth in university enrolments (Healy, 2009b).

Given such developments in a given year, it is possible to envisage a continuing state of fluctuating numbers in a globalising world. A review of Australia's higher education offerings has made its own recommendations along these lines:

> A relatively low proportion of Australia's higher degree students are international students compared with other OECD countries. It has been in the provision of undergraduate education that Australia has excelled. But times have changed and, with looming shortages of academic staff and the new imperative to build international research networks, it is time to consider how increases in higher degree enrolments from high-performing international students might be encouraged (Bradley, 2008).

Whatever the numbers of students that reach Australian tertiary institutions, there is a need to consider those institutions' offerings for international higher degree by research students. The only surety we can exercise any control over is the guarantee of the quality of the offerings and their appropriateness for the needs of those who make up the international market. In a globalizing world, this is of no small importance, but equally, in relation to research training, the quality of supervision of higher degree research students is a measure of that quality.

We have taken up understandings of globalization of cultural practices as they pertain to supervisory practices of students studying for a research degree in a country that is not their country of citizenship. These students are usually categorized as international students, and we have framed our discussion of the issues pertaining to these students in relation to poststructuralist theorizing with conceptualizations of discursive practice, subjectivities, silences and resistance to inform our discussion, drawing particularly on the work of Foucault (1973; 1974; 1976; 1980a; 1980b).

Poststructuralist theorizing analyses power relations in relation to discursivity. This is based on an argument drawn from Foucault's (1980a) suggestion of 'regimes of truth', that is that discourses organise our perceptions, our ways of knowing, making some things visible and others invisible, some things true and others false. Discourse as a *noun* refers to ways in which particular ways of speaking have been institutionalized and thus become constitutive of people and their actions (Davies and Harré 1991/92). Discourses are constituted by exclusions as well as inclusions, by what can be said as well as what cannot be said, so that ways in which individuals or groups are included or excluded function as normalization. Discourse as *practice*, or *discursive practice*, is the ways people constitute themselves and are constituted by others (Davies and Harré 1991/92). *Subject* refers to ways people think about themselves and ways they act, and it refers to discourses and practices that pre-exist us to which they are accountable. Subjectivity, then, is a product of discourses and practices to which all people are subject.

Marginalization can be understood as being a result of particular constructions of subjectivities through discursive practices, that is, normalization. Normalization is understood as suggested by Gane and Johnson (1993: 'the establishment or institutionalization of those disciplines, knowledges and technologies that lay the ground for the emergence of the autonomous, self-regulating subject' (p. 9). If we accept that normalization is a technique which gives rise to marginal groups taking up hegemonic discourses then it is possible to argue that these discourses are not imposed by authority-based restrictions, but that they seduce, manipulate and encourage normalization. A key focus of ours in this chapter is an examination of normalizing processes that arise through tensions arising from discourses of research degree that are central to them, including those who produce education policy, and those that are marginal—in this instance international research degree students.

Individuals, through learning the discursive practices of a society, consciously or unconsciously position themselves within those practices in multiple ways, and develop subjectivities both in concert with and in opposition to others. Thus, although a person's subjectivity is constructed for them, it *becomes* them as they actively take up subject positions and they are only able to construct themselves within discourses that are made available to them. Since meaning is not fixed, though, the availability of subject positions is always in a state of flux. If society is perceived of as being constantly created through discursive practices then it is possible to see the power of these practices—not only to create and sustain the social world but also to see how that world can be changed through the refusal of certain discourses and the generation of new ones. Thus, through the analysis of discourses, poststructuralists develop their understanding of the relations between persons and their social worlds (Davies, 1989) which has important implications in conceptualizing social change implemented through the generation of counter-hegemonic discourses.

GLOBALIZATION

Metadiscourses framing policies of internationalization are facilitated by shifts to techno-economic paradigms in commercial enterprise that is now recognised as globalization. This in itself is a stimulus to current debate that positions the phenomenon in the most recent of events in world history or traces it back through to the beginning of recorded time as humankind has colonized the world. Increasing knowledge regarding the use of tools, and now especially electronically-based tools, has brought technological developments a long way beyond the major impacts of the development of the wheel. The list of such developments is strikingly long, too long to be enumerated here, but suffice to say that it provided the basis for the Industrial Revolution which allowed Henry Ford to design his mass production processes and ultimately brought us to the present pass of globalization, the hallmark of which is the so-called Knowledge Age (Zeegers and Barron, 2010).

As globalization of research higher degree studies becomes the focus of universities around the world, discursive practices of supervision and the supervision of international students then can be understood as essential aspects of producing economically important commodities. This economic importance is exemplified by the notion that the design and advertizing of this product called research higher degrees may attract considerable investment. We are not advocates of using the term *product* in relation to education, and in another space would be critical of such nomenclature. Here we are drawing on neoliberalist discourses that have been generated by governments that have had the effect of framing education as a product.

Discourses of higher education have increasingly positioned the field within discourses of economics, of cost-effectiveness in relation to inputs and outputs, in an environment of declining government funding to universities. The current phase of internationalisation has seen international students in Australian higher education grow from 21,000 in 1989 to over 185,000 in 2008: 'Australia ranked as the fifth largest recipient of overseas higher education students among OECD countries in 2005 and the third largest English-speaking destination for overseas students behind the United States and the United Kingdom' (Reserve Bank of Australia, 2008, cited in Bradley, 2008, p. 87), with over 80 per cent of international students in Australian higher education are from Asia, including 21 per cent from mainland China with 3.6% of these in higher degrees by research Bradley (2008, p. 92). . In relation to the national economy, enrolments of international students in the early years of the 21st century are worth 13.7 billion Australian dollars (Bradley, 2008, p. 87).

All of this occurs at the very time that discourses of globalization have become privileged in discursive formations of modern economics. The idea of globalization carries with it a complexity that is viewed by some not as any sort of homogeneous entity but rather as an 'umbrella term for a myriad of social processes' which are 'differentially propagated depending on human interests and resources'(Rowan, Bartlett and Evans, 1997). Others question whether it is even globalization more of a sort of heightened internationalization of commercial and financial institutions and structures that have emerged in the wake of rapid advances in technology (Hirst and Thompson, 1996). At another extreme others warn us of the imminent demise of the nation-state as the basic political unit in the face of its increasing irrelevance in a changed world context (Luard, 1990). When pushes for Australian universities' internationalization are positioned within such discourses of globalization, this has significance in relation to the positioning of international postgraduate experience as well in that they construct issues, as well as the subjectivities of the students themselves, in ways that are of no small import as far as the supervision of international postgraduate students are concerned. We consider the very words that frame discussions of globalization, higher education domestic and international students generally and postgraduate students in particular, are most telling in the structuring of the experience of students.

The matter of correctly labelled globalization or hyper-internationalization is itself worthy of some consideration. If it is indeed a matter of heightened internationalization, then individual cultural markers have a significant role to play in ways in which international research higher degree students are supervised. If it is a matter of nation-states being redundant within the phenomenon of globalization, then discourses of cultural markers are backgrounded while privileged western discourses of postgraduate studies are foregrounded. There are therefore major changes in the possibilities for educational as well as commercial endeavour, and postgraduate study in western universities, a system of higher education in which Australia has a significant part to play, is a part of that.

A major change that is to be negotiated is that of 'the global redistribution of political power and cultural legitimation, the deterritorialization and decentring of power in the West, the transformation in the nature of the forces of production, and the emergence of new forms of cultural criticism' (Aronowitz and Giroux, 1991, p. 15). That deceptively simple term, *globalization*, encompasses a complexity of social processes, shifts in spatial forms of organization and activity with seemingly consistent transcontinental patterns. It involves a stretching and deepening of social relations by institutions across space and time, producing a connectedness between places separated by the entire globe. Integral to all of this, of course, is the Internet. Yet discourses which employ the concept of *globe*, rather than *countries*, or *nations*, for example, serve to naturalise phenomena in ways which mask universal diversity, let alone differences. New developments in unprecedented flows of populations and electronic interconnectedness of families, of villages, of cities, of countries, all gathered under the umbrella term of *globalization*, construct images of homogeneity. Realities of diversity within these populations across the globe exist as silences, rendered invisible as to important ontological and epistemological positions of millions of people in hundreds of countries in the world as discourses of heterogeneity are foregrounded.

Our universities are generally quite explicit as to what is expected of any research higher degree undertakings: original work, independence in relation to study; a maintenance of standards of postgraduate research work; a sense of research methodology; conventions for production of such work, and so on (Cryer, 1997), all of which is to be conducted within discourses of supervision couched in reasonable, comfortable tones, such as evinced by Connell (1985). While this is coming increasingly under question, (Barron and Zeegers, 2002; Grant and Graham, 1994; Green and Lee, 1999; Zeegers and Barron, 2008), there is no real sense of alternative paradigms as anything other than suggestions positioned on the margins of dominant discourses. We suggest that a number of possibilities exist within present discourses that may be exploited for their timeliness and relevance to domestic as well as international research higher degree student supervision.

Later in this chapter we look at possibilities for disrupting or resisting particular subjectivities through discursive formation. The notion of *discursive formation* is suggested by Foucault (1972), who argues that the world is completely interwoven with discourses. Accepting this notion means that the possibilities of counter-hegemonic discourses need to be examined in terms of positionality within these discourses and the ways in which others are positioned. The Australian push to frame education as a product which has value in the international market place can also been in other western countries such as the United Kingdom and the United States. Discourses that underpin notions of educational market economies can be understood as the same discourses that have been mobilized by neoliberalism and manifested in the political agendas of Thatcher in the UK, Reagan and G. W. Bush in the US (van der Wende and Westerheijden, 2001), and Howard in Australia through the Department of Education Training and Youth Affairs (Department of Education Training and Youth Affairs, 2000):

> Throughout the world there has been a move to mass higher education associated with higher diversity of institutions and programmes and a large increase in the number and size of universities. This expansion of higher education promoted the rise of a variety of modes of course delivery...All these developments pose challenges for the efficacy of institutional quality controls...Australia's national policy environment encourages universities to seek greater commercial opportunities and align themselves more closely with industry needs (p. 1).

Hence, a discursive formation may be discerned as universities have appropriated discourses of commercialization and commerce itself, which has come to be synonymous with private funding. Universities have as a result looked to what they perceive as untapped markets to sell their product. The new funding formula introduced to Australia in 2001, known as the Research Training Scheme (RTS) overtly encourages universities to draw on fee-paying international participation. The reward is a potential win from funding formulae based in part on completion of higher research degrees, including those of international students. Hodson's (2001) report on the UK experience in this regard could also be read as the Australian experience. In both countries reduced government funding per student has been implemented at the same time as have increases in quality assurance and assessment procedures. It is tempting to enter into a debate about the worthiness or otherwise of conservative modernization, but this is beyond the scope of this chapter. Rather, we raise the issue as framed by Apple (2001), who points out that:

> Conservative modernization has radically reshaped the common sense of society. It has worked in every sphere – the economic, the political, and the cultural – to alter the basic categories we use to evaluate our institutions and our public and private lives. It has established new identities (p. 194).

Massification of Higher Education

These new identities have been constructed in the context of the massification of higher education in Australia, identified by Moses (1997) and Skilbeck (1993) where a 432% increase in the total number of students, under-and postgraduate, in higher education has positioned universities as having moved from an elite to a mass higher education system. Skilbeck (1993) defines the point at which this transition occurs as being when the participation rate is in the range of 15% to 25% of the population of school leaving age (p. 19), and figures since 1993 have vindicated this perception. Hodson (2001) reports a similar experience in the UK. This massification has had the effect of squeezing the higher education funding purse with a net reduction in funding per student to the sector. Of some concern in relation to this is that the range of student backgrounds implied by such an assault on traditional elites of higher education would suggest the sorts of non-white, non-male, non-middle class populations among student postgraduate research cohorts that would give rise to a number of different positionings of students within postgraduate research activities. We also suggest that there is a consequent need for a range of postgraduate research pedagogies to be employed (Barron and Zeegers, 2002).

Within the new framing of education as a product and the funding-squeezed environment Australian Universities have been prompted to seek collaborations with other universities in Australia and with international partners, and attracting fee paying students. Collaborations within Australia are limited in that this merely divides a limited recruitment pie in new ways. As this is a small country with declining population growth there is also a limit to any potential growth in a local fee paying higher degree population (Böhm et al., 2002). International collaboration and the attraction of international fee paying students can thus be understood as the only real sources of additional income for universities.

One major possible advantage of opening university doors to international students could have resulted in the valuing of diversity through the contribution of a wide range of perspectives. As Morey and Kitano (1997) state, 'A multicultural curriculum provides a more comprehensive, accurate, intellectually honest view of reality' (p. 1). However, as Hodson (2001) points out, competition between the US, the UK and Australia operates in a climate of scarcity, so that the pressing needs for funds mean that universities are pushed to adapt their curriculum to fit the market. This in and of itself is neither good nor bad, in educative terms. The tension for institutions in the higher education sector is where to position themselves in regard to short-term financial gain and long term quality maintenance (Levine and White, 1961). The challenge for educators then is to ensure that changes to curriculum and curriculum delivery remain imbued with educational imperatives rather than sacrificing education quality to the forces of the market.

The increase in quality assurance and assessment procedures has also meant that discursive productions of subjectivities have been framed within notions of surveillance, normalization and disciplinary power. Here we draw on the notion that within Panoptical discourses (see Foucault, 1980a; 1980b; 1991) the individual who does not fit average profiles, and thus is in some way abnormal, is constantly under surveillance, watched by an authority who remains unseen. One of the effects of the Panopticon is 'to induce in the inmate a state of conscious and permanent visibility that assures the autonomous functioning of power' (Foucault 1991, p. 201). Within research training (education) areas this has been manifested in ways of supervising that act to construct normative models of being and behaving for students and supervisors alike.

The resultant masks of homogeneity thus constructed apply no less to international research higher degree supervision, yet in some ways loom as a sort of Star Trek-type of *Last Frontier* in that discourses of international research higher degree supervision have constructed this as part of an inviolate academic tradition. Research higher degree pursuit in western universities then emerges as a discursive field in which it is by no means evident that western forms of knowledge production are in any way decentred, as suggested by Aronowitz and Giroux (1991) regarding the effects of globalization. Research higher degree supervision has its own particular forms of production and distribution of knowledge processes and protocols. International research higher degree students from non-western institutions arriving at Australian universities will not only find their situation at odds with assertions of decentring western forces; they will also find their situations marginalized within privileged Oxbridge traditions of research higher degree supervision that accord their prior learning and academic achievements the status of inferior forms of knowledge production, if indeed there is any recognition of their having knowledge at all. They will find no space in which any sort of dialogic engagement with western and non-western postgraduate supervision traditions is possible.

CONSTRAINTS ON CONSTRUCTS: THE FORCES OF POSTGRADUATE STUDIES

We have not even found spaces in which a questioning of such supervisory traditions may occur as far as supervision of domestic research higher degree students are concerned(Barron and Zeegers, 2002; Zeegers and Barron, 2000; Zeegers and Barron, 2008). We are not alone in suggesting that this of any more importance than dealing with issues of international postgraduate study (Bruce and Bromeld, 1999; Grant and Graham, 1994; Knight, 1999; Ryan, 2000), but we do contend that the issues in relation to international research higher degree students need to be dealt with as well. Given the supervision problems that domestic research higher degree students face as being of some urgency, there is even more need for supervisors of international research higher degree students to question the relevance of what has became traditional discourse to inform their practice. Supervisory practices embedded in Oxbridge discourses of homogenous elites have not been entirely relevant since the 1993 massification of higher education which has produced a flow-on to higher research degree student demographics, yet they continue as if that change had never occurred (Barron and Zeegers, 2002). These have in effect structured ways in which supervisors of both domestic and international research higher degree students will engage in their own practices of supervision and dealings with subject disciplines and knowledge formations.

We would argue that, within poststructuralist theories the individual is constructed by the discourses that are available. The individual also resists certain discourses, but the effects of normalization operate so that individuals will privilege particular constructions of their subjectivity. According to Foucault (1980a; 1980b), the power for current, hegemonic conservative discourses to be oppressive arises when one way of knowing is understood to be the 'truth', but this can be resisted by declining to take up normalising discourses. Although we find this suggestion not to engage in normalizing techniques appealing, we also see that international research higher degree students may not be able even to identify what these are, let alone how resistance might be possible in practice. Although it may be in some utopian sense a good idea to avoid normalizing practices, embeddedness in discursive practices of research higher degree and its institutions will probably mean that this cannot in reality be achieved. The question then is not whether to avoid such forms of institutionalized behaviours. It is rather to educate international students and their supervisors to question taken for granted truths, so that normalized and normalizing behaviours are critiqued for their effects in terms of hegemonies and the possibilities of resisting dominant discourses. Cherryholmes (1988) states that dominant discourses determine what counts as true, important, relevant and what gets spoken and who speaks. Oppositional discourses are seen as discourses offered by those who resist and contest the dominant interpretation of *truth*.

SILENCES: THE LITERATURE OF POSTGRADUATE STUDIES

One such force in this sort of *truth* production is the International English Language Testing System (IELTS). The cost of acquisition of English language proficiency, coupled with the now virtually compulsory IELTS score for entry to Australian institutions is bought at a high price, and demand drives the price and the value upwards rather than otherwise. This is part of what is described as the next focus for marketing activities for the corporate sector (Dahringer et al, 1994), being on services, which currently account for 30% of world trade, as 'the site for the next great battle for global corporations' in the form of telecommunications, business services, entertainment, banking, finance, insurance, tourism and *education*' (p. 146. Italics added). Indeed, the English Language Intensive Courses for Overseas Student (ELICOS) industry in the financial year of 2000-2001 alone generated a turnover calculated as the exact amount of that year's national Budget surplus (Cox, 2001). With the Test of English as a Foreign Language (TOEFL) now redundant as far as most western universities are concerned, there is a general trend to the minimum level acceptable for entry to these universities set at Band 6 in at least one of the four macro skills of Reading, Writing, Listening and Speaking. It is important to note that an international student does not need to be at this level in all of the areas in all universities. Some will accept a Band 6 score in

Speaking or Listening, for example, as indicating a proficiency in the English language that can accommodate the demands of university study.

We would suggest that it is an unusual university that sets its assessment tasks as purely oral. The privileged form of assessment is that of formal academic writing, and one with which even native-speaking English students, who can be rated as being above IELTS Band 9, have difficulty. Academic writing, whatever the language of its conduct, has its own situations, its own registers, and its own codes concepts in terms of descriptors articulated by Halliday and Hassan (1985), each of which is to be negotiated via sophisticated linguistic conventions to satisfy stringent requirements for academic success. In research higher degree studies, the sophistication reaches even higher levels, and these within the essentially private educational acts transacted between supervisor and student (Barron and Zeegers, 2002).

Table 1 is a set of descriptors for the various Bands (Farquhar, 1999, p. 123):

Table 1. IELTS bands: Description of relevant English proficiency

BAND	DESCRIPTION
6. Competent user:	Has generally effective command of the language despite some inaccuracies, inappropriacies and misunderstandings. Can use and understand fairly complex language, particularly in familiar situations
7. Good user:	Has operational command of the language, though with occasional inaccuracies, inappropriacies and misunderstandings in some situations. Generally handles complex language well and understands detailed reasoning.
8. Very good user:	Has fully operational command of the language with only occasional unsystematic inaccuracies and inappropriacies. Misunderstandings may occur in unfamiliar situations. Handles complex detailed argumentation well.
9. Expert user:	Has fully operational command of the language: appropriate, accurate and fluent with complete understanding

Even a cursory glance at the Band 6 descriptors suggests the skills described as being hopelessly inadequate as a basis for the task of the international postgraduate in setting up a research project within Oxbridge conventions. The emphasis on 'familiar contexts' belies the need for the production of original work that will generate new knowledge, or even use existing knowledge in new ways. A Band 6 international student will have enough trouble accessing the scholarly works of leading researchers even to generate a review of the literature, let alone generate new literature in the form of an examinable thesis. Even so, such Bands and their descriptors tend to be accepted uncritically as IELTS examiners are bound to secrecy as part of their training. With only a small number of IELTS examiners world wide (that is, approximately 2,000) there is a limit to the knowledge that enrolment officers have when they accept international students for postgraduate candidature.

Thus is generated a demand for implicit faith in a single testing device by those not initiated to IELTS, constructing a major barrier to international students' research higher degree successes as application to and acceptance by a western university is not necessarily predicated on shared understandings of what the various Bands indicate about a candidate, nor about how ratings in one band coheres with ratings in others. It ignores concepts of threshold language levels that may heavily influence a non-native English speaker's ability to respond to English language encountered, especially in unfamiliar settings (see for example Lin, 2002). It generates a truth about the student, without any real questioning of how that *truth* has been constructed.

This sort of combination of academic language conventions and a preferred system of testing language proficiencies constitute a major discursive apparatus underpinning discourses of international research higher degree students before they ever arrive at the western university that has enrolled them, embracing them as integral to the institution's internationalization program within discourses of globalization. Its blatant masking of language difficulties is a problem consistently identified by western supervisors of international research higher degree students. Even more telling, it is represented as a construction of problems that the students themselves have. It is not represented as a fault within the testing system as a predictor of academic success at the levels set at all, and generally comes under headings of *Lack of English Language Proficiency* in the literature on problem aspects of supervising international research higher degree students. The student is constructed as deviant from the norm, or as lacking ability, or both, despite an educational background (albeit a non-western one) that has produced this higher research degree candidate.

This then creates a sort of 'regime of truth' where these are constructed as problems that the students themselves need to address, albeit with the assistance of *English for Academic Purposes* courses designed and delivered by the relevant university. The most culturally sensitive writers in the field outline what they perceive as problems arising from a lack of English language proficiency, and recommend immediate attention to this deficiency in their students (Ballard and Clanchy, 1991; Bartlett and Mercer, 2001; Bruce and Bromeld, 1999; Knight, 1999; Sillitoe and Crosling, 1999). Even where lack of language proficiency is acknowledged as more than matters of grammar, spelling and lexis, the argument still turns back onto students as needing some form of instruction in what are presented as the correct western forms.

A reading of the literature points up disorders of discourse (Wodak, 1996) where ontological and epistemological factors as to what constitutes knowledge and the presentation of it in research higher degree endeavours simply do not mesh. We see an urgent need for genuine dialogic interaction with such material, which implies much more than an attempt to account for non-western constructs of knowledge. There is some important work to guide us in this, especially in relation to diverse forms of academic writing and scholarly works across cultures (Kaplan, 1966). While critiques of such work suggests that such identified forms more properly belong to cultures than languages themselves (Clyne, 1994), such perspectives present possibilities of resisting discourses of deficit as constructing subjects to be attended to in terms of making them More Like Us, if not Completely Like Us. Yet we still use benchmarks against which we are able to measure deficits, or deficiencies in people, that we may strive to fix, or remedy, or for which to compensate. Western responses to alternative discourse styles still marginalise the non-western with disparaging comments about the Other research higher degree students, such as 'learning at the feet of the Master', as if this is somehow anathema to authentic teaching and learning.

A review of a number of *English for Academic* types of courses that have been developed for international students at undergraduate and research higher degree levels (Zeegers, 2003) has pointed up glaring discourses of deficit where such things as statements comparing American and Mexican children (Samovar and Porter, 1995), show that the latter 'are usually not as competitive as white children' (p. 243), and a bland assertion that in the cultures of China, Japan and Korea 'learning is passive, and students are expected to do a great deal of rote memorization' (p. 146). They tend towards picking up rather uncritically claims in relation to strong emphases in Oriental patterns of discourse as non-assertive and indirect, evidenced by a more oblique writing style that relies on implication, and a weakness in relation to academic debate among Japanese students, for example, because of loss-of-face concerns (Hinds, 1987), and such works as that of Myers' (1981) explanation of cultural differences between Africa, a big country with many cultural groups, and western ways. Samuelowicz (1987) for example, in another article so often used by those giving advice to international postgraduate students, refers to international students as being 'accustomed to be passive recipients of knowledge' (p. 125), with Malaysian students characterized as having good memories but not analytical minds, lacking initiative and reluctant to participate in class (p. 123).

Constructed in such ways as being inferior by the very people who are to work with them as part of the western postgraduate experience, international students are then given as academic exercises this sort of literature, compelling in its invitations to take up the discourses for themselves. This is done even as they are to perform as researchers within systems of supervisory protocols that are based discourses of collegiality and mentorship. Having been castigated for prior experience based on learning at the feet of the master, they are now to engage in more of the same as inculcation processes are brought into play.

INCULCATION

Even where cultural differences and expectations between international research higher degree students and their supervisors are sympathetically outlined, they are followed up with exhortations that western epistemologies and ontologies be 'inculcated' in international students (Knight, 1999; Smith, 1999). Disorders of discourse are thus inextricably networked with discourses of deficit. Inculcation as applied to notions of values does not carry with it any suggestion of parity of esteem regarding these values. Rather, it suggests that students are unable to distinguish for themselves when it comes to conflicting sets of values. Samuelowicz (1987) refers to 'reproducing orientation', seen as evidence of a surface approach to study based on rote learning, memorising facts to be reproduced as demanded by established practices within Asian education systems (p. 123). Within Western systems, memorization and rote learning as surface learning have received bad press from Rousseau (1762) to Dewey (1933) to Freire (1970). Yet applying the same constructs to non-western systems may not be as valid as it may appear on the surface (see for example Zeegers, 2010).

A closer examination of this as it applies to Chinese learners serves to illustrate the point. There is a general recognition that the academic achievement of Asian students in western institutions is high (Cortazzi and Lixian, 2001; Ho, 2001; Watkins and Biggs, 2001) a paradox indeed if the purported rote learning deficiency is so distasteful to devoted educators. The supervisor will inculcate distaste, for example, for Confucian-based approaches to learning as repetitive, using memorization as a method to recall and a most valuable tool on the path to knowledge (Watkins and Biggs, 2001). The previously Confucian-based student will learn that their entire educational and thus cultural value system of such learning that has helped them to arrive at research higher degree levels of study is, in the context of Western tradition, rote memorization being synonymous with surface learning, producing no internalized understandings and hence no knowledge. The student is to have this inculcated, and learn to denigrate their own academic traditions, even if they are centuries long with a remarkable record of stability and continuity across generations (Hofstede, 1986).

They will also have been inculcated with the belief that the only valued path to knowledge is the western one, even if their whole Confucian-based learning tradition has produced students who outperform westerners throughout the world, especially in Science and Mathematics (Watkins and Biggs, 2001, p. 3). Watkins and Biggs (2001) examine research that shows the apparent paradox resolved as Chinese teachers and students utilising memorising and learning as complementary, interlocking processes, actually developing understanding through processes of memorization (p. 6). This is not characteristic of the surface learning normally ascribed to memorization. Ignoring such evidence means that discourses of inculcation are unimpeded, and no resistance by supervisors or their students is really possible.

Hence, privileged discourses construct international research higher degree students as subjects within a 'cultural-deficit' discursive field (Ninnes, Aitchison and Kalos, 1999), one that constructs silences in which challenges to stereotypes can be engaged by neither student nor supervisor as taken-for-granted values remain inviolate. What is more, they construct deliberate and systematic attempts to reduce variations between international higher degree research students in a globalizing world, framed entirely by western-based discourses of academic skills. The foregrounding of these is relentless, effectively privileging western academic discourses over any other, and presuming that any prior knowledge that international research higher degree students may have simply does not exist or is not worth knowing. It treats them as starting from The Year Zero, and from that point there is a void of ignorance so vast that it may appear impossible to fill it with the requisite knowledge in Western terms. In relation to features identified by Kaplan (1966), being able to synthesise points of view, to reach an harmonious resolution of tensions within disagreements and discontinuities, itself a highly skilled undertaking, is given no recognition whatever. Being able to construct a sonata-like statement of theme to be teased out in the body of the work and brought back to a satisfying concluding whole, another highly skilled undertaking, is similarly ignored. Each and all of the Kaplanesque skills of academic discourses, except for the English one, exist so far on the margins of academic discourse as to be non-existent.

A refreshing difference in approach is that of Ryan (2000), whose guide to teaching international students includes a chapter on postgraduates. Her work (Ryan, 2000) is aimed at academic staff, those who 'recognise that the first step towards [improving their teaching of international students] is to improve their …practices and to change some of what they currently do or believe', advising such staff to position themselves as 'an anthropologist of your own culture' (p. 5). Suggestions of academics themselves taking up alternative discourses enable questioning of traditions that have so much been appropriated by discipline foci that these have themselves become naturalized within the academe. Such self-anthropological positions may give rise to interesting results, possibly a different reading of western approaches to research and research studies, perhaps even along the lines suggested by Kuhn (1961/1970).

We doubt that this would ever happen. It would require a perhaps too painful an examination of the discourses that construct western practice. Far easier is to put the international student in this position of self-doubt. Mei's story (Aspland, 1999; Ryan, 2000) comes to mind, as she struggles with being positioned by one supervisor as 'stupid' only to encounter a different one who acknowledges that she is not so. In her case, it has been a matter of her own education background being constructed as 'passive', and she herself therefore as lazy; 'dependent' upon her supervisor, and therefore immature; a 'low level thinker', and therefore a poor achiever (Aspland, 1900, p. 37). Nonetheless, having had a number of such myths debunked as part of her experience with her new supervisor, she was still to learn to study in western ways, taking up a subject position of having to become a more acceptable western-type critical thinker than one who tries to understand the knowledge and wisdom of those who had already blazed a knowledge path before her. What is more, she herself acknowledges this gratefully, as she states she is slowly learning to get better at western ways of thinking, thereby herself taking up normalizing discourses as she proceeds on the path of western education success.

Globalization nevertheless suggests that we are no longer locked into neo-colonialist discourses that position students like Mei in such ways. It assumes that these discourses have been well and truly, not to mention rightfully, debunked. Appreciation and celebration of multiculturalism positions educational undertakings as part of discourses of inclusion, of welcome diversity. This goes beyond practical concerns like helping international postgraduate students to learn to function in what we have dubbed *Academic English* as soon as possible—it goes into the depths of culture. Yet we still take the step of offering supplementary courses based on concepts of deficits—international research higher degree students to be treated, remediated, or somehow fixed to overcome constructed barriers of non-western academic traditions. This can only happen where such discourses are privileged.

Resisting the Paradigm

We question the inevitability of moving from the point of defining academic undertakings in terms of western models, and urge resistance to the pressure to shape international research higher degree students according to practices inherent in such processes. First of all, we question the assumptions underlying constructs of non-western teaching and learning. Such assumptions privilege westernized ontological and epistemological systems in universities and construct international research higher degree students as being subjects of their own education rather playing an active role in shaping it. When we enrol international research higher degree students in our universities, we are engaging in more than the teaching of a set of what (Luke, 1991) might question as being 'neutral competencies' (p. 140). This is done as part of higher education in western countries, including Australia, on a massive scale, not least of which is impelled by pushes within globalization discourses for universities to internationalise. Even teasing out certain cultural backgrounds within constructs of what it means to be an international research higher degree student (for example African, Malaysian, Confucian-based) and then lumping certain types, such as oriental cultures, together is not helpful. A study of Korean and Japanese international English language students (Bitchener, 2002) suggests these two socially and culturally similar backgrounds demonstrated dissimilar interactional behaviour in language learning (p. 10). Puleo and Hird (2002) have explored Japanese learner responses to different teaching strategies in the light of learning styles theory and concluded that the fact of being Japanese did not exclude students from decision-making tasks within Australian educational institutions. Rather, it meant that the teaching styles would have to be adjusted to suit the learners.

Similarly unhelpful is the lumping together of all international research higher degree students as some sort of postgraduate cohort regardless of the discipline or subject areas of their study. Research higher degree supervisors have not yet even come to interrogate the protocols of their own discipline areas so that we still have the bifurcation of physical sciences and social sciences research. Any social science researcher is aware of just how much justification they are required to undertake for their own research in relation to just how far it departs from discursively constructed benchmarks of the physical sciences.

RESEARCH TRADITIONS

Discourses of western research traditions construct a positivist as one who uses the hypothetico-deductive approach to attempt to prove or disprove hypotheses, presuming an objective reality that may be observed, documented and tested by a dispassionate, objective researcher who is not in any way involved in the experiments conducted. They construct a social scientist as one who will reject the very possibility of such a position, and instead of setting hypotheses to be proved, will research on the basis of questions to be explored via careful observation of a social world of which they are very much a part (see also Zeegers and Barron, 2010). While the work of Kuhn (1961/1970) has put paid to much of the claims of science made by the so-called objective stance of positivist and hypothetico-deductive approaches, the tradition continues. This is in spite of questions regarding the claims of the approach in relation to producing new discoveries, new theories, new universal knowledge based on the ideal of scientists as disinterested, objective people making careful observations and conducting experiments to produce rigorously analysed data.

Charlesworth (1982) takes up this idea as a myth, part of ritual behaviour of the scientific community which is so far removed from what it says it is that it tells the experimenters not only *what* to look for but also *how* to look for it (p. 30). It suggests something quite other than the ideal of an independent observer waiting for nature to reveal itself in some sort of manifestation scientifically discovered. Chalmers (1982) argues that 'there is just no method that enables scientific theories to be proven true or probably true', citing Feyeraband's contention 'that science has no special features that render it intrinsically superior to other branches of knowledge such as ancient myths or voodoo' (pp. xv-xvii) (see also Zeegers and Barron, 2008). The field of science is itself a contested field, with claims and counter claims as to the truth or universal laws, not as objective as has been presented. Such contention does not come up in the literature on international research higher degree student supervision.

The point that we are arguing here is that the sort of questioning of privileged scientific research discourses that Kuhn (1961/1970) makes possible effectively destroyed the power of Baconian-based convention over academic research, and thereby opened up new discursive fields for the social scientist to exploit, if only they have the courage to do so. Even then, there are small pockets within western academic communities that, in the completeness of their taking up the voodoo/myth discourses, have pioneered new forms of knowledge generation and dissemination. There are theses submitted, examined and found acceptable as meeting requirements of social science research that, in regard to their research rigour and knowledge production, claim validity while their dissemination within the academe takes the form of narratives, poetry, film, CD-ROM. There is a similar development in the production of academic books, all serving to inform the research activities of others in new stimulating, exciting and interesting ways. These are not rejected as failures on ontological and epistemological grounds in relation to the production of original work and new knowledge. Quite the reverse is the case. Research communities are witnessing spaces opening up even more as such creative works come onto the scene as valid research undertakings.

POSSIBILITIES FOR THE FUTURE

We currently have a situation where the form that dominates is a research process incorporating the production of a thesis AND a process of examination, both of which are to be engaged in western discourses of knowledge production and dissemination, including protocols of supervision and originality, independent student work (so why have a supervisor at all?) within a framework of quite private actions and behaviours based on supervisor beliefs and theories, properly tested or otherwise (Barron and Zeegers, 2002). All of this is in place, sacrosanct and unquestioned in a context where, if the government-commissioned forecasts of international student markets over the next two decades are correct, we can expect to see an increase in the number of international students that will serve to inflate the research higher degree student numbers as a matter of course. The figures suggested are an increase of the current 102,000 international students to 996,000 in 2025, with the average for individual universities rising from 2,500 to 23,000 (Böhm et al, 2002, pp. vi-vii). In the context of western countries' declining population growth, this means that if we are serious about building research capacity, international research higher degree students are the means by which universities may develop that sort of critical mass required for vibrant, dynamic research cultures necessary in a globalizing world where it is crucial to pursue wider-ranging research interests than would otherwise be possible.

We look to the suggestive possibilities of communities of practice (Lave and Wenger, 1994) and as part of these, Lave and Wenger's notion of Legitimate Peripheral Participation as providing useful models to explore (Zeegers and Barron, 2000; Barron and Zeegers, 2002). Within communities of practice, roles of various members at various stages of their activities and progress may be systematically supported, with good theory to underpin the communities' endeavours. The position of the supervisor as mentor, within a framework suggested by Lusted's (1986) discussion of the role of pedagogy may be further explored. Within such a framework any number of possibilities may be canvassed: using pedagogic conversations (Palmer, 1998); confronting power relations issues (Bartlett and Mercer, 2001; Green and Lee, 1995; 1999); engaging reflective practice (Schön, 1987; 1990), and so on. These are models already in place, and we can adapt them to suit the changing requirements of higher degree research students generally.

Even so, details within such models need to be worked out. We argue that there is a need to go further and acknowledge the international higher degree research students and their supervision have particular needs that are not currently being acknowledged, let alone addressed. We argue that the language problem needs to be tackled in earnest. Band 6 is far too low a level in any of the macro skills for a higher degree research student whose first language is not English and who is required to produce a thesis written in English. A number of strategic decisions need to be made. A major one is an insistence on Band 9 proficiency levels before undertaking a higher degree research in English. That can be done in Australia as part of the degree, with credit points and/or exemptions negotiated for the extra-thesis work involved. We also argue that this needs to be done as part of properly constituted and accredited ELICOS courses, or their equivalents, with systematic and rigorous overseeing of all centres that teach such accredited courses.

At the same time, given the very electronic tools that have made the globalization phenomenon possible in the first place, associate supervisors may be employed from the students' countries of origin to assist in the supervisory process, making it more public and thereby more accountable in relation to cultural sensitivities and academic language conventions. This would give rise to international higher research degree students being supervised by a panel of experts which include experts from their own countries of equal standing with Australian supervisors, connected by electronic information and communication technologies.

We argue further that extensive interpreter/translator facilities must be established, staffed by trained multi-lingual academics who will be designated advisors to international higher research degree students where they have opted for English as the medium for their research activities. Even so, international higher degree research students need not have only English as the language for producing a thesis. Their own languages need not be considered inadequate to such a task, unless we are to position all non-English languages as inferior. Theses are currently produced in German, French, Spanish, Italian, Chinese, Japanese and so on, with no adverse effect on the academe as a whole. Present requirements for all theses to be examined by international experts suggests that mechanisms are in place for non-English speaking examiners to be used for this purpose, and their numbers may be extended to provide for a number of non-English based international examiners of international higher research degree students. Given the increased and increasing numbers of non-western-based higher research degree student enrolments, the availability of a number of qualified supervisors in a range of languages to enable the whole of the degree to be undertaken in languages other than English must be forming and growing all the time.

If the forecasts are correct, the importance of supervisory approaches that are relevant to and supportive of international higher degree research students cannot be underestimated. We cannot go on as we have been, relying on the strength of discursive elements to force a climate of inculcation of western knowledge production systems. We argue that the current state of affairs requires a radical rethinking within discourses of higher research degree supervision. It is along these lines that we present the following as an alternative reading of current discourses (borrowing from Hofstede, 1986), an example of the suggestive possibilities of discourse analysis:

> The western research higher degree student derives from a relatively recent education tradition that, in its emphasis on the production of original work, encourages them to be blatant in their questioning of all that established scholars have done before, rejecting and proving wrong the work of their cultural sages, and reading all the literature they encounter with a critical eye as part of their seizing upon any chance to find gaps in culturally-

constructed knowledge that their work may fill. They expect to work independently from their supervisors, constructing their own research projects with minimal supervision, and so in this isolation are expected to become masters themselves in their fields without ever having really proved that they have been able to internalise the work of more experienced and knowledgable predecessors. In such ways, they may be considered intellectually arrogant and culturally destructive, conditioned never to learn how to generate and disseminate knowledge in the subtle, nuanced and respectful ways of non-western traditions. Their own restricted language background constrains them to think entirely within the cultural parameters of that language and never to explore alternative ways of knowing or being. It is incumbent upon international research higher degree students abroad to try to accommodate these backgrounds as politely as possible, while affirming the validity of their own educational backgrounds as appropriate for their own needs as higher degree research students.

REFERENCES

Apple, Michael W. Educating the "Right" *Way: Markets, Standards, God, and Inequality.* New York and London: Routledge Falmer, 2001.

Arambewela, Rodney. "Right Ticket for Research." Postgraduate Report, Campus Revue, 2003.

Aronowitz, Stanley, and Henri A. Giroux. *Postmodern Education: Politics, Culture and Criticism. Minneapolis:* University of Minnesota Press, 1991.

Aspland, Tania. "You Learn Round and I Learn Square: Mei's Story." In Supervising Postgraduates from Non English Speaking Backgrounds, edited by Y. Ryan and O. Zuber-Skerritt, 25-39. Buckingham: Open University Press, 1999.

Australian Broadcasting Commission. "Indian students in $78m snub to Australia"Dec 30, 20092009 Retrieved May 30, 2010 from http://www.abc.net.au/news /stories/2009/12/30/2782416.htm

Ballard, Brigid, and John Clanchy. *Teaching Students from Overseas: A Brief Guide for Lecturers and Supervisors.* Melbourne: Longman Cheshire, 1991.

Barron, Deirdre, and Margaret Zeegers. "'O' for Osmosis, 'P' for Pedagogy: Fixing the Postgraduate Wheel of Fortune." (2005) accessed September 17, 2010 http://www.le.ac.uk/teaching/teaching/focus/postgrad.html.

Bartlett, Alison, and Gina Mercer, eds. Postgraduate Research Supervision: Transforming (R)Elations. New York: Peter Lang, 2001.

Bitchener, J. "Language Learning Opportunities Provided by Japanese and Korean ESL Learners During Negotiated Interaction." *EA Journal* 20, no. 1 (2002): 8-16.

Böhm, Anthony, Dorothy Davis, Denis Meares, and David Pierce. "Global Student Mobility 2025: *Forecasts of the Global Demand for International Higher Education.*" Sydney: IDP Education, 2002.

Bradley, Denise. *Review of Australian Higher Education Final Report.* Australian Commonwealth Government. Canberra. December. 2008.

Bruce, Christine S., and Gerald H. Bromeld. "Encouraging Student-Directed Research and Critical Thinking in Nesb Students." In *Supervising Postgraduates from Non English Speaking Backgrounds*, edited by Y. Ryan and O. Zuber-Skerritt, 156-66. Buckingham: Open University Press, 1999.

Chalmers, Alan F. What Is This Thing Called Science?: *An Assessment of the Nature and Status of Science and Its Methods*. 2nd ed. Melbourne: University of Queensland Press, 1982.

Charlesworth, Max. *Science, Non-Science, and Pseudo-Science*. Geelong: Deakin University Press, 1982.

Cherryholmes, Cleo H. *Power and Criticism: Poststructural Investigations in Education*. New York: Teachers College Press, 1988.

Clyne, Michael. *Inter-Cultural Communication at Work: Cultural Values in Discourse*. Melbourne: Cambridge University Press, 1994.

Connell, Robert W. "How to Supervise a PhD." *Vestes* 2 (1985): 38-41.

Cortazzi, Martin, and Jin Lixian. "Large Classes in China: 'Good' Teachers and Interaction." In *Teaching the Chinese Learner: Psychological and Pedagogical Perspectives*, edited by D. A. Watkins and J. B. Biggs, 115-34. Hong Kong and Melbourne: Comparative Education Centre and ACER, 2001.

Cox, Christine. "Welcome Address." Paper presented at the 14th EA Education Conference: Innovations in ELICOS for the 21st Century, *Manly, NSW*, October 18-20 2001.

Cryer, Pat. Handling Common Dilemmas in Supervision: *Issues in Postgraduate Supervision, Teaching and Management: A Series of Consultative Guides No 2*. London: Society for Research in Higher Education, 1997.

Dahringer, Lee D. et al "Consumer Involvement in Services: An International Evaluation." In *Globalization of Consumer Markets*: *Structures and Strategies*, edited by S. S. Hassan and E. Kaynack, 138-49. New York: International Business Press, 1994.

Davis, Bronwyn, and Rom Harre. "Contradictions in Lived and Told Narratives." *Research on Language and Social Interaction* 25 (1991/92): 1-36.

Dewey, John. How We Think. Chicago: Henry Regnery, 1933.

Farquhar, Mary. "'Third Places' and Teaching English for Research Purposes." In *Supervising Postgraduates from Non- English Speaking Backgrounds,* edited by Y. Ryan and O. Zuber-Skerritt, 119-30. Buckingham: The Society for Research into Higher Education and the Open University Press, 1999.

Foucault, Michel. *The Archeology of Knowledge*. Canada: Tavistock, 1974.

———. *The Discourse on Language*. New York: Harper Colophon, 1976.

———. The Foucault Reader Edited by Paul Rabinow. London and Ringwood, Vic: Penguin, 1991.

———. *The Order of Things: An Archeology of the Human Sciences*. New York: Vintage, 1973.

———. "Truth and Power." In *Power/Knowledge: Selected Interviews and Other Writings 1972-1977*, edited by C. Gordon, 109-32. New York: Pantheon, 1980.

Foucault, Michel. "The Eye of Power." In *Power/Knowledge: Selected Interviews and Other Writings 1972-1977,* edited by C. Gordon, 146-65. New York: Pantheon, 1980.

Friere, Paulo. Pedagogy of the Oppressed. New York: Seabury, 1970.

Gane, Mike, and Terry Johnson, eds. *Foucault's New Domains*. London and New York: Routledge, 1993.

Grant, Barbara, and Adele Graham. "'Guidelines for Discussion': A Tool for Managing Postgraduate Supervision." In *Quality in Postgraduate Education,* edited by O. Zuber-Skerritt and Y. Ryan, 165-77. London: Kogan Page, 1994.

Green, Bill, and Alison Lee. "Educational Research, Disciplinarity and Postgraduate Pedagogy: On the Subject of Supervision." In *Supervision of Postgraduate Research in Education: Review of Australian Research in Education No. 5,* edited by A. Holbrook and S. Johnstone, 207-23. Coldstream: Australian Association for Research in Education, 1999.

Halliday, Michael, and Ruqaiya Hassan. Language Context and Text: Aspects of Language in a Social-Semiotic Perspective. Geelong: Deakin, 1985.

Harloe, Michael, C.G. Pickvance, and John Urry, eds. Place, Policy, and Politics: Do Localities Matter? London and Boston: Unwin Hyman, 1990.

Healy, Guy. "Overseas student enrolments in Australia at record high" The Australian Feb 26, 2009, Retrieved September 17, 2009 from: http://www.theaustralian.com.au/news/nation/overseas-students-rise-to-record-high/story-e6frg6nf-1111118973485 (2009a)

Healy, Guy. "Overseas enrolments up" The Australian Sept 23, 2009, Retrieved May 25, 2010 from: http://www.theaustralian.com.au/news/overseas-enrolments-up/story-e6frgcoo-1225778337400 (2009b)

Department of Education, Training and Youth Affairs (DETYA), Higher Education Division. "The Australian Higher Education Quality Assurance Framework." Canberra: Commonwealth Government, 2000.

Hirst, Paul, and Grahame. Thompson. Globalization in Question. London: Polity Press, 1996.

Ho, Irene T. "Are Chinese Teachers Authoritarian?" In *Teaching the Chinese Learner: Psychological and Pedagogical Perspectives*, edited by D. A. Watkins and J. B. Biggs, 99-114. Hong Kong and Melbourne: Comparative Education Centre and ACER, 2001.

Hodson, Peter, and Harold Thomas. "Higher Education as an International Commodity: Ensuring Quality in Partnerships." *Assessment and Evaluation in Higher Education 26,* no. 2 (2001): 101-12.

Hofstede, Geert. "Cultural Differences in Teaching and Learning." *International Journal of Intercultural Relations* 10 (1986): 301-19.

Kaplan, Robert B. "Cultural Thought Patterns in Intercultural Education." *Language Learning* 16, no. 1 and 2 (1966): 1-20.

Knight, Nick. "Responsibilities and Limits in the Supervision of Nesb Research Students in the Social Sciences and Humanities." In *Supervising Postgraduates from Non English Speaking Backgrounds*, edited by Y. Ryan and O. Zuber-Skerritt, 93-100. Buckingham: Open University Press, 1999.

Kuhn, Thomas. *The Structure of Scientific Revolutions.* 2nd ed. Chicago: University of Chicago Press, 1970.

Lash, Scott, and John Urry. *Economies of Signs and Space.* London: Sage Publications, 1994.

Lave, Jean, and Etienne Wenger. Situated Learning: Legitimate Peripheral Participation. New York: Cambridge University Press, 1994.

Levine, S., and P. White. "Exchange as a Conceptual Framework for the Study of Inter-Organisational Relationships." *Administrative Science Quarterly* 5, no. 4 (1961): 583-601.

Lin, Zheng. "Discovering Efl Learners' Perception of Prior Knowledge and Its Roles in Reading Comprehension." *Journal of Research in Reading* 25, no. 2 (2001): 172-90.

Luard, Evan. *The Globalization of Politics: The Changed Focus of Political Action in the Modern World.* London: Macmillan, 1990.

Luke, Alan. "*Literacies as Social Practices.*" English Education October (1991): 131-47.

Lusted, David. "*Why Pedagogy?*" Screen 27, no. 5 (1986): 2-14.

Morey, Anne, and Margie Kitano. *Multicultural Course Transformation in Higher Education.* Boston: Allyn and Bacon, 1997.

Moses, Ingrid. "Redefining Academic Roles: In Support of Teaching." In *Australia's Future Universities,* edited by J. Sharpham and G. Harman, 175-96. New South Wales: University of New England, 1997.

Myers, L. J. "The Nature of Pluralism and the African American Case." *Theory into practice* 20 (1981): 1-22.

Ninnes, Peter, C. Aitchison, and S. Kalos. "Challenges to Stereotypes of International Students' Prior Education Experience: Undergraduate Education in India." *Higher Education Research and Development* 18, no. 3 (1999): 323-42.

Palmer, Parker J. *The Courage to Teach: Exploring the Inner Landscape of a Teacher's Life.* San Francisco: Jossey Bass, 1998.

Puleo, A-M., and B. Hird. "The Effectiveness of Decision-Making Tasks for Japanese Esl Learners." *EA Journal* 20, no. 1 (2002): 24-41.

Rousseau, Jean Jacques. Émile. Paris: Garnier, 1762.

Rowan, Leonie, Leo Bartlett, and Terry Evans. "Prologue." In *Shifting Borders: Globalisation, Localisation and Open and Distance Education*, edited by L. Rowan, L. Bartlett and T. Evans, 3-4. Geelong: Deakin University Press, 1997.

Ryan, Janette. *A Guide to Teaching International Students.* Oxford: Oxford Centre for Staff and Learning Development, 2000.

Ryan, Yoni, and Ortrun Zuber-Skerritt. "Supervising Non English Speaking Background Students in the Globalised University." In *Supervising Postgraduates from Non English Speaking Backgrounds,* edited by Y. Ryan and O. Zuber-Skerritt, 3-11. Buckingham: Open University Press, 1999.

Samovar, L. A., and R. E. Porter. *Culture and Education: Communication between Cultures.* 2nd ed. USA: Wadsworth, 1995.

Samuelowicz, Katherine. "Learning Problems of Overseas Students: Two Sides of a Story." *Higher Education Research and Development* 6, no. 121-134 (1987).

Schön, Donald A. Educating the Reflective Practitioner: Toward a New Design for Teaching and Learning in the Professions. San Francisco: Jossey Bass, 1987.

———, ed. *The Reflective Turn: Case Studies in and on Educational Practice.* New York: Teachers College Press, 1990.

Sillitoe, Jim, and Glenda Crosling. "Thesis Planning and Writing: A Structured Approach." In Supervising Postgraduates from Non English Speaking Backgrounds, edited by Y. Ryan and O. Zuber-Skerritt, 167-74. Buckingham: Open University Press, 1999.

Skilbeck, Malcolm. "Opening Address." Paper presented at the The transition from elite to mass higher education, Canberra 1993.

Smith, Doug. "Supervising NESB Students from Confucian Educational Cultures." In *Supervising Postgraduates from Non English Speaking Backgrounds*, edited by Y. Ryan and O. Zuber-Skerritt, 146-56. Buckingham: Open University Press, 1999.

van der Wende, Marijk, and Don Westerheijden. "International Aspects of Quality Assurance with Special Focus on European Higher Education." *Quality in Higher Education* 7, no. 3 (2001).

Wikipedia. (2010). Violence against Indians in Australia controversy Retrieved May 25, 2010, from http://en.wikipedia.org/wiki.

Wodak, Ruth. *Disorders of Discourse*. New York: Longman, 1996.

Zeegers, Margaret. Focussing on format: Focus groups and ELICOS evaluation. *EA Journal: Winter* (2003): 17-23.

Zeegers, Margaret. " Let's Get Critical: Observations on a Non-Literate Text and Context." *Changing Education: A Journal for Teachers and Administrators* 1, March (1996): 22-24.

Zeegers, Margaret. "Lessons to be Learned from the Other: Teacher Educaiton in Papua New Guinea" In K.Karras and C.C. Wolhuter (Eds), International *Handbook of Teacher Education Worldwide* Vol II: Athens: Atropos. 2010. 829-848

Zeegers, Margaret, and Barron, D. "Discourses of deficit in higher degree research supervisory pedagogies for international students". *Pedagogies: An International Journal,* 3, no. 2 (2008): 1-16.

Zeegers, Margaret , and Deirdre Barron. "More Than an Apprenticeship Model: Legitimate Peripheral Participation and the Postgraduate Research Conference." In *Proceedings of Making Ends Meet: Quality in Postgraduate Research Conference,* edited by M. Kiley and G. Mullins, 179-88. Advisory Centre for University Education, University of Adelaide, Adelaide, (2000).

Zeegers, Margaret, and Deirdre Barron. "To Registrate and/or Deregistrate: Getting onto and Off the Postgraduate Supervisor Register." *International Journal of Learning,* 10, (2003): 721-776.

Zeegers, Margaret, and Deirdre Barron. *Gatekeepers of Knowledge: A Consideration of the Library, the book and the Scholar in the Western World.* Oxford, Cambridge and New Delhi: Chandos Publishing. 2010.

In: Progress in Education. Volume 26
Editor: Robert V. Nata, pp. 53-74
ISBN 978-1-61324-321-3
© 2011 Nova Science Publishers, Inc.

Chapter 3

THE EFFECTIVENESS OF BEHAVIORAL AND ECLECTIC INTERVENTION PROGRAMS FOR 6.5-14 YEARS OLD CHILDREN WITH AUTISTIC SPECTRUM DISORDERS: A CROSS-CULTURAL STUDY

Maria K. Makrygianni,[*][1] *Angeliki Gena*[2] *and Phil Reed*[1]

[1]Swansea University, U.K
[2]University of Athens, Greece

ABSTRACT

The effectiveness of behavioral intervention programs for children with Autistic Spectrum Disorders has been the subject of several studies. However, most of the studied programs were usually from UK and USA, although these types of programs exist in many more countries. Additionally, there is lack of cross-cultural studies, which could indicate to what extent the findings from the studied programs can be generalized and the impact of cultural environment to the effectiveness of intervention programs. The study in this chapter constitutes one of the first cross-cultural studies on the effectiveness of intervention programs for children with Autistic Spectrum Disorders. It compares the effectiveness of both behavioral and eclectic intervention programs for 6.5-to 14- year old children with Autistic Spectrum Disorders, from Greece and UK/Republic of Ireland, in a period of nine months. Some of the developmental factors that were assessed were the non-verbal IQ, language understanding, adaptive behavior, repetitive and stereotypic behaviors and other developmental difficulties of the children. The findings of the study indicate, that (a) the ABA and eclectic programs in English speaking countries were equally effective, (b) the Greek ABA programs were almost equally effective as the programs in the English speaking countries and superior to the eclectic Greek programs, (c) the Greek eclectic programs were less effective than all the other programs both in Greece and UK/Republic of Ireland.

---

[*] Address for correspondence: Maria K. Makrygianni, Milonos 23-25, 11745. Athens, Greece. Tel: +30 6936492959.

INTRODUCTION

There has been a growing interest in cross-cultural issues related to Autism Spectrum Disorders (ASD). There are several studies on the prevalence, diagnosis, and education of children with ASD, in different cultural environments (e.g., Tanoue, Oda, Asano, and Kawashima, 1988; Wilder, Dyches, Obiakor, and Algozzine, 2004; Williams, Glasson, Wray, Tuck, Helmer, Bower, and Mellis, 2005; Zhang, and Ji, 2005; Zionts, and Zionts, 2003). However, there are no cross-cultural studies addressing the effectiveness of intervention programs. The vast majority of the studies conducted in the field of ASD have not taken into account variables associated with race or culture (Connors, and Donnellan, 1998; Dyches, Wilder, Sudweeks, Obiakor, and Algozzine, 2004). Rather, they have mainly focused on the effectiveness of intervention programs on American, and Western European populations of children with ASD (Forehand, and Kotchick, 1996; Rogers, and Vismara, 2008).

Nevertheless, cultural issues could well moderate the effectiveness of intervention programs (Rogers, and Vismara, 2008). Different home values, family traditions, and socio-cultural experiences, as well as cultural differences in expectations about child independence, parental authority, and the availability of educational services, could significantly influence the applications of interventions, as well as their effectiveness, the teachers' input, and the family's contribution on the child's progress (Dyches et al., 2004; Gonzalez, Brusca-Vega, and Yawkey, 1997; Utley and Obiakor, 2001, Ysseldyke, Algozzine, and Thurlow, 2000).

To the best of our knowledge, there are currently no studies that compare the effectiveness of intervention programs for children with ASD from different cultural environments. The present study aspires to contribute towards this direction, providing some comparative data from intervention programs in Greece, and the U.K./Republic of Ireland. As this is one of the first studies to assess the effectiveness of Greek intervention programs for children with ASD (Kaderoglou, 2000), it provides a thorough description of those programs, and a comparison of some of their features with those of intervention programs from English-speaking countries (UK, and Republic of Ireland). The English-speaking sample was chosen as a comparison sample because it is the most commonly studied in this field.

The types of programs that were chosen for comparison purposes were those based on ABA (Applied Behavior Analysis), and eclectic programs. The ABA programs are based on the principles derived from ABA research, and constitute the most widely studied intervention approach in autism research (e.g., Anderson, Avery, DiPietro, Edwards, and Christian, 1987; Bibby, Eikeseth, Martin, Mudford, and Reeves, 2002; Birnbrauer and Leach, 1993; Eldevik, Eikeseth, Jahr, and Smith, 2006; Reed, Osborne, and Corness, 2007b). The eclectic intervention programs include features from different intervention approaches, such as TEACCH, PECS, interactive models, and ABA teaching techniques. Eclectic programs were chosen because they are the most commonly used control group on previous studies, as well as the most commonly employed educational intervention (e.g., Eldevik et al., 2006; Howard, Sparkman, Cohen, Green, and Stanislaw, 2005; Reed et al., 2007b).

Unlike most of the previous studies (e.g., McEachin, Smith, and Lovaas, 1993; Smith, Eikeseth, Klevstrand, and Lovaas, 1997), the present study extended the outcome measures further than IQ, adaptive behavior, and language test scores. Specifically, the present study assessed the progress of the children with ASD on the developmental domains where the core difficulties of ASD are located (e.g., social interaction, communication, and restricted, repetitive, and stereotyped behavior), on the developmental domains that have been studied from some previous researchers (such as intellectual abilities), and some which cover additional developmental aspects. This approach to children's developmental progress could help produce a more rounded picture of the children's abilities at the beginning of the study, as well as their progress across time. Additionally, given that the intervention programs, and some family features are inter-correlated, and influence the children's progress (Gabriels, Hill, Pierce, Rogers, and Wehner, 2001; Moes, and Frea, 2002; Osborne, McHugh, Saunders, and Reed, 2007; Robbins, and Dunlap, 1992; Robbins, Dunlap, and Plienis, 1991), the present study also included, and assessed some family factors (family status, routines, family support, parent-child relationship, and parental stress).

Of course, cultural differences constitute a very wide field, which is difficult to assess completely. In the current study, the measurement of cultural factors was based on questionnaires that were already used for other purposes in the present study. Such factors included family routines, family support, parental stress, parent-child relations, marital status, and educational background. These factors do not refer directly to cultural differences, but their outcomes could be partly attributed to such differences. Specifically, family support that comes from relatives is related to family relationships, and they can differ from country to country, while the support from professional and social organizations has to do with their availability in each society, and their role. Additionally, the level of family support is related to social norms, and family factors, which can differ, and, at the same time, influence the parent expectation for support. Similarly, this factor could explain any potential differences in stress levels, especially stress related to parent, and family problems, and in parent-child relationships. Lastly, these factors could be a reflection of the attitude of community towards individuals with special educational needs, and especially ASD (Danseco, 1997).

Summing up, the purpose of the current study was to carry out a cross-cultural study about the effectiveness of behavioral analytic versus eclectic intervention programs in Greece, and UK/Republic of Ireland. Specifically, the aims of the study were: (a) to examine cultural differences between a Greek, and an English-speaking sample, (b) to describe community-based ABA and eclectic programs in Greek and English-speaking countries and c) to compare their effectiveness.

METHOD

Participants

The participants in the current study were recruited from Greek, English, and Irish intervention programs of behavior analytic or eclectic types, which specialize in children with ASD. The participants were selected on the basis of the following criteria: (a) the children had to have an independent diagnosis of autism, the diagnosis of PDD was also accepted because it is one of the most common diagnoses for children with ASD in Greece; (b) they had to be between 6.5 and 14 years old at the time of baseline assessment; (c) the participants had to be free of any other major medical condition that may adversely affect their development; (d) the children had to be enrolled in either a behavioral or an eclectic intervention program for children with ASD; and (e) they had to not receive any other major intervention during this study.

For the recruitment of the participants from Greek schools, three well known private ABA programs, and four state funded eclectic programs were approached. From these seven schools, which were initially contacted, six (three ABA, and three eclectic) agreed to participate in the present study by sending an information sheet, and consent form to the parents of their pupils. From the parents that were invited to participate in the study, approximately 70% (27 children) consented to participate. This response rate is considered satisfactory given the extensiveness of the questionnaires (approximately 90-120 minutes, twice in nine months), and that parents had no affiliation with the researchers.

Thus, at baseline administration of the tests, the sample consisted of 10 children from ABA interventions, and 17 children from eclectic interventions. Nevertheless, some parents did not complete the questionnaires either at baseline, or at follow-up assessment, and some children changed school during the nine months of the study (see Figure 1). This resulted in the final sample to be consisted of 7 children from ABA intervention programs, and 14 children from eclectic programs. The drop-out rate from the study was 30% from ABA programs, and 18% from eclectic program (see Figure 1).

Regarding the participants for the English-speaking sample, they came from ABA schools in London, and the Republic of Ireland, and eclectic programs in England and Wales. From the twelve schools that there were contacted, and invited to participate in the present study, five schools (two ABA, and three eclectic schools) expressed an interest to participate by sending the information sheet, and the consent form to the parents of their pupils. The response rate from the ABA programs was an approximately 80% (13 children), and a 10% (15 children) from the eclectic programs. Thus, at baseline administration of the tests, the sample consisted of 15 children from ABA interventions, and 13 children from eclectic interventions. The response rate from eclectic schools, and the parents in them, was quite low. However, this seems to be common in the U.K., and colleagues who do research on the educational field in UK attest similar difficulties.

From the parents who agreed to participate in the study, some did not complete the baseline or the follow-up questionnaires, and one child from an ABA program had changed schools when the follow-up assessments were carried out. Furthermore, there was a problem with some parents' and teachers' completion of the questionnaires.

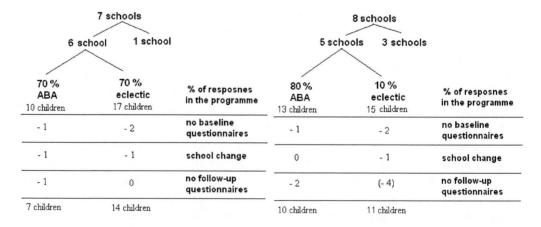

Figure 1. Schematic representation of attrition rate in Greek (left) and English-speaking (right) samples.

Table 1. Comparison of Greek- and English-speaking samples on children's baseline characteristics

	Greek-speaking	English-speaking		
	mean (SD)	mean (SD)	t	P
Age	120.90 (24.77)	128.05 (27.98)	0.876	0.386
IQ (Leiter)	39.76 (10.11)	39.63 (10.65)	0.040	0.968
language (PPVT) raw scores	10.52 (14.24)	18.94 (30.65)	1.114	0.273

For these reasons, all children for whom there were enough baseline and follow-up data were included in the study, despite some missing data (e.g., some uncompleted questionnaires from parents or teachers). Thus, finally, the English-speaking sample consisted of 11 children in the ABA group, and 10 in the eclectic group. The attrition rate from the study was 23% for ABA programs, and 27% for eclectic programs (see Figure 1).

Obviously, the participants in the present study were not randomly assigned to the groups, but they were well matched in some of their baseline developmental characteristics (see Table 1). Specifically, the Greek and the English-speaking sample were matched on age, intellectual abilities, and language understanding, but not in autistic severity, and adaptive skills; the Greek sample was consisted of milder cases, with lower adaptive behavior abilities (see Table 5).

Settings

The participants were recruited from behavioral and eclectic programs, which specialized in children with ASD and/or PDD. A brief description of the included programs is presenting in the following paragraphs.

English and Irish ABA Intervention Programs: All ABA programs included in the present study provide full-time education for young pupils who have moderate to severe autism, and related disorders. Their aims were to provide high quality special education based on scientifically proven educational methodology (ABA), and ongoing training to their families. They also provided a supportive and nurturing environment where children, staff, and parents work together, respecting and helping each other, in order to address, in an on-going basis, children's individual needs, so that each child could achieve their fullest possible potential.

As regards the quality of the programs, information exists only for the English ABA program, which had recently been inspected. The report of the inspectors characterized the standard of the school related to welfare, health, and safety of the pupils, as outstanding, and the school overall as: "good with excellent features". All the ABA schools were run by a principal, who was qualified and experienced. They consisted mainly of ABA tutors, who were already trained, or were being trained. They also had a consultant psychologist, a supervising behavior analyst who advised the tutors, and assisted in their training and professional development, as well as a speech-therapist, and an occupational therapist, who had short sessions with each child, every week, according to their needs, and always using the principles of ABA.

The ABA consultant drew up an Individual Education Plan (IEP) for each child in accordance with the general curriculum of the school, but which was designed for each child individually, according to his/her needs. Their programs were constantly updated to reflect children's progress, and changing needs. The IEP took into consideration all areas of development, including: communication skills, social skills, self-help skills, sensory issues, and academic skills. Lastly, the children's parents were also consulted about the IEP, and informed about their children's progress.

The ABA programs were providing intense, highly structured learning, based on a minimum of one-to-one tutor:pupil ratio. All the included programs were using discrete trial teaching, and basic principles, and teaching methods of ABA, which were implemented by ABA tutors, and supervised by a consultant behavior analyst. However, at certain times, such as group and structured play, a range of approaches could additionally be used, depending on the child's learning needs.

Finally, all ABA programs recognized that parents should have an active role in their child's education, and for this reason they were encouraged to be involved in their children's programs, by attending IEP meetings, attending programs review meetings, and actively generalizing skills learned in school to the child's other environments.

English eclectic programs: The English eclectic intervention programs were special schools for children with ASD from primary age to secondary-school age. Their aim was to provide a high-quality and relevant education, designed to meet the specific needs of children, in a structured, safe, and stimulating environment, with a well-balanced and flexible curriculum. In this atmosphere, the children were encouraged to develop effective communication, social and independence skills, and achieve their academic potential.

Both of the included programs were of high quality. One of them had been accredited with Autism Accreditation, an autism-specific quality assurance program, since 1994, and is annually reviewed in order to maintain its accreditation, while the other one had been inspected recently, and had very good reviews for its effectiveness, and the teaching quality. Both schools followed the Code of Practice 2001 (*Education Act 1996*), and ensured that all the requirements stated in it were fully met. They ensured that all pupils received their entitlement to a broad and relevant curriculum, which is differentiated according to each pupil's individual needs. Their curriculum included subjects which interested the pupils, and the content was delivered in a very practical and concrete manner, to maximize learning. Some of the subjects were English, mathematics, science, history, geography, modern foreign languages, art, design, and technology, physical education, music, ICT, religious education, personal, social, and health education, and community-based education. Additionally, the pupils in these schools were helped to develop social and communication skills, and to learn how to behave appropriately in school and out in the community. Emphasis was also placed on providing opportunities for social inclusion, leading to increased independence.

Both schools had high staff-student ratio, and even more individual support was provided when necessary. In each class, there were a class teacher, and support staff, while for some subjects (e.g., music), the children received specialist teaching. The work of the teachers was supported by speech therapists, and psychologists when necessary.

Parents in both of the included eclectic programs were considered partners in the education of their child. The students had a contact book, which was used for the communication of the teachers with the parents, while once-every-term there were activities in the schools such as consultation, and parents' association evenings, but there was not further contact or co-operation in children's educational programs, like in ABA programs.

Greek ABA Intervention Programs (Gena, 2007): All the included ABA programs were private centers, which offered psycho-educational programming to children, home-programming services (parent-training at home), and family support services (psycho-educational support, parent counseling, and support groups for the siblings of the students). Parents' co-operation constituted an important part of the programs, which provided information to parents about ASD, and ABA, and encouraged them to attend their child's sessions, and to be actively involved in their treatment, as co-therapist.

The daily program of each child in these centers was individualized, in order to address his/her specific deficits, and the problems in each of the major developmental areas. Usually, it was divided into small sessions, during which many tasks were taught, with small breaks in between them. Success in a task was considered satisfactory when the child's performance reached 80% accuracy, and generalization across various stimulus, and behavioral conditions. The intervention program goals were updated weekly, according to the daily documented data, provided by therapists.

Initially, intervention was provided in the format of one-to-one sessions, but group sessions were introduced to encourage social interaction, and communication skills. Augmentative communication (specifically PECS) was used when necessary. Speech and language therapy was carried out by the therapists, as part of the daily program of the children, under the guidance of speech and language therapists, and always using ABA techniques.

The ABA programs had three levels of administration: a) an educational director, and b) an executive director in each school, who both were well-trained professionals, with experienced in the administration of ABA programs; as well as c) supervisors, program managers, and therapists. Most of the therapists had either studied psychology or other related fields, and they had received training, and on-going supervision in the use of behavior analytic procedures (theory, and practice).

Greek Eclectic programs: The Greek eclectic programs in this study were state special schools, which adopt an 'eclectic' approach in teaching, including features of many different intervention approaches, such as interactive models, TEACCH approach, MAKATON, PECS, and ABA techniques. All children from this type of programs, in this study, were attending a morning school-based program of 3 to 4 hours per day, for five days per week. The aims of these programs were the development of children's personality, the improvement of their abilities, and skills in order to be included in mainstream classes, and their preparation for semi-autonomous living. The teaching was based in the National Curriculum (European Commission, 2009), and was organized in four units: speaking, psycho-motor, and cognitive abilities, and emotional organization.

The state special schools were usually directed by a senior teacher with extensive educational experience. The staff consisted of teachers, with either specialization in children with special educational needs, or educational experience. Other professionals who worked in the eclectic programs were speech therapists, physical education teachers, school nurses, and, in some cases, social workers, and psychologists. The intensity of the provided therapies was usually quite low, and for this reason many parents were seeking additional hours of therapies (mainly speech therapy), from other sources.

These schools, in principle, work with the support of the Centre for Diagnosis, Assessments, and Support, but in practice, their staff could offer very little in the special schools program, because of the large number of schools, and children that they service. As regards the family support, there was very little provision, and this generally was restricted to contact between the therapist, and the teachers, and some information-giving meetings with the families during the school year.

Materials

This study used scales to measure the progress of the children on the developmental domains, where the core difficulties of ASD are located (e.g., social interaction, communication and restricted, repetitive and stereotyped behavior), on developmental domains that have been studied from some previous researchers (such as intellectual abilities), and on some other general developmental aspects. The questionnaires that were used in the study were the: Leiter International Performance Scale (Roid and Miller, 1997); Peabody Picture Vocabulary Test (third Edition; PPVT; Dun and Dunn, 1997); Autism Behavior Checklist (ABC; Krug, Arick, and Almond, 1980); Vineland Adaptive Behavior Scale (VABS; Sparrow, Balla, and Cicchetti,1984, 2005); Strengths and Difficulties Questionnaire (SDQ; parents and teachers versions) (Goodman, 1997; 1999); Developmental Behaviour Checklist (DBC; Einfeld and Tonge, 2002); Repetitive Behavior Scale-Revised (RBS; Lam, 2004); and a questionnaire with some demographic questions, and questions about the history of the child, and his/her interventions.

The factors related to the family were the parent-child relationship, the support of the family from different sources, the satisfaction with the intervention program, parental stress, the family routines, and some demographic information about the family. The scales that were used were: the Questionnaire on Research and Stress–Friedrich (QRS; Friedrich, Greenberg, and Crnic, 1983); Parent-Child Relationship Inventory (PCRI; Gerard, 1994); Family Support Scale (FSS; Dunst, Jenkins, and Trivette, 1984); Family Routines Inventory (FRI; Boyce, Jensen, James, and Peacock, 1983; Jensen, James, Boyce, and Hartnett, 1983); and Parent Satisfaction Scale (based on Huntingdon Client Satisfaction Scale: Clare and Pistrang, 1995).

The factors related to the school that were studied were the teachers' self-efficacy (Teacher efficacy scale-short form: Hoy and Woolfolk, 1993), the teachers' qualifications and experience, the intensity and the structure of the intervention, and an informal evaluation of the co-operation with the parents.

For the Greek sample, most of these scales (all except SDQ, and DBC) were translated in Greek, and back to English by two independent persons, before they were used, so as to ensure that the translation did not affect the integrity of the checklist. The translated scales had satisfactory internal consistency, with Cronbach's alpha coefficient to range from 0.728 to 0.954. Due to the comparison across cultural groups, a criterion for the selection of the scales above was also the scales to be cultural free, and to have been used with no problems in other countries.

Procedure

The first step of the study was obtaining ethical approval from the Ethics Committee of the Department of Psychology, at Swansea University. After this was obtained, the search for the sample started by contacting schools in Greece, U.K., and Republic of Ireland. In order a child to be included in the study, his or her parents had to sign a consent form, approving their and their child's participation in the study. For their participation, there was no monetary compensation. More information about the recruitment procedure is provided in the 'participants' section, above. Given the recruitment procedure, the assignment of the children in the groups was not random, and it was based on the parents' decision about the program that they wanted for their child. However, although the allocation to the group was not random, the children's characteristics did not appear to influence their group assignment, and the groups were well matched on age, IQ, and language understanding, at the beginning of the study (see 'participants' section).

The next step was the conduct of the baseline assessments. Two of the scales were administered directly to the children, by the first author, who was trained to administer them. Those scales were the Leiter International Performance Scale, and the Peabody Picture Vocabulary Test (third Edition), for the assessment of the intellectual and language understanding abilities of the children, respectively. The administration of these scales was taken about 60 to 120 minutes, depending on the severity of the autistic condition, and the age of the child. The rest of the scales, for the baseline assessments of other developmental aspects, and the family and intervention factors, were given to parents by the teachers with the contact details of the researcher, offering the parents the opportunity to seek out help or guidance, if it was required. Those scales were: ABC, VABS, QRS, PCRI, FSS, FRI, SDQ, RBS, and the questionnaire with some demographic questions, questions about the history of the child, and about the interventions that the child had received, and was receiving. Their completion took approximately 90-120 minutes, and they had to be returned to the teachers. The teachers were used as mediators, because it was noticed that this was increasing the likelihood that parents responded. Finally, two more questionnaires were given to the main teacher, who was providing the intervention to the child: the SDQ, and the DBC.

Approximately nine months after the baseline assessments, the author revisited all, but one, of the schools to conduct the follow-up assessments of the children. The follow-up assessments included the evaluation of the intellectual and language abilities of the children, as assessed with the Leiter International Performance Scale, and the PPVT, the administration of SDQ, and DBC to teachers, and the administration of ABC, VABS, QRS, SDQ, and RBS to parents. Apart from the aforementioned questionnaires, the parents had also to complete a questionnaire about their satisfaction from the program/school, and the services that they had received from it. The teachers had to complete, additionally, some questionnaires about their qualifications, and their efficacy as teachers. As mentioned above, one of the English eclectic schools (5 children) was not visited by the author for the children's follow-up assessments of IQ, and language (for financial reasons). However, all the rest of the scales were given to the parents, and teachers for the follow-up assessments.

Data Analysis

The statistical procedures that were chosen for the comparison of the two groups (English-Greek speaking at baseline), when the independent variable was continuous, was the independent sample t-test, and when the independent variables were categorical, was the chi-square test (Pearson chi-square). For the comparison of the effectiveness of the ABA and eclectic programs from the Greek and English-speaking samples on different developmental domains, all the data had to be changed into a common metric system, which could allow the comparison amongst them. The common metric system that was chosen was to be used is *Eta squared*, which is a form of effect size, which assesses the magnitude of the intervention's effect. It is used with paired samples (in this case baseline and follow-up data, and it is obtained by the following formula, where *t* is the *t* value from paired samples t-test (baseline-follow-up) and *df* are the degrees of freedom (Pallant, 2007).

$$EtaSquared = \frac{t^2}{t^2 + df}$$

The guidelines for interpreting the *Eta squared* values are that values between 0.01 and 0.06 describe a small effect, values between 0.06 and 0.14 describe a medium effect, and values higher than 0.14 describe a large effect (Pallant, 2007).

RESULTS

The presentation of the results starts with the outcomes from some family and intervention factors, which could indicate cultural differences between the English-speaking and Greek-speaking sample.

Demographic Characteristics, Family Factors and Intervention Programs

Table 2 displays the demographic information about the participants' family. The single:married parents ratio was slightly higher in the sample from U.K. and Republic of Ireland, than for the Greek sample, which is reasonable because the U.K. has more single-parent families, and higher divorce rates, than Greece (Lanzieri, 2008). Despite this fact, the difference was not statistically significant. Additionally, most of the participants from both groups had one sibling; in the Greek sample the percentage of only children was a little higher, but not significantly so. The educational level of parents from the two groups did not differ significantly, but it was slightly lower in the Greek sample, with more parents having ceased their education in primary school. Significant differences were not indentified between the two samples on employment status, either.

Table 3 contains more information about the children's family, such as: family support, parents' stress, the parent-child relationship, and the family routines. These factors do not refer directly to cultural differences, but their outcomes could be a partial reflection of those differences. The results about family support from the parents in both groups indicate almost equal levels of support from all sources. As regards the parents' stress, no statistically significant difference was found between the two groups. Another family factor that was assessed was the parent-child relationship, and on this factor there was a statistically significant difference ($p=0.047$) in satisfaction with parenting. Specifically, it is noticed that the British and the Irish parents were significantly less satisfied with parenting than the Greek parents. The last factor in Table 3 is the family routines, where there is no sign of difference between the English and Greek-speaking samples.

Table 2. Demographic characteristics of the families by group

FAMILY		English-speaking	Greek-speaking	Pearson x^2
marital status :	Married	15	19	5.271
	Single	3	2	
number of siblings:	0	2	6	3.910
	1	12	12	
	≥2	5	3	
father's education:	primary school	0	4	7.875
	secondary school	7	9	
	college/university	9	8	
	postgraduate studies	2	0	
mother's education:	primary school	1	1	7.007
	secondary school	7	10	
	college/university	5	10	
	postgraduate studies	5	0	
				Yates correction
father's occupation:	Employed	16	20	0.007
	Unemployed	1	0	
mother's occupation:	Employed	16	17	0.057
	Unemployed	2	4	

*$p<0.05$, **$p<0.01$.

Table 3. Other family characteristics by group

FAMILY		English-speaking[5] (SD)	Greek-speaking[6] (SD)	t
family support[1,2]:	total in FSS	39.21 (16.4)	31.38 (12.1)	1.731
	partner	2.15 (1.26)	1.92 (0.97)	0.638
	informal kinship	2.02 (1.15)	1.43 (0.92)	1.806
	formal kinship	2.42 (1.82)	1.45 (1.46)	1.867
	social organizations	2.12 (1.16)	1.68 (0.88)	1.358
	professional services	2.42 (1.08)	2.21 (1.20)	0.569
Stress[3,4]:	total	31.21(12.9)	33.10 (8.65)	0.518
	parent and family	11.64 (5.97)	11.33 (4.50)	0.175
	pessimism	8.79 (2.08)	9.38 (2.01)	0.846
	child characteristics	8.86 (4.26)	9.76 (3.03)	0.735
	physical incapacity	1.93 (1.73)	2.62 (1.28)	1.356
PCRI[1,2,7]:	parental support	47.80 (11.89)	41.38 (9.48)	1.802
	satisfaction with parenting	41.47 (10.40)	48.90 (10.9)	2.061*
	involvement	36.87 (14.60)	45.43 (8.63)	2.031
	limit setting	45.93 (10.47)	44.71 (6.69)	0.427
	autonomy	43.27 (11.71)	42.05 (5.40)	0.420
	role orientation	44.93 (16.06)	54.14 (9.68)	1.979
family routines[1,2]		52.05 (11.54)	47.29 (11.32)	1.317

*$p<0.05$, ** $p<0.01$ [1]NABA=9 [2]Neclectic=10 [3]NABA=8 [4]Neclectic=6 [5]N=14-19 [6]N=21 [7]PCRI=Parent Child Relationship Inventory.

Table 4 displays results from the comparison of the intervention programs. The intervention programs in the English-speaking countries had higher intensity than the Greek programs, which was expected given that the daily program of the special schools in UK and Republic of Ireland lasts longer (6-6.5 hours/week) than the Greek (4-4.5 hours/week). This difference in weekly intensity of the program seems to consist of extra hours of one-to-one sessions, while the intensity of the group sessions were quite similar in the intervention programs from the studied countries.

As regards the number of staff who was involved in the children's educational program, no statistically significant differences were found between the groups. The staff from different countries had similar qualifications, similar general educational experience, and experience with children with ASD, and equal levels of general and personal teacher efficacy.

Lastly, findings about the relationship between parents and the intervention programs in Table 4 indicate that Greek parents were more satisfied from the intervention programs, than the British and Irish, but the British and Irish teachers were more satisfied from their co-operation with the parents. Despite these differences, none of them was significant.

Table 4. Characteristics of the intervention programs by group

INTERVENTION		English-speaking [1]	Greek-speaking [2]	Statistic [3]
Intensity		29.76 (2.22)	23.85 (5.11)	4.764**
hours / day 1-to-1 sessions		3.72 (1.39)	2.12 (1.58)	3.029**
hours / day group sessions		2.22 (1.58)	2.50 (1.20)	0.567
number of therapist per child		3.24 (1.61)	3.44 (0.53)	0.525
STAFF		English-speaking [4]	Greek-speaking [5]	
staff qualifications(f):	psychology	2	8	4.890
	education	7	10	
	other	4	2	
	no qualification	1	0	
level of degree (f):	none	1	0	1.476
	BA	7	11	
	MA, MSc or 2 BA	6	9	
years of educational experience		8.38 (9.24)	11.60 (7.70)	1.005
years of experience with ASD		3.86 (3.53)	4.81 (3.41)	0.753
general teacher efficacy		19.21 (6.19)	20.70 (4.74)	0.793
personal teacher efficacy		24.43 (2.06)	25.05 (2.78)	0.709
age of therapist		34.43 (11.18)	36.35 (9.97)	0.506
other interventions:	≥ 1	10	14	5.200
(f)	0	8	7	
parental satisfaction[6,7,8]		29.05 (12.10)	34.86 (9.45)	1.323
teacher-parents co-operation[9,7,10]		2.38 (0.81)	2.04 (0.72)	1.131

*p<0.05, ** p<0.01 [1] $N_{English-speaking}$=9-20 [2]$N_{Greek-speaking}$=16-21 [3]statistic = Pearson chi-square (x^2) for categorical variables and t-test for continuous variables [4]$N_{English-speaking}$=15-20 [5]$N_{Greek-speaking}$=13-15 [6]N_{ABA}=9 [7]$N_{eclectic}$=6 [8] $N_{Greek-speaking}$=21 [9]N_{ABA}=2 [10] $N_{Greek-speaking}$=12 f= frequency.

Participants and Their Developmental Profiles

Table 5 and Figures 2-4 provide information about the participants, and give an idea about the developmental profile of the children, when the baseline assessments were carried out. The data in table 5 show that the English and Greek-speaking samples did not differ significantly on age, mean age that the problem was first noticed by parents, and the mean age at which it was diagnosed.

It has already been mentioned, that the two samples were matched on IQ and on language understanding. The British and Irish children had statistically higher adaptive behavior abilities (VABS total, $t(28) = 6.74, p < 0.001$; communication $t(30) = 6.10, p < 0.001$; daily living skills, $t(30) = 7.29\ p < 0.001$; socialization, $t(30) = 3.07, p < 0.01$); but, at the same time, they were more severely autistic (total autistic severity, $t(27) = 3.05, p < 0.005$).

Table 5. Sample characteristics by group

SAMPLE	English-speaking [1]	Greek-speaking [2]	Statistics
gender (boys/girls)	19/2	19/2	0
mean age at baseline (SD)	128.05 (27.98)	120.90 (24.77)	0.876
mean age first noticed a problem (SD)	18.56 (8.51)	21.05 (6.82)	0.987
mean age when autism diagnosed (SD)	38.71 (14.62)	35.50 (15.39)	0.646
autistic severity (ABC) (SD)	56.29 (20.51)	84.50 (26.56)	3.054**
adaptive behavior (SD) (VABS standard scores)	52.20 (11.37)	28.70 (7.64)	6.736**

*$p<0.05$, ** $p<0.01$ [1]= Pearson chi-square(x^2) [2]= F value.

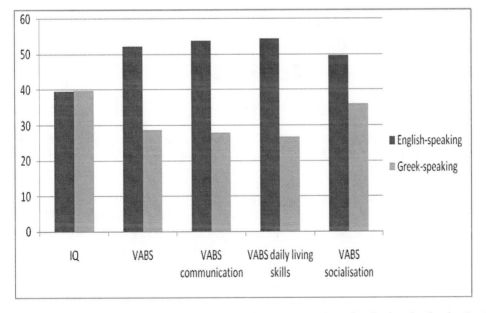

Figure 2. Graphic representation of the mean scores of IQ and VABS total and subscales for the Greek and British/Irish samples.

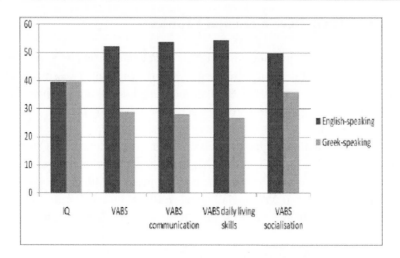

Figure 3. Graphic representation of the mean scores from the subscales of the Repetitive Behavior Scale for the Greek and British/Irish samples.

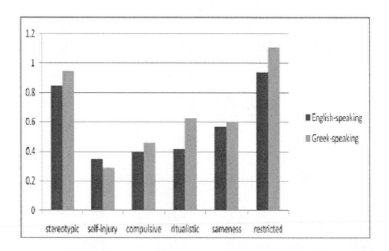

Figure 4. Graphic representation of the mean scores from parents and teachers versions of Strengths and Difficulties Questionnaire (total, peer problems and prosocial behavior) for the Greek and British/Irish samples.

Additionally, British and Irish children had slightly lower repetitive behaviors than Greek children (stereotypic behaviors $t(31)=0.598$, compulsive behaviors $t(31)=0.304$, ritualistic behaviors $t(31)=1.047$, perseverance to sameness $t(31)=0.151$, and restricted interests $t(31)=0.671$, all $ps > 0.05$), except self-injury behaviors ($t(31)=0.396$, $p> 0.05$), which were slightly higher than the self-injury behaviors in the Greek group. However, this significant difference could be due to the fact that very few children engaged in self-injury and that the samples were relatively small, which practically means that even the presence of only one child with self-injury could skew the results.

Lastly, the results from parents and teachers' SDQs and their subscales of peer relationships and prosocial behaviors, at baseline shows no significant difference between the two groups (total SDQ-P $t(34)=0.306$, SDQ-T $t(35)=0.687$; peer relationships SDQ-P

$t(34)=0.290$,   SDQ-T $t(35)=0.065$;   prosocial   behaviors   SDQ-P $t(34)=0.200$,   SDQ-T $t(35)=0.611$, all ps>0.05).

In general, these findings indicate that, although the children from UK/Republic of Ireland had statistically significant higher adaptive behavior abilities, they had significantly higher autistic features. Between the two samples, no significant differences were found in the children's difficulties in their relationship with peers, in their prosocial behavior skills and in their restricted repetitive behaviors.

Effectiveness of Intervention Programs

Table 6. Effect sizes (Eta squared) of ABA and eclectic intervention programs in Greek and English-speaking countries

	English-speaking		Greek-speaking	
	ABA	Eclectic	ABA	Eclectic
IQ	*0.147*	*0.367*	(0.139)	(0.005)
VABS total	(0.046)	*(0.768)*	(0.122)	*(0.414)*
ABC total	0.127	*0.345*	(0.011)	(0.091)
SDQ-P total	0.048	0.05	*0.593*	(0.082)
SDQ-T total	0.083	(0.004)	0.048	(0.038)
DBC total.	*0.457*	(0.122)	*(0.260)*	0.049
VABS daily living skills	0.012	*(0.371)*	*(0.142)*	*(0.188)*
PPVT raw scores	*0.299*	*0.213*	*0.406*	*0.348*
VABS communication	*(0.556)*	*(0.505)*	(0.006)	*(0.469)*
DBC communication disturbances	*0.514*	(0.049)	(0.134)	(0.006)
VABS socialization	*(0.395)*	*(0.185)*	0.010	*(0.310)*
SDQ-P peer problems	0	(0.013)	(0.036)	0.010
SDQ-Pprosocial behavior	*0.250*	(0.016)	*0.184*	0.043
SDQ-T peer problems	0.017	0.041	*(0.188)*	(0.017)
SDQ-T prosocial behavior	0.013	*0.368*	*(0.397)*	0.019
DBC social relating	*0.311*	(0.090)	*(0.790)*	(0.042)
DBC disruptive behavior	0.010	(0.093)	0.109	0.078
Stereotypic	(0.030)	0.002	*0.628*	(0.107)
Self-injury	(0.042)	0.067	0.091	(0.017)
Compulsive	(0.033)	0.014	*0.233*	0.002
Ritualistic	*0.267*	*0.257*	0.100	0.054
Sameness	*0.444*	*0.154*	*0.446*	0
Restricted	0.065	*0.340*	*0.410*	0.032
Stress Parent and family problem	*0.233*	*0.188*	0.001	*0.149*
Stress-Pessimism	*0.568*	*0.176*	*0.399*	0.006
Stress-Child characteristics	(0.008)	*0.356*	*0.416*	0.002
Stress-Physical incapacity	0	0	(0.048)	0.013
Stress total	*0.328*	*0.253*	*0.192*	0.050

( )=the change was not to the desirable direction (decrease of a skill or increase of a problem/disturbance) , numbers in bold=large effect size (>0.14).

The last, but not least, aim of the present study was to compare the effectiveness of the ABA and eclectic programs from the Greek and English-speaking samples on different developmental domains. For this reason, all the data were changed into a common metric system, which could allow their comparison. The common metric system chosen was the *Eta squared*. Table 6 presents the effect sizes of all the studied developmental and family factors for each intervention program separately. The large effect sizes are presented with numbers in bold, while changes in an undesirable direction (e.g., decrease of a skill, or increase of a problem/disturbance) have been placed in brackets. Thus, ABA programs in English-speaking countries had 13 large effect sizes, 11 of which were to the desirable direction, and 3 medium effects, all to the desirable direction. The eclectic programs from the English-speaking countries had 15 large effect sizes, 11 of which to the desirable direction, and 4 medium, 1 of which to the desirable direction. The Greek ABA programs had 15 large effect sizes, 10 of which to the desirable direction, and 6 medium, 3 of which to the desirable direction. Lastly, the Greek eclectic intervention programs had 6 large effect sizes and 4 medium one, from which only two large effect sizes and 1 medium were to the desirable direction.

CONCLUSION

This study investigated ABA and eclectic programs from Greece and UK/Republic of Ireland, under the same experimental design, which could allow their comparison, and provide some information about cultural differences and the generalizability of the findings from Greek samples.

The first aim of the study was to check for cultural differences, as they are reflected in the family. The results from this first part of analysis, in general, did not show many differences between the samples from the studied cultural environments. Specifically, the findings indicated that the structure of the family (marital status and number of children) did not differ strongly between the Greek and British/Irish samples. The English-speaking group had slightly higher educational background, while some differences were also found in parent satisfaction related to parenting. The English-speaking sample had lower parent satisfaction from parenting, and slightly lower involvement with their children's activities, which could possibly attributed to cultural differences, and the quite child-oriented Greek family (Maratou-Alipranti, 1995; Maratou-Alipranti, 1999). Apart from these, no differences were found between countries, in employment status, family support, parent stress, limit setting, autonomy, and role orientation.

As regards the intervention programs in Greek and English-speaking countries, the analysis showed that the programs from the studied countries were quite similar, and their differences were confined to their intensity, and not to quality and functional factors, such as the staff qualifications, experience, and self-efficacy. These findings shows that the Greek programs, which were quite representative of their type (ABA, eclectic) in Greece, could be used as reference, and for comparison in future research.

Another issue that was studied was the developmental profile of the children from the Greek and UK/Republic of Ireland, which were matched originally on age, IQ, and language understanding. The analysis brought out some differences, which could constitute an interesting field for further analysis. Specifically, the children from UK/Republic of Ireland had higher adaptive behavior abilities, and, at the same time, had significantly higher autistic features. Between the two samples there were no real differences found in the children's difficulties in their relationship with peers, in their prosocial behavior skills, and in their restricted repetitive behaviors. The last finding does not support the findings of Papageorgiou et al. (2008) about the cross-cultural heterogeneity of the restricted repetitive behaviors and interests. However, the two studies compared Greek children with children from different countries (North America, UK and Republic of Ireland), where the difference in findings could be attributed. Thus, none of these results can be broadly generalized and further research is required about restricted repetitive behaviors cross-culturally.

Regarding the significant differences between the groups in the Vineland Adaptive Behavior Scale, there are no cross-cultural data in autistic populations to be compared. However, most of the previous studies (Magiati, Charman, and Howlin, 2007; Reed, Osborne, and Corness, 2007b; Sallows and Graupner, 2005) report higher VABS standard scores than the scores of the Greek groups in this study. At the same time, most of those studies assessed younger children, and some of them higher functioning ones, when both age and level of functioning constitute factors which have impact on VABS outcomes (Carter et al., 1998; Perry et al., 2008). These reports could simply justify the presence of low VABS standard scores, but they cannot give an answer about the difference between the two studied autistic populations. A possible explanation could be the difference in the language and communication abilities of the children, which according to the data were a little lower in the Greek sample, but not statistically significant. However, the level of significance of the difference could have been influenced by the presence of the 'floor effect'.

The observed significant differences in developmental profiles between the groups could be either a real difference between the studied countries, or could possibly be explained by the different focus on the intervention programs (e.g., on behavioral problems, autistic features or adaptive abilities), or on children's up-bringing, which could be culturally related. A single study is certainly not sufficient to reach definite conclusions about possible differences in developmental profiles of children from different countries, but it reveals an interesting field for further research.

The last aim of the present study was to compare the effectiveness of community-based ABA and eclectic programs in Greek and English-speaking countries. The analysis of the effectiveness of the four programs indicates, firstly, that ABA and eclectic programs in English speaking countries were equally effective. Secondly, the Greek ABA programs were almost equally effective as the programs in the English speaking countries. Thirdly, the Greek eclectic programs were less effective than all the other programs. Between the ABA programs, the Greek programs were a little bit better than the British/Irish programs in addressing restricted repetitive stereotypic behavior, and in decreasing parental stress related to children characteristics, while the English–speaking programs were a little bit better in general developmental factors, communication, and social skills. These findings could be possibly explained by the different focus of the programs. Between the eclectic programs the difference is significant, and the programs from the English speaking countries as well as the Greek ABA programs were significantly more effective than the Greek eclectic programs.

These findings are quite interesting, but like most applied research in early intervention, the present study had some limitations, which have to be noted. Firstly, the sample size was relatively small, which is a problem for the statistical power of the outcomes, but similar to other studies on the field. Additionally, some small differences among the samples may not have been depicted due to the small sample sizes, yet the differences that were revealed may not be doubted. Secondly, the participants were not randomly assigned to the groups, but at least they were matched on age, IQ and language understanding.

Two other limitations were that the administrator of the test was not blind to the child's program, and many instruments had to be translated for the needs of the study since there was no standardized Greek versions of them. For this reason, the scales which were chosen were cultural free or translations of them had been previously used with no problems in other countries. The duration of the study was short (nine months), but similar to that of some previous studies (Ben-Itzchak and Zachor, 2007; Eikeseth et al., 2002; Reed et al., 2007a; Reed et al., 2007b). Additionally, there was not a direct control of the quality of the intervention programs, but some of the programs in Britain had recently been inspected and had received good reviews, and some of the Greek programs are well-known in Greece for their quality, while all of them are representative to the existing community based programs for children with ASD in Greece.

Apart from the above limitations, this study also has some strength compared to the previous ones, and those are the presence of a control groups, the high ecological validity because of the use of community-based programs, as well as the assessments of a wide range of developmental and family factors.

Another strong point was the use of the same measures for all of the children, both at baseline and follow-up assessments, minimizing the misleading assumptions regarding the tests. Finally, the present study is the first cross-cultural study on the field of effectiveness of intervention programs for children with ASD. This new direction, towards which the present report aims to contribute with its findings, could be quite promising. Cross-cultural studies, apart from recording the education of children with ASD around the world, could also be quite informative. They could show different applications and adjustments of the same type of programs in different countries and their outcomes, which may be different to the findings that everybody knows through the English literature.

Additionally, in cases like in the present study, where the cultural differences are not significant, a cross-cultural study could provide the space for interesting comparisons of programs' effectiveness.

REFERENCES

Anderson, S.R., Avery, D.L. DiPietro, E.K., Edwards, G.L., and Christian, W. P. (1987). Intensive home-based early intervention with autistic children. *Education and Treatment of Children, 10,* 352-366.

Ben-Itzchak, E., and Zachor, D. A. (2007). The effects of intellectual functioning and autism severity on outcome of early behavioral intervention for children with autism. *Research in Developmental Disabilities, 28,* 287-303.

Bibby, P., Eikeseth, S., Martin, N. T., Mudford, O. C., and Reeves, D. (2002). Progress and outcomes for children with autism receiving parent-managed intensive interventions. *Research in Developmental Disabilities, 23*, 81-104.

Birnbrauer, J.S., and Leach, D.J. (1993). The Murdoch early intervention program after 2 years. *Behaviour Change*, 10 (2), 63-74.

Boyce, W. T., Jensen, E. W., James, S. A., and Peacock, J. L. (1983). The family routines inventory: Theoretical origins. *Social Science and Medicine, 17(4),* 193-200.

Carter, A.S., Volkmar, F.R., Sparrow, S.S., Wang, J.J., Lord, C., Dawson, G., Fombonne, E., Loveland, K., Mesibov, G., and Schopler, E. (1998). The Vineland Adaptive Behavior Scales: Supplementary norms for individuals with autism. *Journal of Autism and Developmental Disorders, 28,* 287-302.

Clare, L., and Pistrang, N. (1995). Parents' perceptions of portage: Towards a standard measure of parent satisfaction. *British Journal of Learning Disabilities, 23,* 110-117.

Cohen, H., Amerine-Dickens, M., and Smith, T. (2006). Early Intensive behavioural Treatment: Replication of the UCLA Model in a Community Setting. *Developmental Behavioral Pediatrics, 27 (2),* S145-S155.

Connors, J.L., Donnellan, A.M. (1998). Walk in beauty: Western perspectives on disability and Navajo family/cultural resilience. In H. I. McCubbin, E. A. Thompson, A. I. Thompson, and J. E. Fromer (Eds). *Resiliency in Native American and immigrant families* (pp159-182). Thousand Oaks: Sage.

Danseco, E.R. (1997). Parental beliefs on childhood disability: insights on culture, child development and intervention. *International Journal of Disability, Development and Education, 44,* 41–52.

Dunn, L., and Dunn, L. (1997). *Peabody Picture Vocabulary Test-III.* Circle Pines, MN: American Guidance Service.

Dunst, C.J., Jenkins, V., and Trivette, C.M. (1984). Family support scale: reliability and validity. *Journal of Individual, Family, and Community Wellness, 1,* 45-52.

Dyches, T.T., Wilder, L.K., Sudweeks, R.R., Obiakor, F.E., and Algozzine,B. (2004). *Multicultural Issues in Autism. Journal of Autism and Developmental Disorders, 34 (2),* 211-222.

Einfeld, S.L., and Tonge, B.J. (2002). *Manual for the Developmental Behaviour Checklist: Primary Carer Version (DBC-P) and Teacher Version (DBC-T). 2nd ed.* Melbourne: Monash University Centre for Developmental Psychiatry and Psychology.

Eldevik, S., Eikeseth, S., Jahr, E., and Smith, T. (2006). Effects of low-intensity behavioural treatment for children with autism and mental retardation. *Journal of Autism and Developmental Disorders, 36 (2),* 211-224.

European Commission (2009), "The Education System in Greece 2007/08", Eurybase, The Information. Database on Education Systems in Europe, Directorate-General for Education and Culture, Eurycide. Retrieved September 11, 2009 from http://eacea.ec.europa.eu/ressources/eurydice/eurybase/pdf/0_integral/EL_EN.pdf

Forehand, R., and Kotchick, B. A. (1996). Cultural diversity: A wake-up call for parent training. *Behavior Therapy, 27,* 187-206.

Friedrich, W. N., Greenberg, M. T., and Crnic, K. (1983). A short-form of the Questionnaire on Resources and Stress.American *Journal of Mental Deficiency, 88,* 41–48.

Gabriels, R. L., Hill, D. E., Pierce, R. A., Rogers, S. J., and Wehner, B. (2001). Predictors of treatment outcome in young children with autism: A retrospective study. *Autism, 5,* 407-429.

Gena, A. (2007) *Theory and practice in behaviour analysis.* Athens: Gutenberg. (Γενά, Α. (2007). *Θεωρία και πράξη της ανάλυσης της συμπεριφοράς.* Αθήνα: Gutenberg.)

Gerard, A. B. (1994). *Parent-Child Relationship Inventory Manual.* Los Angeles, CA: Western Psychological Services.

Gonzalez, V., Brusca-Vega, R., and Yawkey, T. (1997). *Assessment and instruction of culturally and linguistically diverse students with or at-risk of learning problems: From research to practice.* Boston: Allyn and Bacon.

Goodman, R. (1997). The Strengths and Difficulties Questionnaire: A research note. *Journal of Child Psychology, Psychiatry, and Allied Disciplines, 38 (5)*, 581-586.

Goodman, R. (1999). The extended version of the Strengths and Difficulties Questionnaire as a guide to child psychiatric caseness and consequent burden. *Journal of Child Psychology, Psychiatry, and Allied Disciplines, 40 (5)*, 791-799.

Howard, J., Sparkman, C., Cohen, H., Green, G., and Stanislaw, H. (2005). A comparison of intensive behaviour analytic and eclectic treatments for young children with autism. *Research in Developmental Disabilities, 26*, 359-383.

Hoy, W. K., and Woolfolk, A. E. (1993). Teachers' sense of efficacy and the organizational health of schools. *The Elementary School Journal, 93 (4)*, 355-372.

Jensen, EW., James, S.A., Boyce, W.T., and Hartnett, S.A. (1983). The family routines inventory: Development and validation. *Social Science and Medicine, 17(4)*, 201-211.

Kaderoglou, L. (2000). *Home based early intervention in high functioning autistic children.* Presentation to the International Special Education Congress, 24-28 July 2000, University of Manchester.

Krug, D. A., Arick, J. R., and Almond, P. J. (1980). Behavior checklist for identifying severely handicapped individuals with high levels of autistic behaviour. *Journal of Child Psychology and Psychiatry, 21*, 221-229.

Lam, K.S.L. (2004). *The Repetitive Behavior Rating Scale – Revised: Independent validation and the effects of subject variables.* Unpublished doctoral dissertation, The Ohio State University, Columbus.

Lanzieri, G. (2008). *Population and social conditions (Eurostat),* European Communities. Retrieved August 2009 from http://epp.eurostat.ec.europa.eu/cache/ITY_OFFPUB/KS-SF-08-081/EN/KS-SF-08-081-EN.PDF.

Magiati, I., Charman, T., and Howlin, P. (2007). A two year prospective follow up study of community based early intensive behavioural intervention and specialist nursery provision for children with autism spectrum disorders. *Journal of Child Psychology and Psychiatry, 48 (8),* 803-812.

Maratou-Alipranti, L., (1995). Defining Family Obligations in Greece. In J. Millar, and A. Warman (Eds). *Defining Family Obligations in Europe, Social Policy Papers.* University of Bath, Report No 24,129-154.

Maratou-Alipranti, L. (1999). *Διαγενεακές σχέσεις στη σύγχρονη εποχή:Τάσεις και οι νέες φάσεις του κύκλου ζωής.* Proceedings of the 3rd Panhellenic Educational Conference: Family in modern society, Komotini, May 1999.

McEachin, J.J., Smith, T., and Lovaas, O.I. (1993). Long-term outcome for children with autism who received early intensive behavioral treatment. *American Journal on Mental Retardation, 97(4)*, 359-372.

Moes, D. R., and Frea, W. D. (2002). Contextualized behavioral support in early intervention for children with autism and their families. *Journal of Autism and Developmental Disorders*, 32, 519-533.

Osborne, L., McHugh, L., Saunders, J., and Reed, P. (2007). The effect of parenting behaviours on subsequent child behavior problems in Autistic Spectrum Conditions. *Research in Autism Spectrum Disorders, 2*, 249-263.

Pallant, J. (2007). *SPSS survival manual (3rd ed.)*. London: Open University Press.

Paneque, O.M., and Barbetta, P.M. (2006). A study of teacher efficacy of special education teachers of English language learners with disabilities. *Bilingual Research Journal, 30,* 171-193.

Papageorgiou, V., Georgiades, S., and Mavreas, V. (2008). Brief report: Cross-cultural evidence for the heterogeneity of the restricted, repetitive behaviours and interests domain of autism: A Greek study. *Journal of Autism and Developmental Disorders, 38(3)*, 558-561.

Perry, A., Cummings, A., Geier, J. D., Freeman, N. L., Hughes, S., LaRose, L., Managhan, T., Reitzel, J., and Williams, J. (2008). Effectiveness of intensive behavioral intervention in a large, community-based program. *Research in Autism Spectrum Disorders, 2,* 621–642.

Reed, P., Osborne, L.A., and Corness, M. (2007a). Brief Report: Relative effectiveness of different home-based behavioural approaches to early teaching intervention. *Journal of Autism and Developmental Disorders, 37(9)*, 1815-1821.

Reed, P., Osborne, L., and Corness, M. (2007b). The real-world effectiveness of early teaching interventions for children with autistic spectrum disorders. *Exceptional Children, 73(4),* 417-413.

Remington, B., Hastings, R., Kovshoff, H., Degli Espinosa, F., Jahr, E., Brown, T., Alsford, P., Lemaic, M., and Ward, N. (2007). Early intensive behavioral intervention: outcomes for children with autism and their parents after two years. *American Journal on Mental Retardation, 112(6)*, 418-438.

Robbins, F. R., and Dunlap, G. (1992). Effects of task difficulty on parent teaching skills and behavior problems of young children with autism. *American Journal on Mental Retardation, 96,* 631-643. 334.

Robbins, F. R., Dunlap, G., and Plienis, A. J. (1991). Family characteristics, family training, and the progress of young children with autism. *Journal of Early Intervention, 15,* 173-184.

Rogers, S. J., and Vismara, L. A. (2008). Evidence-based comprehensive treatments for early autism. *Journal of Clinical Child and Adolescent Psychology, 37,* 8-38.

Roid, G.H., and Miller, L.J. (1997). *Leiter International Performance Scale--Revised*. Wood Dale, IL: Stoelting.

Sallows, G., and Graupner, T. (2005). Intensive Behavioral treatment for Children With Autism: Four-Year Outcome and Predictors. *American Journal On Mental Retardation, 110 (6)*, 417-438.

Smith, T., Eikeseth, S., Klevstrand, M., and Lovaas, O.I. (1997). Intensive behavioral treatment for preschoolers with severe mental retardation and pervasive developmental disorder. *American Journal of Mental Retardation. 102 (3)*, 238-249.

Sparrow, S. S., Balla, D. A., and Cicchetti, D. V. (1984). *Vineland Adaptive Behavior Scales: Interview Edition, Survey Form Manual*. Circle Pines, MN: American Guidance Service.

Sparrow, S. S., Balla, D. A., and Cicchetti, D. V. (2005). *Vineland Adaptive Behavior Scales Second Edition Survey Forms Manual*. Circle Pines, MN: American Guidance Service.

Tanoue, Y., Oda, S., Asano, F., and Kawashima, K. (1988). Epidemiology of infantile autism in southern Ibaraki, Japan: differences in prevalence in birth cohorts. *Journal of Autism Developmental Disorders, 18(2)*, 155-166.

Utley, C.A., and Obiakor, F.E. (2001). *Special education, multicultural education, and school reform: Components of quality education for learners with mild disabilities*. New York: Charles C. Thomas.

Wilder, L. K., Dyches, T. T., Obiakor, F. E., and Algozzine, B. (2004). Multicultural Perspectives on Teaching Students with Autism. *Focus on Autism and other Developmental Disabilities, 19,* 105-113.

Williams, K., Glasson, E., Wray, J., Tuck, M., Helmer, M., Bower, C., and Mellis, C. (2005). Incidence of autism spectrum disorders in children in two Australian states. *Medical Journal of Australia, 182(3)*, 108-111.

Ysseldyke, J.E., Algozzine, B., and Thurlow, M. L. (2000*). Critical issues in special education, 3 rd Ed* . Boston, MA: Houghton Mifflin Company.

Zhang, X., and Ji, C.Y. (2005). Autism and mental retardation of young children in China. *Biomedical and environmental sciences, 18(5)*, 334-340.

Zionts, L.T., and Zionts, P. (2003). Multicultural aspects in the education of children and youth with autism and other developmental disabilities: Introduction to the special issue. *Focus on Autism and other Developmental Disabilities, 18*, 2-3.

In: Progress in Education. Volume 26
Editor: Robert V. Nata, pp. 75-96

ISBN 978-1-61324-321-3
© 2011 Nova Science Publishers, Inc.

Chapter 4

EVALUATION AND ACCREDITATION: LONG TERM CHALLENGES FOR HIGHER EDUCATION

*Mario Letelier, Rosario Carrasco, Danae de los Ríos,
Claudia Oliva and María José Sandoval*
Universidad de Santiago de Chile

ABSTRACT

The main focus of this article is evaluation, its relevance, complexity and potential, in the perspective of higher education accreditation. Accreditation, institutional and at program level, has a history of twenty years in Chile, through sequential stages. In parallel, the Universidad de Santiago de Chile-USACH has been involved in self-study and systemic evaluation since 1997. The senior authors of this article, in different roles, have participated in this experience, which is the basis of the studies and results here reported. As highlighted in the recent Annual Meeting of the Middle States Commission on Higher Education in the U.S., evaluation is a key factor for fostering quality, accountability, and institutional learning. Two main subjects of evaluation are considered critical: institutional effectiveness and student learning. The USACH experience, as much as the national one, has shown the authors a concern for academic goals and their usually qualitative and subjective nature, since the absence of measurement implies seldom certainty that the goals have been really met. The Chilean National Accreditation Commission (CNA) is at present revising its institutional accreditation criteria in order to pass from a "declarative" stage to a "demonstrative" one. In this, to demonstrate means to show evaluated results. Evaluating is often compounded by a lack of clear purposes of evaluation subject or object, by use of inappropriate instruments, by mismanagement of political variables, and by a lack of the necessary means for recording and storing relevant information. Here the authors present, in a systematized way, the results of exploring several areas of evaluation within the perspective of quality assurance. These areas include learning outcomes, accreditation's impact on institutions, and graduates' follow-up, among others. This experience has led to the development of a general evaluation model, which considers political, technical, financial and operational variables. The model is the outcome of a varied experience on evaluation that includes different subjects, such as public program's performance, learning outcomes, undergraduate programs, graduate programs, higher education institutions, and alumni and employers' assessment of professional education relevance. In this article some conclusions are drawn that intend to show and stress the big relevance and complexities of systemic institutional evaluation as a unique tool for quality assurance and, particularly, for strengthening institutional integrity. Integrity means, among other things, the capacity of stating goals and verifying results in a consistent way. Practice has led these authors to believe that the former implies developing institutional capacities of which many universities seem to be unaware of.

INTRODUCTION

This paper highlights evaluation's relevance, complexity and potential in the perspective of higher education accreditation. Though evaluation is considered a key factor in fostering quality, accountability, and student learning, the experience of the Universidad de Santiago shows that evaluation is often compounded by a lack of clear purposes of evaluation subjects or objects, undermining the certainty that these goals have been fully met.

The authors present the results of some evaluation experiences within the perspective of quality assurance, related to learning outcomes, accreditation impact on institutions, and graduate follow-ups, among others. These initiatives have led to the development of a general evaluation model, also described in this article, which considers political, technical, financial and operational variables.

Some conclusions are drawn in order to stress the relevance and complexities of systemic institutional evaluation as a tool for quality assurance and for strengthening institutional integrity, understood as the capacity of stating goals and verifying results in a consistent way.

BACKGROUND

Quality Assurance and Accreditation in Chilean Higher Education

Chile started a massive educational reform in the early eighties which involved, among others, the creation of new higher education institutions. Until 1981, the country had eight universities, besides some institutes, academies and other institutions, which enrolled 120,000 students. The higher education system was known as highly selective and homogeneous with a limited offer of educational programs, only oriented to upper and middle class families and students, corresponding to an elitist type of educational system (Trow, 1973).

The educational reform triggered several changes, including a re-organization of the two national universities and the incorporation of educational fees. In addition, considering the limited amount of higher education programs, the reformers pursued an expansion allowing for the creation of new universities, professional institutes and technical training centers. The reform was highly successful in this regard, since several groups started new higher education institutions that slowly captured the emerging demand for higher education.

Ten years after this reform, the country had more than 300 higher education institutions: 60 universities, 81 colleges and 161 vocational colleges (SIES, 2010). Those were offering diverse academic programs, addressing the shy but increasing demands for massive higher education. Up to 1990 the new institutions were under the supervision of the older universities (those that existed prior 1981), which assessed teachers, students and program quality until the new institutions would gain autonomy.

The arrival of a democratic coalition in 1990 triggered an in-depth revision of the prevailing monitoring mechanisms. As a result, a new licensing system for higher education institutions was created, installing the Higher Education Council (Consejo Superior de Educación-CSE) as the public institution in charge of the licensing process for new institutions, through accreditation-like procedures. Between 1990 and 2007, CSE was in charge of 209 licensing initiatives, allowing the entrance of new players into the educational arena.

In 1998 the educational system was increasingly shifting towards a mass system: more than 406,553 students were attending the 251 higher education institutions (SIES, 2010). The increasing access was perceived as a positive outcome, but there was a rather pessimistic view regarding the quality of the new educational institutions. Social skepticism was growing because the public observed that once institutions were granted autonomy, there was freedom to act with a reckless approach to educational matters, leading in some cases to weak academic standards.

The public skepticism was not only regarding new institutions but also the older or traditional universities, especially some of the regional branches of the national universities. In addition, families and students were demanding reliable information of the quality of these institutions and their educational programs. Therefore, there was a need for greater academic accountability for all institutions, regardless of their origin or dependency.

The need for greater accountability among higher education institutions became a reality in 1999 with the creation of the National Commission for Undergraduate Accreditation (Comisión Nacional de Acreditación de Pregrado-CNAP). The CNAP was created with the purpose of setting the foundations of an accreditation system for institutions and undergraduate programs, and designing a national quality assurance system. The nature of CNAP was experimental in nature because there was limited knowledge and expertise to start an accreditation process (CNAP, 2007). Therefore, CNAP was built as a transition agency to build a comprehensive accreditation system.

Until 1999, very few universities had developed self-evaluation processes. Among those we can highlight the experience of Universidad de Concepción and Universidad de Santiago, which were some of the few universities with experimental processes of self-evaluation, generating the initial capability to assess key educational activities. Those universities were pioneers in the system feeding with rubrics, documents, and surveys that were important for the development of the whole accreditation system.

CNAP assumed several challenges including the creation of institutional standards for accreditation. To build them, CNAP conducted a detailed search of accreditation experiences around the world, particularly from Europe and the US. Once the standards were defined, CNAP created a process for conducting accreditation, providing several instruments to guide institutions through accreditation. The installation of the experimental system involved a self-study process and external audit by national and international professionals, which required the training of peer evaluators, using the human resources of the licensing system in this task.

Between 1999 and January 2007, CNAP had completed 380 voluntary accreditation processes out of the more than 560 undergraduate programs engaged in this initiative. CNAP experience was quite successful in several aspects, particularly introducing an important, although incipient, capability of self-regulation in an important segment of educational institutions that were able to install self-evaluation capability within their own communities.

As for the institutional accreditation, CNAP started to conduct experimental and voluntary processes at the beginning of 2003 by assessing institutional management and teaching processes, together with assessment of elective areas chosen by each institution, namely research, graduate programs, community engagement or lifelong learning (CNAP, 2007). In 2004, once the experimental phase ended, the evaluation criteria and procedures were revised in order to apply this process to other institutions, and by 2007 more than 60 institutions had engaged in this activity.

As an experimental initiative, CNAP was a rich experience for the installation of the National Accreditation Commission (Comisión Nacional de Acreditación-CNA), the agency that merged in 2007 all accreditation initiatives, including institutional and program accreditation. Unlike CNAP, the new accreditation agency emerged with a new law that aimed to install a national quality assurance system, compelling institutions and programs to strengthen their self-regulation capabilities, introducing formal and obligatory accreditation processes. CNA is now in charge of undergraduate, graduate and institutional accreditation; the authorization of accreditation agencies; and the creation of a public higher education information system.

The new agency has maintained the fundamental resources installed through CNAP, especially manuals, orientations and standards, although there has been an attempt to assess and adjust the available instruments. Since 2008, the new commission has merged all the existing procedures, pursuing a more coherent approach to all those processes, considering the relations between institutional and program accreditation initiatives. In parallel, the commission has started a review of the impact of the accreditation system aiming to improve its quality.

The Commission has come to the conclusion that the accreditation process has been positive for institutions but not fully oriented to educational outcomes. So far, universities and colleges have become smart in formalizing institutional procedures but less competent regarding the assessment of educational outcomes. As noted by Letelier et al. (2009), though the new quality assurance system considers the assessment of educational outcomes, feedback and improvement, this concept has proven to be elusive for some institutions with weaker academic standards. Therefore, there is a need of shifting the quality assurance system towards the assessment of students' learning.

Therefore, through CNA, the Chilean higher education system is attempting to initiate a new stage of quality assurance, moving institutions to a value-added approach. Unfortunately, there is limited knowledge regarding students learning at the higher educational system but several institutions are moving into that direction. Hereafter, the authors explain the case of Universidad de Santiago, which could be considered as a leading institution regarding the assessment of students' outcomes.

Quality Assurance Process at the Universidad De Santiago

The Universidad de Santiago started its second institutional self-evaluation process in 2007. The university faced this process with significant pressure since the first accreditation experience was not quite successful, giving the university a modest accreditation result.[1] The university was internally pressured to improve its years of accreditation, keeping its recognition in the mandatory and elected domains.

At the same time, the law that created the National System of Quality Assurance in Higher Education and the National Accreditation Commission was pushing in the direction of quality assurance, a novel experience for many, if not all, higher education institutions, including the Universidad de Santiago. Therefore, the university needed to change its approach to self-evaluation, pushing faculties and administrators under a new assessment approach.

The university leaders decided to start the self-evaluation process with a new vision of quality. Unlike the previous accreditation process, there was a wide consensus that the university lacked a proper quality assurance approach, conducting its main activities with a rather formal and bureaucratic approach. As a result, university leaders created a quality assurance commission, representing the first action for the creation of an institutional quality assurance system. This commission had to define a quality assurance model and an implementation strategy, defining managerial activities.

The commission was integrated by representatives of different academic units, key administrators and technical crew. Two of the authors were part of this commission, acting as technical members and coordinators of the process. Until 2007, the Universidad de Santiago had discussed quality in many of its documents, including its Strategic Plan and the Educational Model, but it did not have a quality assurance system for the improvement of its main processes.

The institutional model of quality was created under the influence of two international perspectives of quality assurance. The first was linked to accreditation, which has a long tradition in higher education and intends to ensure quality and social relevance of academic activities. The second influence came from the industrial area and refers to quality management based on the ISO 9000 norm, which establishes the minimum requirements an organization has to accomplish in order to operate with efficiency, customer satisfaction and continuous improvement capability.

Once the system and its regulations were approved at the institutional level, a new structure based on this quality model was implemented within the university units, and the self-study process was oriented under this new perspective of quality. This required the creation of commissions in charge of the different areas of evaluation: undergraduate education, institutional management, graduate education, research, and community engagement.

The assessment of the five accreditation areas was done according to the institutional quality assurance system, which established that each area had main processes associated with regular institutional activities. It was necessary to define purposes, goals, outcomes and impact indicators, queries and improvement plans that derived from the assessment, which could enable the necessary corrective and preventive actions required to overcome the university's weaknesses and enhance its strategic priorities.

---

[1] In Chile institutional acreditation provides a minimum of two and a maximum of seven years of accreditation. Institutions should assess at least two mandatory areas or domains: institutional management and undergraduate education. Institutions can assess three additional domains: research, community engagement and graduate education

Under this new framework, the mechanisms of quality assurance were related to the procedures that cautioned the application of the Institutional Quality Assurance Model and were supposed to lead to the continuous improvement of its processes. The main processes of the university were selected by using the following criteria:

- Representation of core functions associated to key institutional activities
- Agreement with CNA principles and requirements
- Features which ensure the involvement of all relevant participants

A relevant issue in this outlook was the commitment to the identification and evaluation of impacts for all the university's areas and processes. This required that all areas and processes had to be displayed in a standard way in accordance to the National Accreditation Commission's requirements, and therefore structured and evaluated with a common format of main processes that contained the following information:

- Name of the process
- Purposes and goals
- Activities of the process
- Measurement of indicators
- Evaluation and learning

Each institutional process was described and assessed using this format. Purposes were understood as the direct product of the university's activities, expressed as expected outcomes of the processes, and description of goals, which respond to the impacts among the community. Activities described the sequence of main tasks of each process and the functions of different linking mechanisms. A summary of quality assurance mechanisms included a description of activities, human, material and economic resources, and the regulations that governed the development process.

In addition to indicators for measuring progress, each process was assessed and analyzed according to the results obtained from the measurement of indicators and the surveys applied to key informants, determining causes, strengths and weaknesses. The evaluation established areas to be improved and thereby intended to reduce the gaps between expected and obtained outcomes and impacts. Finally, quality sources were defined and consulted throughout the self-evaluation process.

Though the Universidad de Santiago has been involved in self-study and systemic evaluation since 1997, the self-evaluation process carried out in 2007 represented a series of challenges for the institution. First of all, the evaluation of the different accreditation areas proved to be quite complex. Those working in each area had to come to agreement as to the definition of purposes, goals, expected results, impact indicators, methodology for measuring the performance of these indicators and improvement plans.

Besides the difficulty in achieving this agreement in each of the areas assessed, those involved in the self-evaluation effort were faced to a new evaluation language which included new terms, such as "outcomes" and "impacts". This meant that the commission members had to learn the meaning and modeling of outcome and impact indicators for each area, which had commonly been absent or very implicit in the institutional practices.

This proved to be especially true for the case of the undergraduate education, since teaching has been typically assessed by using more traditional perspectives of assessment which don't necessarily evidence learning outcomes, such as generic and specific skills. Therefore, a more intense work toward monitoring educational gains needs to be installed within higher education institutions.

Alumni and employers' commitment with the self-evaluation process was limited. Therefore, if the Universidad de Santiago expects to count with reliable and systematic information of its academic impacts, it should pay more attention to its work with employers and alumni. The self-evaluation process demonstrated that the university has a rather casuistic and unsystematic relationship with these stakeholders.

The challenges that emerged throughout the self-evaluation process pointed out the necessity of implementing demonstrative evaluation criteria regarding academic goals, rather than declarative criteria, in order to foster quality, accountability and institutional learning. So far, the University has initiated some experimental projects to assess educational outcomes through MECESUP (Programa de Mejoramiento de la Calidad y Equidad), a state initiative that aims to improve educational quality and equity. MECESUP has been a major funding initiative that has been providing resources for enhancing higher education effectiveness since 1999.

EVALUATION OF ACADEMIC OUTCOMES: THE CASE OF MECESUP

MECESUP, the program for improving quality and equity in higher education has been a major educational initiative in Chile. Starting ten year ago, the program was originally oriented to enhance infrastructure in universities and colleges. After five years of implementation, MECESUP made its own evaluation, redirecting its efforts and resources to enhancing institutional capabilities toward educational improvement. Since 2005, MECESUP is more narrowly focused on quality, accountability, and institutional learning.

Over the past years, the Universidad de Santiago has developed several projects oriented to enhance institutional effectiveness and student learning, moving from a declarative to a demonstrative process of assessing students' outcomes. In the next paragraphs, the authors explain two important initiatives: one implemented in the engineering faculty and another developed within the university to assess the impact of MECESUP projects oriented to enhance students' outcomes developed within the whole university. Both experiences can be understood as experimental efforts to enhance institutional capability to assess educational outcomes.

Assesing Students Skills in the Engineering Faculty

The engineering faculty and its departments are one of the oldest schools of the university, recognized as a key educational resource. For years, its departments have developed activities in the field of scientific and technological innovations. Nonetheless, these initiatives have not emphasized innovations for their professional education. Different academic departments have struggled with academic innovation skills, without producing systematic changes related to curriculum design, teaching practices, certification systems, flexible curriculum and a stronger relationship with the workplace.

Before this project was proposed, the departments of the engineering faculty did not count on strategic information to identify academic priorities, implement corrective measures, evaluate or re-design innovations that improved their education, or support job placement of undergraduates and graduates. In addition, there was a lack of basic skills in assessing outcomes and impacts, and in providing technical advice related to academic improvement and innovations.

For this reason, the innovation and improvement cycles have had low impact on the faculty and its departments, and the accumulation of know-how has been quite limited. The future academic innovations should include systematic changes in teaching practices, investments, management, and the acquaintance of students to new educational focuses, which should be planned and in accordance to the continuous improvement processes.

In order to address these weaknesses, the faculty decided to create a technical unit capable of installing the capability to improve key educational processes. The project included this unit due to two main reasons: first, the academic challenges posed by the implementation of the quality assurance system and the supervision of the quality cycle and second, the need to build expert capacity in supporting the faculty's academic management. The new unit was designed to assist the curricular administration throughout the following activities:

- Strengthening curricular development.
- Strengthening learning and impact assessment.
- Developing an adequate community engagement.
- Developing minimum conditions required for achieving curricular innovations.
- Carrying out the specific objectives mentioned in USA0605.

The unit was created in 2008 with three professionals that were in charge of the activities mentioned above. Since its creation, this unit has achieved results in a) curricular redesign and quality assurance and b) learning assessment.

The unit worked first redesigning the graduate profiles and establishing a graduate profile common to the entire faculty's engineering study programs. After this activity was completed, and as part of the institution's quality cycle, these profiles were assessed by alumni and employers. This unit organized workshops to assist in the revision and update of each department's alumni and employers databases. As part of the validation of the profiles, this unit submitted a survey to a group of alumni of each engineering study program.

In a second stage, the technical unit carried out an experimental assessment of several skills that are part of the educational goals of the university's engineering programs. The following learning outcomes were included:

- Autonomous learning
- Application of knowledge to engineering problems; Problem solving; System modeling
- Engineering design
- Group work

- Effective communication
- Ethical behavior
- Social responsibility

A first step of the evaluation process consisted of reviewing the engineering graduate profiles. This revision suggested that all these profiles make explicit some of these desirable learning outcomes. In addition, each study program was revised in order to identify courses related to the development of generic skills, attitudes and values.

Given that the methods used in assessing skills vary in reliability, feasibility of implementation, cost and predictive capacity, and that the methods selected should consider these aspects as well as the objectives of the evaluation, evaluators expertise, and the general context of the evaluation, the methods finally chosen to assess group work and effective communication were the self-report, peer-report and direct observation.[2]

The assessment of these outcomes required a matrix containing the capacities associated with each outcome. Each capacity was then associated with knowledge, skills and attitudes. Subsequently, assessment items were elaborated for each of these capacities. In total, 15 instruments were created to assess the learning outcomes mentioned above:

- Questionnaire to determine the role assumed in group work situations
- Co-evaluation questionnaire for assessing group work
- Self-evaluation questionnaire for assessing group work
- Global evaluation of group work
- Checklist to determine effective communication expressed in a resume
- Engineering problem used to assess group work and effective communication
- Rubric used to assess written report of the engineering problem
- Checklist of effective communication
- Observation guideline for assessing group work
- Opinion survey on ethical behavior
- Multiple choice test about knowledge of personal and professional ethics and social responsibility
- Case of an ethical dilemma
- Checklist used to assess ethical dilemma
- Questionnaire for the assessment of autonomous learning
- Engineering problems: application of knowledge to engineering problems, problem solving and system modeling.

These instruments were finally applied to 30 students belonging to electric engineering, chemical engineering, mechanical engineering and industrial engineering, who were in the final stage of their studies or had graduated.

According to the results obtained, over 50% of the students were capable of assuming a specific role inside the group (as a leader, thinker or conciliator) and were flexible enough to

---

[2] Some of the instruments considered for assessing these outcomes were anecdotal reports, checklists, rating scales and attitude scales.

change roles. This would indicate a professional capable of acquiring different roles, acting according to the work requirements.

As for written communication, the results indicated that there is a poor capacity to communicate through written texts. In addition, the rubric applied to a report showed that the students achieve a better performance in communicating academic ideas related to their career.

Oral communication was assessed observing a simulation of engineering problem solving, which required the use of a checklist. The results indicated that students express well their ideas in a verbal form, use an adequate voice and language, and listen to their peers, even when gestural and corporal expression is lower.

The overall evaluation suggests that students have the basic skills to communicate in an effective manner, though there would only be a partial achievement of this skill since they would excel better at communicating technical issues. According to the assessment results, this skill would not be developed across the curriculum, and only three programs have a specific course on communication.

The results suggest that students would excel at good ethical behavior, though it was not possible to infer if this is only a consequence of their formal education. The students assessed indicated scarce knowledge on personal and professional ethics, but the majority would possess knowledge on social responsibility. In the case of a professional dilemma, the results were lower than expected, which would indicate an insufficient comprehension of ethical problems associated to the profession.

A considerable percentage of students would tend to learn in an autonomous form, with higher autonomy in verifying and achieving their learning outcomes, adopting an analytical position of themselves. Consequently, it is possible to assume that the academic grades are not the only official guideline that can be used to verify learning achievement. In addition, co-evaluation results were coherent with the above mentioned results. In contrast, the assessment results suggest that they would be less autonomous in establishing learning objectives.

Finally, students were asked to address a global engineering problem related to manufacturing that allowed the application of knowledge in engineering basic sciences. The students had to answer theoretical issues and also had to be capable of solving a problem using the concept of modeling system and, simultaneously, be capable of answering questions that emerged throughout the exercise. The students achieved an adequate performance on the application of knowledge, obtaining on a $1 - 7$ scale, an average score of 5.0. In contrast, system modeling registered a weaker performance, obtaining 2.7. Finally, problem solving also obtained a low achievement, with an average score of 3.8.

This experience has shown that schools and departments at the Universidad de Santiago have been poorly oriented to assessing educational outcomes, assuming that the pure presence of a curriculum would be a guarantee of educational effectiveness. The engineering faculty has created a specific unit to enhance its monitoring capability, installing a team of three professionals that are revising courses, minors and majors. In addition to that, the departments are slowly introducing information of key stakeholders in their educational decisions.

At the same time, the faculty is starting to develop its own system to assess educational outcomes, generating a first attempt to assess some skills required among young engineers. This process has been novel within the university context, since the university as a whole has not created a similar unit to monitor educational outcomes at the central level. The engineering faculty's experience will be an important input to other departments interested in assessing learning outcomes, and, therefore, its results will feed the university as a whole.

In the next section we explain a second initative developed within the University to enhance the quality assurance capability.

Developing an Assessment Model for the Measurement of Outcomes and Impacts of MECESUP Projects on Student Learning

In 2008, the Ministry of Education made a call to present projects to assess the impact of MECESUP programs on student learning. This initiative was a great challenge for all the universities since there was a significant lack of national know-how on this issue. The Universidad de Santiago presented a proposal, which was approved by MECESUP, together with other 13 initiatives.

The main objective of this project was to strengthen the institutional management capacity related to learning outcomes of undergraduate and graduate students. More specifically, it intended to assess the impact of MECESUP projects approved during 1999-2004 by the Universidad de Santiago.

Though it is possible to affirm that these projects have achieved tangible progress, the assessment of its effects on student learning has been unknown, and has turned out to be highly complex. It is important to note that these projects did not count with impact assessment criteria based on the institutional quality assurance model at the time they were formulated. In addition, the governmental assessment of MECESUP program indicated that for the period 2000-2003 these projects only considered quantitative indicators but lacked qualitative indicators that could measure some of its long-term effects.

The Universidad de Santiago made the assumption that the outcomes and impacts of MECESUP projects were subject to the influence of external variables, all of which suggest that it is unlikely to isolate the outcomes and impacts of MECESUP projects. This project took into account the university's definition of quality as well as the notion of quality applied in national public policies.[3]

Since this project was meant to be aligned with the focus of quality assurance adopted by the university, it considered the definition provided by the university's system and quality unit, which states that quality, is the degree in which the characteristics of an entity fulfill the requirements of the stakeholders (http://www.dcs.usach.cl/index.php?id=28). Though the stakeholders can be understood as internal and external participants, this assessment stressed the assessment of the internal parts, mainly, the faculty and students.

Complementary to this definition, the government's budget department-DIPRES, underlines that the impacts imply a significant improvement in the target population which, in some cases, is sustainable over time (http://www.dipres.cl/572/articles-37416_doc_pdf.pdf).

---

[3] For example, the institutional, undergraduate and graduate self-evaluation processes represent a process used for identifying strategic priorities that, in turn, lead to the creation of a MECESUP project. At the graduate level, research projects that are being carried out in parallel with a MECESUP project, can contribute to these projects outcomes. Finally, other MECESUP projects of previous years could also be complementary as to the objectives, activities and expected impacts.

As to the definition of student learning, it used the classification of learning outcomes established in the university's educational model, which distinguishes main areas of knowledge, abilities, skills, and attitudes and values.

In contrast to the projects developed by other universities, the Universidad de Santiago chose a qualitative methodology to verify the achievement of outcomes and impacts on student learning. It included the revision of institutional documentation, interviews to project directors and project collaborators, focus-groups with graduate students and an opinion survey applied to undergraduate students.

Though this study has not yet finished, its researchers have come across several difficulties in leading the assessment of these projects. A first difficulty has been that these projects did not include an identification of specific learning outcomes expected to be developed, and in most of the cases they only refer to very general types of learning outcomes, making an implicit mention of these results a challenge for the definition of assessment standards.

This challenge could be related to the emphasis of MECESUP contributing to the universities infrastructure and equipment during the period 1999-2004. At an institutional level, these projects did not count with an institutional educational model that could guide the selection of priority learning outcomes that were consistent with the learning categories of knowledge acquisition, abilities, skills, and attitudes and values.

Another omission in the formulation of these projects, and that has added another obstacle, has been the poor characterization of the student target population, which hampers the definition of the student population affected by the project's innovations. As for the records of each project, the documentation for some of them was incomplete, and there were inconsistencies in the information of different documents that affected the project's internal coherence, therefore raising doubts about valid data to be assessed.

It has also become evident that the university needs to improve its institutional capacity to monitor immediate results derived from these projects, and especially the assessment of the contribution made to the teaching and learning process. Follow-up enquiries applied to the student target population have not been regularly applied, and therefore indicate a weakness in assessing the degree of students' satisfaction with the educational innovations implemented in each project, and in assessing the project's contribution to student learning.

Finally, the indicators used in these projects would indicate a satisfactory achievement of its purposes. Nonetheless, these indicators give an account of quantitative measurements and scarcely complement these with a qualitative assessment that can better explain and put in context the numerical results.

Both MECESUP projects described above represent a great opportunity for the installation of quality assurance capabilities in the Universidad de Santiago. More specifically, the feedback obtained throughout these initiatives has already provided relevant information for the review of the evaluation criteria applied by CICES. A clear expression of this contribution lies in the revision and update of the Center's general evaluation model, which is described in the following section.

General Evaluation Model

The assessment experiences have led the authors to the development of a general evaluation model. This model should be understood as a theoretical-empirical model. On one hand, it intends to mirror the state of the art in evaluation as it is conceived in education, psychology, management and other disciplines, and on the other hand, it includes ideas from multiple assessment experiences such as opinion surveys, assessment of university students' competencies, internal and external evaluation of undergraduate, graduate and institutional accreditation processes, among others.

The assessment model is integrated by three components: general concepts, methodology and resources. The first component includes:

- Definition of evaluation
- Types of evaluation entities
- Evaluation criteria
- Subjects and objectives of the evaluation
- Available evidence
- Forms of measurement
- Standards

General Concepts

Evaluation is defined as a process applied to specific entities which implies defining an evaluator who determines objectives and criteria, gathering evidence of the accomplishment of objectives, applying one or more forms of measuring accomplishment of objectives, and making contrasts between measurement outcomes and pre-established standards. As for *types of evaluation entities*, this must be considered in a very general form, including concrete and abstract entities such as people, programs, institutions, projects, public policies, products, etc.

Evaluation entities can be assessed by different perspectives or by *evaluation criteria*. These criteria are established by the evaluator according to evaluation needs. Relevant educational evaluation criteria include: efficacy, quality, pertinence, equity, efficiency, integrity, economy and sustainability.

Evaluation *subjects* refer to those who evaluate, such as institutions, units, people, etc, and those that are in charge of establishing the evaluation objectives. This model recognizes two types of *objectives: functional and direct*. The functional objectives refer to the reasons for assessing an entity or program. Functional objectives can define resources, evaluation methods, evaluators, etc. Some functional objectives are: to certify, hire, promote, approve, intervene, and diagnose, among others.

The direct objectives refer to the evaluation of certain characteristics or attributes of the evaluation object as, for example, a person's abilities, competencies, knowledge, performance; a library's resources; an academic unit's efficiency, etc. In the academic realm, defining the evaluation objectives can be a very complex task since the functional objectives can be guided by implicit institutional policies and can be misinterpreted if they affect people.

Available evidence refer to records of the evaluation objectives such as available written texts, reports, projects, resolved problems, portfolios, tests, surveys, interviews, focus groups, etc. Some of the most common *forms of measuring* in education are: scores, expert opinions, indicators, checklists, etc. As for the *standards*, these are desirable degrees of accomplishment which are determined by tentative or accepted criteria (for example, minimum score required, positive opinions, minimum values of indicators).

Methodology

This assessment model applies a general methodology that can be used in any kind of evaluation, and considers a general sequence of 12 steps, including:

- Identification of the entity or object to be evaluated
- Definition of the evaluators, objectives and evaluation criteria
- Identification of the logical frameworks that can be applied: functional or political framework, process logical framework, operational logical framework, others
- Specification of the variables to be evaluated
- Design and/or selection, pretest and validation of instruments and evaluation procedures
- Definition of protocols for the application
- Definition of comparison standards
- Application of protocols, instruments and procedures
- Measurement and elaboration of results
- Application of standards
- Reports
- Evaluation of the evaluation

Many of these 12 steps are complex and require experience for their application. The efficacy of the evaluation relies on the internal consistence between the objectives, procedures, instruments and how these are used. The application of logical frameworks is suggested to facilitate this coherence.

A logical framework is an expression of the desired causality between something proposed and what is effectively achieved. It begins with the purposes, which are expressed as desired outcomes, and goals, which express the expected impacts. The purposes and goals define the activities necessary for their achievement, which are supported by human, material and financial resources, as well as the required organization. The implementation of these activities leads to the accomplishment of certain results, which are not necessarily the same as the expected outcomes.

It is assumed that the greater the coherence between the expected outcomes and those effectively achieved the greater coherence of the process. The outcomes should then lead to impacts that match with the types of outcomes. Finally, the impacts and outcomes should provide feedback to the other components of this causal chain. Nonetheless, it is common that this coherence is weak in higher education, since the activities and resources don't coincide with those required. Therefore, it is not unusual that there is little certainty that the outcomes achieved correspond to the expected. According to this, the following logical frameworks are applied in order to conduct an effective evaluation:

The political or functional logical framework refers to the political or functional objectives of an evaluation. The purposes and goals of the evaluation must be defined, as well as the activities, resources and organization. This framework is associated with the evaluation itself. In a similar way, the *logical framework* refers to certain characteristics of the evaluation objectives that are created through known processes and are possible to model with an appropriate logical framework. Finally, the *operational logical framework* corresponds to a third level of analysis, and it is applied when modeling at an operational level. The modeling is done to strictly adjust to the entity's nature, its characteristics and the direct objectives of evaluation.

The *political or functional* framework answers the question, *"Why is the evaluation done?,"* while the logical framework answers the question, *'How and in what context are the characteristics of the object of evaluation formed?"* At last, the logical operational framework answers the question, "H*ow are the evaluated characteristics defined, modeled and measured?"*

These three logical frameworks are particularly relevant when assessing students' outcomes. It is also possible to identify and use variants of these schemes as appropriate, though there do not seem to be specific rules applied. It is also important to note that in some situations some of these frameworks are irrelevant or not applicable.

Support Resources

Finally, a set of resources have to be associated with this model in order to guide its general concepts and methodology. In particular, there must be a portfolio of relevant experiences that facilitate the multiple stages of an evaluation. This would transform the evaluation model discussed here in a more concrete instrument, instead of a set of theoretical definitions. In other words, the resources embody the empirical evidence of the theoretical model. Nowadays, an important part of these records exist but are still not registered in the desirable format. In the next section, the authors describe an assessment case using the assessment model described in the previous paragraphs.

APPLICATION OF THE GENERAL EVALUATION MODEL IN THE EDUCATIONAL FIELD: THE CASE OF SÚMATE

The authors used the assessment model previously described working with a nonprofit organization called SUMATE, which belongs to Hogar de Cristo, a well known nonprofit organization owned by the Jesuits that has worked for more than five decades with poor individuals and families. SUMATE was created in 1989 to address school rehabilitation needs of children that were excluded from the formal educational system.

At the beginning of 2008, the organization decided to give a new approach to its work, focusing on education and employment programs. SUMATE contacted the Universidad de Santiago seeking advice for the assessment of students' skills. The foundation provided a rich documentation related to formative and summative evaluations conducted in different periods of time. The organization also provided records of the workshops conducted over time providing information about the methodology used to achieve the desired educational outcomes.

A first important aspect of the assessment process was the analysis of the graduate profiles. SUMATE defined five skills that were part of its educational goals. The five skills were communication, self-confidence, commitment, initiative, and civic and social responsibility. Prior to this assessment of learning outcomes, the organization had a general understanding of these skills. Therefore, the first task was to define each skill and its key elements. The assessment team and SUMATE directors came to the conclusion that the first assessment would involve oral and written communication skills, given the complexity and scarce precision of the different definitions.

The assessment proposal used the methodology described in the evaluation model previously described. The assessment considered both the specific contributions of SUMATE to the development of the skill, as well as job demands considered as a whole. This meant that SUMATE analyzed both their employment prospects, mainly according to the perception of employers, as well as the inputs related to the guidance activities provided by SUMATE's program. Both instances offered the information required to analyze the degree of adjustment between the job prospects and the education provided by SUMATE.

The assessment methodology was designed to identify the educational contributions of SUMATE. At the same time, another goal was to create assessment capability in the foundation that should allow a progressive improvement of the methodology, validating its instruments and establishing expected achievement standards. The members of SUMATE established political and process logical frameworks. These included all the SUMATE skills, where communication constituted one of its components (See Appendix 1). Academic or English workshops were not considered because they were not part of the competency-based training program that was expected to be evaluated at the time (See Appendix 2).

Communication skill was defined as the *"capacity to express in oral, written and technical-symbolic form, concepts and questions in a clear, coherent and precise way, adjusting to the idiomatic norms"*. In the case of SUMATE, the skill of communication should be expressed, at least, in the following dimensions and basic skills, which represent the following evaluated variables :

- General oral communication
- Specialized oral communication
- General written idiomatic expression
- Symbolic expression

The tests were applied to SUMATE students and to a control group (students from a similar technical institute) which had not received any reinforcement in this area. The results suggest that SUMATE students performed better in "assisting and understanding listeners" and in the basic skill "correctly incorporating concepts and specialized terms".

Basic capacities are associated with each of the dimensions, which are described below:

Skills	Basic Capacities
General Oral Communication	• Express respect for rules of grammar, phonics and culture • Correctly transmit information • Correctly explain events, situations • Assist and understand listeners
Specialized oral communication	• Correctly incorporate concepts and specialized terms in capabilities 2) and 3) mentioned above
General written idiomatic expression	• Elaborate written texts using rules of *spelling, grammar and logical consistency* • Reading comprehension that allows transfer of information and concepts • Records of background, events, decisions and others • Transmission of information, instructions and others • Write projects and activity reports.
Symbolic expression	• Correctly interpret diagrams, graphics, tables and other symbols. • Correctly use diagrams, graphics tables and other symbols in written and other forms of communication.

In contrast, the students of the control group institute outperformed the SUMATE students in the remaining capacities:

(1) expressing using grammar, phonetic and cultural norms,
(2) correctly transmitting information and
(3) correctly explaining events, situations, etc.

As for the written communication skills, SUMATE students scored higher achieving 56%, whereas the control group achieved 41%. The basic skill related to discourse rules was the only one in which the control group outperformed SUMATE students in almost 20%: SUMATE obtained 52%, while the control group obtained 72% of correct answers.

The results of this assessment exercise have been a significant resource for SUMATE, which is undergoing a serious revision of its educational offer, in the attempt to narrow down the gap between what has been declared as an educational goal and what has been achieved in the formative arena. In addition to that, the assessment efforts have encouraged SUMATE to demonstrate greater accountability of its main educational processes, approaching the organization to the quality assurance culture.

CONCLUSIONS

Evaluation of student learning is becoming a core element in higher education. Until now, Chilean universities and colleges were declaring their efforts regarding student learning, but there was no systematic work on demonstrating this. The University of Santiago has been a pioneer institution in the national context, conducting systemic program evaluations and self-evaluations since 1997. The process has not lacked challenges and complexities, considering a rather weak culture of assessment and accountability within the educational system.

The implementation of a national accreditation system and a recent law oriented to higher education quality assurance has pushed institutions in the direction of demonstrating student learning through assessment. Therefore, colleges and universities are generating mechanisms to assess students´ progress, assuming a value added approach to the higher education process. This effort implies a significant challenge because faculties have needed to agree about professional profiles, identifying skills, capabilities and values that need to be developed over the course of an academic program.

This effort is in many aspects a revolution for academic units since they have been used to teach with a rather mechanic approach. For many years, faculties assumed that the available learning opportunities were enough to develop core academic skills and competencies in different professions. However, the introduction of a quality assurance approach is pushing departments and faculty to demonstrate that substantive learning occurs within higher educational classrooms.

The expansion of the higher educational system has been another influence for this shift, since educational institutions are receiving a more heterogeneous group of students. Thirty years ago, higher education institutions were highly selective but now 40% of the students that finish secondary education are attending universities and colleges. Academic programs have been poorly prepared to address this change and, therefore, teaching and learning have increased scrutiny and supervision.

At the same time, the public's interest in higher education is making institutions more oriented to the demonstrative evaluation of its academic initiatives. Nowadays, tutors, remedial programs, labs and many different educational initiatives are part of the educational cycle and as such, need to get assessed in order to provide concrete evidence that they serve educational purposes. For many years, universities were used to making intuitive evaluations but now, educational leaders and administrators are demanding serious evaluation efforts to grasp their real impact.

This work suggests that the process of assessing student learning is in many ways problematic because educational programs have not been originally designed to be assessed. Many educational programs were created in a rather intuitive manner, lacking precise goals, desired outcomes and performance indicators. For this reason, institutions are becoming aware that there is a need to assess programs and more important than that, there is significant pressure to redesign them so there is a closer connection between the curriculum and the professional profile[4].

The experience of the Universidad de Santiago shows that evaluation efforts are often challenged by lack of clear purposes, by use of inappropriate instruments, by lack of the necessary data and even by mismanagement of political variables. Therefore, evaluation initiatives need to be designed considering both the technical and political aspects. While the technical and political variables are not considered, the impact of assessment efforts will be rather weak.

---

[4]Some international examples of recent experiences on student assessment are the Collegiate Learning Assessment-CLA, which assesses student's ability to think critically, reason analytically, solve problems and communicate clearly and cogently (http://www.collegiatelearningassessment.org/index.html), and the Graduate Skills Assessment-GSA, which assesses critical thinking, problem solving, interpersonal unerstandings, and written communication, applied to students at the beginning and end of their studies (http://www.acer.edu.au/tests/gsa).

The Universidad de Santiago has assumed an approach that calls for the installation of assessment skills within academic units, assuming that those skills or capabilities need to be developed through a closer relation with the participants involved in the teaching and learning process. In our accounts, this is a quite innovative approach since many assessment units are placed at the central level of the university's structure, generating a gap between those that assess and those that need to use assessment results to improve educational interactions.

Finally, it is important to recognize that within the Universidad de Santiago, evaluation has been understood as a learning process. Evaluation efforts have been understood as experiments that are part of the quality assurance cycle. Therefore, new assessment initiatives are welcome as experiences that can help to improve the institutional assessment capabilities.

APPENDIX 1. POLITICAL LOGICAL FRAMEWORK

Purpose

To assess the contribution made by the foundation, throughout their scholarship program, to the development, reinforcement and acquisition of competencies, attitudes and knowledge in the field of communication.

Goals

To assess the methodology of the program in the field of communication, with the objective of improving or replicating it in other programs, as appropriate.

Activities

Create an alliance between SUMATE and CICES to work on the subject of evaluation.
Create assessment instruments.
Apply these instruments
Analyze the results obtained.
Elaborate conclusions.

Organizational Resources (SUMATE)

Define and provide financial resources required in the application of the assessment instruments.
Define human resources: Research Officer, Educational Advisor, and Advisor on integral education.

APPENDIX 2. PROCESS LOGICAL FRAMEWORK

Purposes

To develop competencies, attitudes and knowledge acquisition throughout the scholarship program, such as communication, initiative, self-confidence and commitment.

Goals

To increase the employability provided by SUMATE's scholarship.

Curricular Activities Contained in the Competency Training Plan

Teaching activities	Description	Semester
"Life project" workshop	Workshop carried out by a volunteer of SUMATE program with 10-12 students. It is done in 6 sessions of two hours each. *General objective:* To promote and assess students' motivation throughout workshops that enhance self-awareness and the capacity to reflect on new educational challenges that they are about to begin.	Before entering SUMATE program
Venture team group workshops	Educational workshops carried out by facilitators of SUMATE with 8-9 students. Developed in 8 sessions of two and a half hours each. These are done every two weeks. *General objective:* To enhance the necessary learning outcomes required to achieve the graduate profile in the areas of communication, self-awareness, self-confidence, initiative, commitment and job readiness.	I, II, II y IV
Individual guidance	Individual guidance: 13 hours per month. Follow-up interview every month and a half (an hour and a half each). *General objective:* To enhance the students' learning process throughout a continuous follow-up, in order to ensure their attendance to SUMATE.	I, II, III y IV
"Oral and written expression" workshop	Oral and written workshop with 10-12 students, conducted by volunteers of SUMATE. Composed of 24 sessions, two hours each. *General objective:* To enhance and develop students' skills in communication, in order to strengthen their capacity to listen, establish conversations and express concepts and ideas in a clear, coherent and precise form, whether it be oral or written.	I y II
Cultural workshops	Workshops carried out by volunteers that include issues and exercises dedicated to strengthen communication skills. These include 10 sessions, two hours each.	IV

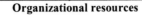

Organizational resources
Human Resources
Facilitators hired by SUMATE in charge of venture group workshops and individual guidance: 12
Volunteers: approximately 120.
Alliances with institutions where SUMATE students can carry out their social work: 10
Infrastructure
Classrooms: 8
Computers for students: 12
Financial Resources
Handbooks for facilitators and students
Materials used in each workshop

Results achieved
Students capable of communicating adequately, both in oral and written form, self-confident in their capacities, capable of defining and achieving their goals, and committed to their tasks and the common good.

Impacts achieved
Quick placement of SUMATE graduates in quality jobs.
Managerial capacity of young graduates' careers.

APPENDIX 3. OPERATIONAL LOGICAL FRAMEWORK

Purposes
To assess the degree of achievement of communication skills.
Goals
Compare the relevance of SUMATE's and the control group's education

Activities
Definition of the skill.
Configuration of the ability.
Design or selection of assessment instruments
Application

Resources
Students.
Experts
Computer media

Results achieved
Effective degree of achievement of the skill according to the instruments and procedures applied.

Impacts achieved
Benefits reported of using this skill.

REFERENCES

Centro de Investigación en Creatividad y Educación Superior (2009). Informe final de evaluación de aprendizajes proyecto MECESUP USA 0605. Universidad de Santiago de Chile, Santiago, Chile.

Centro de Investigación en Creatividad y Educación Superior (2008). Términos de referencia MECESUP USA 0605. Universidad de Santiago de Chile, Santiago, Chile.

Collegiate Learning Assessment. Retrieved May 15, 2010, from http://www. collegiatelearningassessment.org/index.html.

Comisión Nacional de Acreditación de Pregrado (2007). El modelo chileno de acreditación de la educación superior. Ministerio de Educación, Santiago, Chile.

Dirección de Presupuesto. Anexo metodología evaluación de impacto. Retrieved May 10, 2010, from http://www.dipres.cl/572/articles-37416_doc_pdf.pdf.

Graduate Skills Assessment. Retrieved May 15, 2010, from http://www.acer.edu.au/tests/gsa.

Letelier, M., Poblete, P., Carrasco, R. and Vargas, X. (2009). Quality assurance in higher education in Chile. In A.S.P Patil and P.J.J Gray (Eds), *Engineering education quality assurance: A global perspective* (pp.121-132). New York: Springer Science+Business Media.

Sistema Nacional de Información de la Educación Superior. Evolución de la matrícula total de educación superior por género. Retrieved May 10, 2010, from http://www. divesup.cl/sies/wp-content/uploads/2010/01/Evolución-de-la-Matrícula-de-Pregrado-por-Género-1984-2009.xls

Trow, M. (1973). Problems in the transition from elite to mass higher education. Carnegie Commission on Higher Education, Berkeley, California.

Universidad de Santiago de Chile. Concepto de calidad. Retrieved May 10, 2010, from http://www.dcs.usach.cl/index.php?id=28.

In: Progress in Education. Volume 26
Editor: Robert V. Nata, pp. 97-114

ISBN 978-1-61324-321-3
© 2011 Nova Science Publishers, Inc.

Chapter 5

READING GOALS AND TEXT RELEVANCE FOR ASSIGNED COURSE READINGS

Matthew T. McCrudden[*]

Victoria University of Wellington, New Zealand

ABSTRACT

The purpose of this study was to investigate how students determined text relevance for their assigned course readings. *Text relevance* refers to the instrumental value of text information for enabling a reader to meet a reading goal (McCrudden, Magliano, and Schraw, 2010). Undergraduates (n = 38) enrolled in introductory educational psychology course were asked to provide written responses to several open-ended prompts about their goals for the assigned readings, what they focused on while they reading, the strategies they used while reading, and how they evaluated whether they had understood what they read. Readers' responses were analyzed and emergent themes were identified. Readers described an array of different goals, they described using various contextual cues to identify text relevance, described using surface and transformational strategies while reading, and held various beliefs about what constitutes good comprehension. Results are interpreted within the goal-focusing model of relevance. Future directions and educational implications are provided.

INTRODUCTION

University instructors ubiquitously ask students to read for their respective courses. Given the vast amount of information students must read for one class, along with readings for multiple classes and other demands on their time (e.g., work), students must identify text relevance. *Text relevance* refers to the instrumental value of text information for enabling a reader to meet a reading goal (Lehman and Schraw, 2002; McCrudden, Magliano, and

---

[*] Corresponding Author: Matthew T. McCrudden, Victoria University of Wellington, Faculty of Education, PO Box 17-310, Karori, Wellington, 6147, New Zealand. E-mail: matt.mccrudden@vuw.ac.nz. mattmccrudden@hotmail.com.

Schraw, 2010), such as reading to prepare for an upcoming exam. Text information that closely matches readers' goals and enables them to meet their goals is more relevant. Conversely, text information that is tangential or unrelated to readers' goals and does not enable them to meet their goals is less relevant. The purpose of this study was to investigate how undergraduates enrolled in an introduction to educational psychology course determined text relevance for their assigned course readings.

Reading in educational settings is predominantly task-induced, meaning that students read to complete some assigned task, as opposed to self-induced reading, such as reading a magazine for leisure. Task-induced reading can vary in its level of specificity (McCrudden and Schraw, 2007). For example, an instructor can indicate that students should read assigned text because it is a requirement for the course, which is a very general reading purpose. Conversely, an instructor can provide much greater specificity. For example, an instructor can provide reading questions that focus on text content that will be covered in lecture and assessed on a test. In both situations, the instructor is providing relevance cues that signal text relevance. In the first example (i.e., read because it is a requirement), the criteria for determining text relevance is less explicit, such that the student is aware that in a formal classroom setting the assigned readings are connected to the course theme, but there are fewer cues for signaling the comparative relevance of specific topics or concepts in the readings. In the second example (i.e., reading questions aligned with lecture and assessment), the criteria for determining text relevance is more explicit because the students are made more aware of the comparative relevance of specific topics or concepts in the readings.

GOAL-FOCUSING MODEL OF RELEVANCE

McCrudden, Magliano, and Schraw (2010) described an explanatory process model, called the goal-focusing model of relevance (see Figure 1), to explain how students determine text relevance and how this influences reading processes (e.g., strategies) and products (e.g., memory). In task-induced reading situations, personal intentions and given intentions can influence reading goals and outcomes. Personal intentions are internally-generated perceptions and beliefs that readers hold about reading. They can include beliefs about what constitutes comprehension (e.g., standards of coherence; van den Broek, Virtue, Everson, Tzeng, and Sung, 2002) and the value they place on completing an assigned task (e.g., the importance attached to doing well, whether doing well enables the reader to get something else of worth; Pajares, 1996; Wigfield and Eccles, 2000).

Conversely, given intentions are externally-provided cues that can influence readers' goals for reading. Instructors often use cues to help orient readers to a text. Relevance instructions are explicit, given intentions that provide criteria for determining information's relevance to a particular reading task (Lehman and Schraw, 2002; McCrudden et al., 2005; McCrudden and Schraw, 2007). Information that closely matches instructions is more task-relevant, whereas information that does not match the instructions is less task-relevant. Relevance instructions can vary in their specificity (McCrudden and Schraw, 2007), as illustrated in the example described at the beginning of this chapter. McCrudden and Schraw (2007) described two basic types of relevance instructions (see Figure 2) that researchers have used individually or in combination to investigate task-induced reading. Specific relevance instructions typically highlight discrete text elements, whereas general relevance instructions are more likely to highlight broad themes or contexts for reading.

Readers can use relevance instructions to help them identify task-relevant information and strategically process text (Bråten and Samuelstuen, 2004; Cerdán and Vidal-Abarca, 2008; Cerdán et al., 2009; Rouet, Vidal-Abarca, Bert-Erbol, and Millogo, 2001; Wiley et al., 2009), which in turn, influences comprehension.

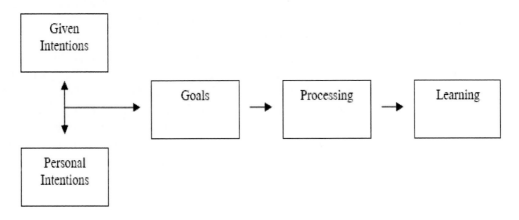

Figure 1. Goal-focusing model of relevance.

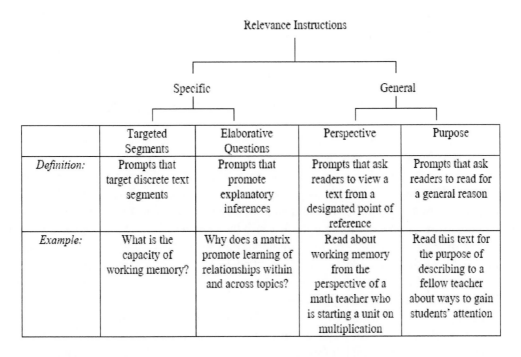

Figure 2. Types of relevance instructions.

According to the goal-focusing model of relevance, reading goals are the product of the bi-directional relation between personal and given intentions. For instance, readers may adjust their standards for determining adequate comprehension based on task demands, such as reading to prepare for a multiple-choice test items that assess fact learning versus concept application. Further, readers may periodically adjust their reading goals as they progress through a text (e.g., Reynolds, Shepard, Lapan, Kreek, and Goetz, 1990).

Successful readers allocate processing resources to more- and less-relevant information in ways that enable them to meet their reading goals (e.g., Cataldo and Oakhill, 2000; Cerdán and Vidal-Abarca, 2008; Cerdán et al., 2009; McCrudden et al., 2005; Rapp and Kendeou, 2007). Further, successful readers typically have greater metacognitive awareness and can self-regulate as they read (e.g., Dunlosky, Rawson and Middleton, 2005; Linderholm, Cong, and Zhao, 2008). They are aware of different strategies and know when and how to use those strategies to meet their reading goals (Perfetti, Landi, and Oakhill, 2005; Reynolds, 1992). Other reader characteristics, such as prior knowledge and motivation, also influence goals and processing (e.g., Alexander, 1997; Guthrie et al., 2004; Taboada and Guthrie, 2006).

Processing subsequently influences performance and learning outcomes. Successful reading comprehension leads to the construction of an integrated understanding of the text (or texts) that enables the readers to meet their reading goals. Thus, in task-induced reading, readers' personal intentions interact with given intentions to produce reading goals, which influence processing and learning.

THE PRESENT STUDY

The purpose of this chapter was to investigate how undergraduates enrolled in an introduction to educational psychology course determined text relevance for their assigned course readings by analyzing students' self-report data. Undergraduates enrolled in one university course were asked to provide written responses to several open-ended prompts about their goals for the assigned readings, what they focused on while they reading, the strategies they used while reading, and how they evaluated whether they had understood what they read. Readers' responses were analyzed and emergent themes were identified.

Four research questions guided this investigation. First, what goals did students describe for the assigned readings? Previous research suggests that readers who receive the same relevance cues can develop a variety of reading goals (McCrudden, Magliano, and Schraw, 2010). In McCrudden et al. (2010), participants who received the same relevance instructions developed different goals for reading and enacted different strategies for meeting those goals. This finding was particularly meaningful because the relevance instructions signaled discrete categories of information (i.e., information about one particular country in a text about four countries). Given that the students in the present student received relevance cues that signaled a broader range of information across multiple readings, it was expected that students would describe a wide variety of reading goals.

Second, what did students describe focusing on when they did the assigned readings? These data were important for providing information about what students focused on because it provided insights into what information was deemed relevant. Although they received relevance instructions in the form of reading questions, it was unclear whether they would focus only on information that was relevant to answering those questions, a broader range of information, or possibly focus on less information or information that was not relevant to answering the questions. This was a particularly interesting question because these data can provide insights into the factors that influence students' decisions for allocating their attention and devoting resources to text information throughout an entire course. These factors may come from various sources including explicit relevance instructions (e.g., reading questions; McCrudden and Schraw, 2007), implicit relevance cues (e.g., content that was or was not covered in lecture; Jetton and Alexander, 1997), reader characteristics (e.g., interest; Schraw and Dennison, 1994), text characteristics (e.g., signaling; Lorch and van den Broek, 1997) and contextual factors (e.g., time constraints). Students' responses would provide insights into the role of the reading instructions and other factors (e.g., anticipation of assessment) in how they determined text relevance.

Third, what strategies did students describe using when they did the assigned readings? Readers use a variety of strategies when asked to read for an assigned purpose (e.g., Linderholm and van den Broek, 2002; *van den Broek, Lorch, Linderholm, and Gustafson, 2001*). For instance, Linderholm and van den Broek (2002) provided participants with an assigned reading purpose (e.g., read for study) before they read a text. They used a think-aloud methodology in which participants verbalized their thoughts as they read. They coded participants' think aloud comments for strategies and found that participants used an array of different strategies as they read. Thus, it was expected that participants in the present study would report using a variety of strategies for the assigned readings.

Lastly, how did students describe what it meant to understand what they had read? Standards of coherence "reflect a reader's knowledge and beliefs about what constitutes good comprehension as well as the reader's specific goals for reading the particular text" (van den Broek, Virtue, Everson, Tzeng, and Sung, 2002, p. 137). This question was included to evaluate how students evaluated their comprehension of the text content in the context of the course. Very little research has investigated readers' beliefs about what constitutes good comprehension in the context of task-induced reading when students are completing assigned readings for a course in which they are enrolled. These data will provide insights into these reader beliefs.

METHOD

Participants and Setting

Participants were 38 undergraduates from the same introduction to educational psychology course, most of which were female ($n = 36$). Participation was voluntary. The majority of participants were education majors, whereas some were psychology majors. The course schedule spanned 14 weeks, with a two-week midterm break during weeks seven and eight. The course met for lecture for two hours and 50 minutes per session, one day a week for 12 weeks. The students completed three tests for the course (week 4, week 10, and week 14). Ninety percent of each student's final grade was based upon their test scores. The other 10% of their final grade came from completion of reading questions. In designing the course, the instructor applied instructional alignment, which is the match between intended learning outcomes, learning activities, and assessments (Eggen and Kauchak, 2010). Intended learning outcomes refer to what instructors expect students to learn (Anderson and Krathwohl, 2001). Learning activities refer to the content delivery and tasks students perform, and assessment of learning corresponds to the measurement of intended learning outcomes and other learning that results from the learning activities. With respect to this course, the instructor, who was the researcher in this study, attempted to align the intended learning outcomes, lectures, study questions, and tests.

Materials

Textbook. The textbook for the course was Eggen and Kauchak's (2010) *Educational Psychology: Windows on Classrooms, (8th ed.)*. This textbook provides an introduction to educational psychology terms, concepts, and ideas, including illustrative examples. The assigned readings consisted of 169 pages from eight chapters on topics including cognitive views of learning, behavioral views of learning, social cognitive theory, cognitive development, constructivism, and motivation.

Tests. Each test consisted of approximately 40 multiple-choice and short-answer items that assessed different levels of understanding including factual knowledge, conceptual knowledge, application, and analysis. Vignettes were also used, in which students read about a classroom scenario and answered questions that pertained to the scenario. Each test built upon the ideas of the former (i.e., cumulative). The content of the tests included information that was covered in lecture only, information that was included in the text only, and information that was covered in lecture and the text.

Study questions. The study questions were similar to the test items and asked students to apply concepts that were covered in the textbook and in the lecture. There were seven sets of study questions ranging from six to 12 items (see Appendix A for example items). The items mainly focused on concept identification and application. One set was due on each of the following weeks: two, three, five, six, nine, 12 and 13. Many of the concepts from the study questions were assessed on the tests, although the items were not identical. Each set of study questions pertained to content in an upcoming lecture. Thus, students had to read the text and complete the study questions prior to the content being covered in class.

On the course syllabus, it was indicated that the study questions were included to help students evaluate their understanding of some of the key concepts that would be assessed on the tests and that these questions were included to provide practice using the ideas from the course and to prepare them for the lectures and tests.

For marking, it was emphasized that their responses could be brief but that they should reflect university-level work, and that they would not lose points for incorrect responses if they had made an effort to answer. It is important to note that there were seven sets of study questions and each set individually was worth a very minimal amount of the total grade for the course (i.e., less than 2%). This was done to enable students to focus on learning the content, yet to provide a small incentive for them to complete the study questions. By aligning instruction, the instructor assumed that the students would see the instrumental value in completing the questions.

Questionnaire. The questionnaire consisted of four open-ended items (see Appendix B for items and instructions), which were generated to reflect the components of the goal-focusing model. The questionnaire was designed to elicit readers' descriptions of their goals for doing the assigned readings, descriptions of what they focused on when they read and the strategies they used, and how they described what it meant to understand their readings.

Procedure

The questionnaire data were collected during week 12. The course instructor distributed the questionnaire to students at the beginning of class and read the instructions aloud, emphasizing that their responses would be strictly anonymous and would not affect their course grades.

To ensure anonymity and the fact that their responses would not affect their course grades, the instructor was absent from the room when students completed the questionnaire and a volunteer from the class collected the responses and placed them in a folder, which would to be given to the instructor after the term had ended and final grades had been submitted.

The instructor emphasized that the purpose of collecting the data was to help university instructors improve course design and to provide feedback on this particular course. Students completed their questionnaires individually; they did not write their names on the questionnaires. Data collection lasted approximately 15 minutes.

Data Analysis

Verbatim transcriptions of the written responses were made before the analysis. The researcher utilized a four-stage scoring process to analyze the responses. This process was repeated for each item on the questionnaire. The first stage involved broad holistic scoring. To begin, the researcher read the transcriptions to get a "holistic sense" of the data (Igo, Bruning, and Riccomini, 2009; Shank, 2006). Next, the researcher extracted descriptive, meaningful phrases that pertained to each item. For example, for item 1, student 19 (s19) wrote, "I look specifically for the information that is relevant to the assignments and try to link what I read in the textbook with what we are taught in the lectures." The second stage involved identifying common descriptive responses. The researcher examined all of the extracted phrases from the first stage for repetition of ideas. For example, for item one, s20 wrote, "To better understand what is presented in class" and s22 wrote, "To get a better understanding of what we are learning about in class". The third stage involved classifying descriptive responses into broader thematic categories. The phrases identified from the second stage were organized into categories of non-repetitive themes. For example, s20's response, "To better understand what is presented in class" and s22's response, "To get a better understanding of what we are learning about in class" were classified as 'augment lecture'. The fourth stage involved generating several broad response categories from the thematic categories.

Tables 1, 2, 3, and 4 provide summaries of the broad response categories for each item, including the broader thematic categories, frequencies, and exemplar quotes.

Table 1. Students' goals for the assigned readings

Response categories / Thematic categories	Definition	Frequency	Exemplar quotes
Assessment			
Complete the assignments	Answer the study questions	19	"To help with finding answers to the weekly assignments" "Looking for answers to the homework questions"
Prepare for the tests	Identify and study information expected to be assessed on the tests	8	"Help my understanding of the topic to study for the tests"
Pass the course	Achieve a grade to fulfill degree requirements	2	"To pass the course"
Build knowledge			
Understand	Understand the content	12	"To understand the content of the readings"
Elaborate/Integrate	Build connections between ideas	7	"To integrate the course material into my own experiences and thoughts"
Know more	Acquire additional knowledge	3	"To know more about the subject"
Augment lecture			
Link text content to previous lecture	Relate text content to lecture content that had been presented	10	"Relate what has been discussed in class to the reading"
Prepare for upcoming lecture	Develop understanding of text content expected in upcoming lecture	8	"To get an idea of what we will be learning in the next class"
Apply content outside of class			
Apply to future job/ my own life	Transfer content to novel situation	7	"[Focus on] things that I can potentially apply in my classroom setting" "To gain knowledge so that I can elaborate on my current understanding about helping people in applied settings"
Use for other courses	Use text content to supplement other courses	2	"[To] use the information in another assignment for another class"

Table 2. What students described focusing on when they did the assigned readings

Response categories / Thematic categories	Definition	Frequency	Exemplar quotes
Context-features			
Assignments	Information pertaining to the assigned study questions	12	"Information related to the assignment questions"
Lectures	Information communicated during class meetings	5	"Relevance to lecture; pick out more important points the instructor has covered in the lecture"
Assigned readings	Pages assigned on the course outline	5	"The assigned course material for that week"
Tests	Information expected to be assessed on the tests	3	"What is relevant to the tests"
Text-features			
Signalled points	Text elements that were demarcated by their physical features/location	12	"I usually focused on the highlighted words" "Things under the headings and subheadings"
Examples	Instances that illustrated concepts	8	"Examples to explain the concepts easily"
Definitions	Key words	4	"Definitions"
Person-features			
Knowledge-building	General attempts to develop a greater understanding of the content	10	"Information that develops my understanding of concepts further"
Familiarity	Focusing on information that was or was not known previously	5	"Anything that looks familiar" "Points or topics that I'm not so familiar with"
Interest	Intriguing information	4	"Things that are of interest to me"

Table 3. Strategies students described using

Response categories / Thematic categories	Definition	Frequency	Exemplar quotes
Surface strategies			
Select	Choosing relevant information	21	"I usually read through it once pulling out key words and then read through again, writing things down on the paper next to me"
Repetition	Repeat an action	10	"I usually read over it more than once. If I don't get a paragraph or page, I will probably read over it a number of times. Once I've read a section I usually go over it in my head so I understand what I've read"
Skim/scan	Read in a cursory way	6	"I mostly skim read it, but keep an eye out for key words that are in the assignment questions. If these key words pop up, then I read that section more thoroughly"
Transformative strategies			
Elaborate	Connect ideas in meaningful ways	14	"I create analogies and plausible scenarios to illustrate the concepts, ones that are relevant to my personal experience" "Thinking of my own examples of [the concepts and] when they might be put into use"
Organize	Group information in meaningful ways	12	"I try to organize the information into a logical structure, often in the form of 'idea-evidence-application' or some other useful variation."
Summarize	Consolidate essential information in reader's own words	5	"Read a couple of paragraphs, then summarize the main points"
Paraphrase	Rephrase using own words	3	"Whatever I don't understand, I try to reword"

Table 4. Students' descriptions of what is meant to understand what they had read

Response categories / Thematic categories	Definition	Frequency	Exemplar quotes
Use			
Apply	Transfer the information to a new setting	20	"When I can directly apply the theories to a practical situation"
Generate own examples	Produce examples to illustrate concepts	4	"Generate my own examples for the facts"
Identify examples	Recognize examples of concepts	1	"Find meaningful examples"
Communicate			
Explain	Clarify meaning to another person	8	"Be able to explain it well enough to someone else"
Paraphrase	Put meaning into own words	4	"To be able to paraphrase the entire passage back to someone else"
Summarize	Consolidate essential information in reader's own words	2	"Be able to retell the information in a summarized version to somebody else"
Discuss with others confidently	Confident in talking about information with others	2	"Have developed coherent knowledge about ideas and concepts which I can comfortable discuss and elaborate on"
Describe	Able to depict information accurately	1	"Able to describe the information in detail"
Retain			
Long-term memory	Store the information in memory for extended period of time	6	"Remember the information over a long period of time"
Know	Familiarity with information	3	"Know the definitions"
Answer test questions	Demonstrate understanding on assessment	1	"To be able to answer test questions without too much thinking"
Other			
Learning is easier	Promotes less effortful learning	1	"Makes learning easier"
Evaluate	Ability to appraise information	1	"To be able to agree or disagree with ideas and concepts"

RESULTS

The first research question was "what goals did students describe for the assigned readings", which was addressed by Item 1. As can be seen in Table 1, many different goals were identified. There were four broad response categories. The first was 'assessment', which described students' goals related to achieving some outcome related to the evaluation of their understanding. This included three thematic categories: 'complete the assignments', 'prepare for the tests', and 'pass the course'. The second broad response category was 'build knowledge', which described students' attempts to develop a greater understanding of the course content.

This included three thematic categories: 'understanding', 'elaborate/integrate', and 'know more'. The third was 'augment lecture', which described students' use of the text to support their understanding of the content covered in the weekly lecture. This included 'link text content to previous lecture' and 'prepare for upcoming lecture'. The fourth was 'apply content outside of class', which described students' attempts to build connections between course content and their lives outside of the class. This included 'apply to future job/my own life' and 'use for other courses'. It is important to note that most students had more than one goal. For example, s33 wrote, "To understand what I am reading, to be able to identify relationships in the information we receive from classes, and to do well on the assignments". This student, and many others, had multifaceted goals when doing the assigned readings.

The second research question was "what did students describe focusing on when they did the assigned readings", which was addressed by Item 2. There were three broad response categories (see Table 2). The first was 'context-features', which described environmental factors external to the text that influenced students' judgments of task-relevance. This included four thematic categories: 'assignments', 'lectures', 'assigned readings', and 'tests'. The second was 'text-features', which described the elements or features of the text that were salient. This included three thematic categories: 'signaled points', 'examples', and 'definitions'. The third was 'person-features', which described characteristics of the students. This included three thematic categories: 'knowledge-building', 'familiarity', and 'interest'.

The third research question was "what strategies did students describe using when they did the assigned readings", which was addressed by Item 3. There were two broad response categories (see Table 3). The first was 'surface strategies', which described activities in which the student processed the information but did not transform it. This included three thematic categories: 'repetition', 'skim/scan', and 'select'. The second was 'transformative strategies', which describe activities in which the student transformed the information in an attempt to make it more meaningful. This included four thematic categories: 'organize', 'elaborate', 'summarize', and 'paraphrase'. It is important to note that many students used a combination of surface and deeper strategies.

The last research question was "how did students describe what it meant to understand what they had read", which was addressed by Item 4. There were four broad categories (see Table 4). The first was 'use', which described the application or utilization of the information. This included two thematic categories (i.e., 'apply' and 'generate own examples') and one additional comment labeled 'identify examples'. The second was 'communicate', which described ways to express the ideas to other people in an understandable way. This included four thematic categories (i.e., 'explain', 'paraphrase', 'summarize', and 'discuss with others confidently') and one additional comment labeled 'describe'. The third was 'retain', which described the ability to store the information in memory. This included two thematic categories (i.e., 'long-term memory' and 'know') and one additional comment labeled 'answer test questions'. The fourth was 'other' with included two comments that did not fit into the other thematic categories.

CONCLUSION

The purpose of this study was to investigate how undergraduates enrolled in an introduction to educational psychology course determined text relevance for their assigned course readings. Four main research questions were addressed. First, readers' goals for the assigned reading were explored. Readers described an array of different goals. The most frequently mentioned goals pertained to assessment. Further, the most frequently identified thematic category was 'answer the study questions'. Clearly, the students acknowledged the value of completing the study questions in the context of the course. Students also commonly identified 'building knowledge' as a goal. Thus, the 'answer study questions' goal appeared to complement the 'build knowledge' goal; suggesting that students may have viewed the study questions as a means to help them learn. Further, the students found the readings to facilitate their understanding of the lectures, as numerous students indicated that they used the readings to help them identify relevant information from the lectures and that the lectures helped them identify relevant information in the readings. It was interesting to note that students established goals of applying the content outside of class. Noticeably, there were no comments indicative of students trying to demonstrate their competence, or conversely, to avoid looking incompetent to their peers or the instructor (Schunk, Pintrich, and Meece, 2008). While it is possible that students espoused these goals, none were mentioned.

Second, what students focused on while they read was examined. Students' comments indicated that they used various contextual cues to identify text relevance but the most frequently mentioned was the assignments (i.e., study questions). The students described using the study questions to select information from the readings. They also mentioned several text features, most prominently signaling. For instance, students noticed bolded print, headings and subheadings, and definitions in the margins. This is consistent with previous research that has shown that text signals increase the salience of the information signaled (Lorch and van den Broek, 1997; Mautone and Mayer, 2001). Further, students described features about themselves that influenced their judgments of text relevance. The most frequently described thematic category was 'knowledge-building'. This suggests that some students were aware of gaps in their knowledge and used the text to fill those gaps (Zhao and Linderholm, 2008). Another possibility is that these students espoused mastery goals (Schunk et al., 2008), and focused on text information that enabled them to meet their goals. This interpretation would be consistent with 'build knowledge' goals that readers described for the assigned readings above.

Third, the strategies students described using when doing the assigned readings were investigated. It is important to note that students commonly described using both surface and transformational strategies. This is important because surface strategies are perquisites of transformational strategies in goal-directed learning. For instance, a reader must select relevant information before generating a summary of key ideas. Thus, the high prevalence of reported surface strategies is not surprising and it is encouraging that they were accompanied by a high frequency of transformational strategies. It is also important to note that students reported using several transformational strategies that have been shown to enhance long-term learning, such as elaboration and organization (Bransford, Brown, and Cockling, 2000).

Lastly, students' standards of understanding were inspected. The most dominant theme for students' descriptions of understanding was 'apply'. These students indicated that they evaluated that they had understood the content when they were able to apply the information. This outcome would appear to be consistent with the nature of an introduction to educational psychology course, particularly when the instructor, as was the case in the present study, communicated that students should be able to use the information after they class had finished. Given this message, it is not surprising that many students described espousing learning goals. Of further importance is the fact that the course assessment was aligned with this message. The intended learning outcomes were aligned with the learning activities and the assessment. When the intended learning outcomes, instruction, and assessment were designed to promote application, the students appeared to develop learning-focused goals (Anderman and Wolters, 2006).

These data can be interpreted within the goal-focusing model of relevance. Consistent with previous research, students used contextual cues to establish goals for reading and for judging text relevance (McCrudden and Schraw, 2007; Schraw, Wade, and Kardash, 1993). Their goals appeared to influence what they focused on, the strategies they used while reading, and their standards for evaluating their understanding of the course content. It also appeared that the broader context in which the readings took place influenced how reader approached the assigned readings. The classroom context could be characterized as instructionally-aligned and designed in a way to promote learning goals. Had the instruction been out of alignment, the findings may have differed. For instance, had the test items focused on lower-level knowledge only, such as memorization of facts and definitions, students may have read differently. Also, if the instructor had promoted performance goals, rather than mastery goals, the students may have espoused different goals and used different strategies. For instance, if the instructor had promoted competition among students, or had not emphasized the importance of learning the content for use after the course had completed, the students may not have describe more learning-focused goals.

In future studies, linking participants' responses to their achievement data would potentially provide more illuminating information about the role of goals, strategies, and standards for understanding learning outcomes. It could be possible to identify different reader profiles which may show relations among these variables. For instance, a student with a learning goal may be more likely to use effortful and deep learning strategies, which may be related to better learning outcomes. The instructor could share these data with students in subsequent classes as a model for these students and to promote their self-efficacy for learning the concepts in the course. Future research should also include observations of the instructor to identify teaching behaviors that influence text relevance for the assigned readings as well as lecture content. It would also be important to conduct in-depth interviews with students to gain more information about their goals and judgments of text relevance.

Retrospective reports of strategy use may not always be accurate or representative of what student actually do when they read as they are sometimes unaware of some of the strategies they use. Thus, future research should have students read an excerpt of an assigned reading using a think-aloud methodology, in which the students verbalize their thoughts while they read. These data could then be coded for different strategies.

The present study has at least two main implications for educators. First, instructors should provide cues for identifying text relevance for assigned course readings. For example, an instructor can provide study questions to help students identify information that the instructor believes to be relevant. It may be beneficial for instructors to provide study questions that prompt students in engage in different kinds of cognitive processes and different kinds of learning (e.g., Graesser and Pearson, 1994). For instance, when content is relatively unfamiliar, it may be more beneficial to provide reading questions that prompt students to build a factual and conceptual understanding, and followed by questions that prompt students to apply the facts and concepts to real-world scenarios, such as case studies.

Second, instructors should attempt to align relevance cues with intended learning outcomes. For instance, an instructor can specifically target assessment-relevant information with relevance cues. However, this is not to suggest that instructors "teach to the test"; rather, by providing cues that are aligned with assessment, students can have a greater task focus and have greater confidence that the use of their time and mental resources are being devoted to activities that promote learning as opposed to doing "busy work". Students can be more motivated to exert effort when they believe that the benefits of doing so outweigh the costs (Wigfield and Eccles, 2000).

In conclusion, these findings provide insights into how students identify text relevance in the context of completing assigned readings for a course and provide insights into their goals for reading, reading strategies, and beliefs about what constitutes comprehension.

APPENDIX A

Examples of reading questions:

1. In simple terms, reading involves decoding (e.g., identifying separate sounds in words and understanding that spellings correspond to pronunciations) and comprehension (i.e., understand meaning of words, sentences, paragraphs, etc.). Assume a beginning reader has not developed decoding skills to the point of *automaticity*. Explain how this will affect the availability of working memory resources for comprehension.

2. Steve, a year 4 student, is working on a drill and practice activity with a computer. Suddenly the screen flashes: "Congratulations, Steve! You just solved the last four problems without an error." A few minutes later the screen again flashed: "Terrific, Steve. You have done it again. You solved four more problems without an error." In the absence of any other information, this best illustrates which reinforcement schedule?

3. You teach reading. You begin class everyday by reading articles that are related to students' interests (assume that the students are interested in the topics you choose).

    a. Explain why reading interesting topics is a good idea from a classical conditioning point of view.

    b.   Using a concrete example, describe how you could use positive reinforcement to increase the number of pages your students read and understand.

4.   A teacher promotes strategy use by saying, "Let's read the next section in our books. After we've read it, we're going to stop and make a one-sentence summary of the passage. This is something each of you can do as you read on your own. If you do, your understanding of what you're reading will increase." Is this teacher emphasizing learning goals or performance goals? Explain.

APPENDIX B

Reading Comprehension

Directions. We are interested in identifying the variables that affect university students' comprehension of their assigned readings for *EDUC 234*. Below are several questions. Some of these questions may seem to have common sense answers, but since we do not want to lead your answers, we request that you provide answers with fine details and examples if possible. Please answer openly and honestly. Everything you tell us is confidential and will *not* affect your grade. Please provide a detailed response to each item.

- Describe your goal (i.e., *what you seek to attain*) when you do the assigned readings for *EDUC 234*.
- *What* do you focus on when you do the assigned readings?
- Describe the *strategies* that you use when you are reading this information.
- Describe what it means to *understand* what you have read.

REFERENCES

Alexander, P. A. (1997). The path to competence: A lifespan developmental perspective on reading. *Journal of Literacy Research, 37*, 413-436.

Anderson, L., and Krathwohl, D. (Eds.). (2001). *A taxonomy for learning, teaching, and assessing: A revision of Bloom's taxonomy of educational objectives.* New York: Addison Wesley Longman.

Anderman, E.M., and Wolters, C. (2006). Goals, Values, and Affect. In P. Alexander and P. Winne (Eds.), *Handbook of Educational Psychology (2nd Edition),* pp. 369-390. Mahwah, NJ: Lawrence Erlbaum.

Bransford, J. D., Brown, A. L., and Cocking, R. R. (Eds.). (2000). *How People Learn.* Washington, D.C.: National Academy Press.

Bråten, I., and Samuelstuen, M. S. (2004). Does the influence of reading purpose on reports of strategic text processing depend on students' topic knowledge? *Journal of Educational Psychology, 96,* 324-336.

Cataldo, M. G., and Oakhill, J. V. (2000). Why are poor comprehenders inefficient searchers? An investigation into the effects of text representation and spatial memory on ability to locate information in a text. *Journal of Educational Psychology, 92,* 791-799.

Cerdán, R., and Vidal-Abarca, E. (2008). The effects of tasks on integrating information from multiple documents. *Journal of Educational Psychology, 100*, 209-222.

Cerdán, R., Vidal-Abarca, E., Martínez, T., Gilabert, R., and Gil, L. (2009). Impact of question-answering tasks on search processes and reading comprehension. *Learning and Instruction, 19*, 13–27.

Dunlosky, J., Rawson, K., and Middleton, E. (2005). What constrains the accuracy of metacomprehension judgments? Testing the transfer appropriate-monitoring and accessibility hypotheses. *Journal of Memory and Language, 52*, 551-565.

Eggen, P. D., and Kauchak, D. (2010). *Educational Psychology: Windows on Classrooms, (8ᵗʰ edition)*. Upper Saddle River, NJ, Merrill Prentice Hall.

Graesser, A. C., and Person, N. K. (1994). Question asking during tutoring. *American Educational Research Journal, 31*, 104-137.

Guthrie, J. T., Wigfield, A., Barbosa, P., Perencevich, K. C., Taboada, A., Davis, M. H., Scafiddi, N. T., and Tonks, S. (2004). Increasing reading comprehension and engagement through Concept-Oriented Reading Instruction. *Journal of Educational Psychology, 96*, 403–423.

Igo, L. B., Bruning, R. H., and Riccomini, P.J. (2009). Should middle school students with learning problems copy and paste notes from the Internet? Mixed methods evidence of study barriers. *Research on Middle Level Education Online, 33*, 1-10.

Jetton, T. L., and Alexander, P. A. (1997). Instructional importance: What teachers value and what students learn. *Reading Research Quarterly, 32*, 290-308.

Lehman, S. and Schraw, G. (2002). Effects of coherence and relevance on shallow and deep text processing. *Journal of Educational Psychology, 94*, 738-750.

Linderholm, T., Cong, X., and Zhao, Q. (2008). Differences in Low and High Working-Memory Capacity Readers' Cognitive and Metacognitive Processing Patterns as a Function of Reading for Different Purposes. *Reading Psychology, 29*, 61-85.

Linderholm, T., and van den Broek, P. (2002). The effects of reading purpose and working memory capacity on the processing of expository text. *Journal of Educational Psychology, 94*, 778-784.

Lorch, Jr., R. F., and van den Broek, P. (1997). Understanding reading comprehension: Current and future contributions of cognitive science. *Contemporary Educational Psychology, 22*, 213-246.

Mautone, P. D. and Mayer, R. E. (2001). Signaling as a cognitive guide in multimedia learning, *Journal of Educational Psychology, 93*, 377-389.

McCrudden, M. T., and Schraw, G. (2007). Relevance and goal-focusing in text processing. *Educational Psychology Review, 19*, 113-139.

McCrudden, M. T., Schraw, G., and Kambe, G. (2005). The effect of relevance instructions on reading time and learning. *Journal of Educational Psychology, 97*, 88-102.

McCrudden, M. T., Magliano, J., and Schraw, G. (in press). Exploring how relevance instructions affect personal reading intentions, reading goals, and text processing: A mixed methods study. *Contemporary Educational Psychology*.

Pajares, F. (1996). Self-efficacy beliefs in academic settings. *Review of Educational Research, 66(4)*, 543-578.

Perfetti, C.A., Landi, N., and Oakhill, J.V. (2005). The acquisition of reading comprehension skill. In M.J. Snowling and C. Hume (Eds.), *The Science of Reading: Handbook of Reading Research*. Oxford: Blackwell.

Rapp, D. N., and Kendeou, P. (2007). Revising what readers know: Updating text representations during narrative comprehension. *Memory and Cognition, 35,* 2019-2032.

Reynolds, R. E. (1992). Selective attention and prose learning: Theoretical and empirical research. *Educational Psychology Review, 4,* 345–391.

Reynolds, R. E., Shepard, C., Lapan, R. Kreek, C., and Goetz, E. T. (1990). Difference in the use of selective attention by more successful and less successful tenth-grade readers. *Journal of Educational Psychology, 82,* 749-759.

Rouet, J.-F., Vidal-Abarca, E., Bert-Erboul, A., and Millogo, V. (2001). Effects of information search tasks on the comprehension of instructional text. *Discourse Processes, 31,* 163–186.

Schraw, G., and Dennison, R. (1994). The effect of reader purpose on interest and recall. *Journal of Reading Behavior, 26,* 1–18.

Schraw, G., Wade, S. E., and Kardash, C. A. (1993). Interactive effects of text-based and task-based importance on learning from text. *Journal of Educational Psychology, 85,* 652–661.

Schunk, D.H., Pintrich, P.R. and Meece, J.L. (2008). *Motivation in education: Theory, research, and applications* (3rd ed.). Upper Saddle Creek, NJ: Merrill/Pearson.

Shank, G. D. (2006). *Qualitative Research: A Personal Skills Approach, 2nd ed.* Upper Saddle River, NJ: Pearson Education.

Taboada, A., and Guthrie, J. T. (2006). Contributions of student questioning and prior knowledge to construction of knowledge from reading information text. *Journal of Literacy Research, 38,* 1-35.

van den Broek, P. Lorch, R. F. Jr., Linderholm, T., and Gustafson, M. (2001). The effects of readers' goals on inference generation and memory for texts. *Memory and Cognition, 29(8),* 1081-1087.

van den Broek, P., Virtue, S., Everson, M. G., Tzeng, Y., and Sung, Y. (2002). Comprehension and memory of science texts: Inferential processes and the construction of a mental representation. In J. Otero, J. A. Leon, and A. C. Graesser (Eds.), *The psychology of science text comprehension* (pp. 131-154). Mahwah, NJ: Erlbaum.

Wigfield, A., and Eccles, J. S. (2000). Expectancy-value theory of achievement motivation. *Contemporary Educational Psychology, 25,* 68-81.

Wiley, J., Goldman, S. R., Graesser, A. C., Sanchez, C. A., Ash, I. K., and Hemmerick, J. (2009). Source evaluation, comprehension, and learning in internet science inquiry tasks. *American Educational Research Association Journal*, 46, 1060-1106.

Zhao, Q. and Linderholm, T. (2008). Adult metacomprehension: Judgment processes and accuracy constraints. *Educational Psychology Review*, Vol 20(2), 191-206.

Reviewed by:
Meiko Negishi, University of North Florida

In: Progress in Education. Volume 26
Editor: Robert V. Nata, pp. 115-131

ISBN 978-1-61324-321-3
© 2011 Nova Science Publishers, Inc.

Chapter 6

ACCREDITATION PROGRAM FOR PERSONAL DOSIMETRY IN BRAZIL

L. F. Nascimento and F. Vanhavere

Radiation Dosimetry and Calibration, SCK-CEN. Mol. Belgium

Workers exposed to ionizing radiation must be insured by a high quality radiation dosimetry. The dosimetric process requires the use of a dosimeter, which is a device used to measure the cumulative amount of radiation that a person is exposed. To evaluate that, each kind of dosimeter has its specific reading mechanism, using a specific physical property.

Whole-body dosimeters for individual monitoring are calibrated to measure the operational quantity personal dose equivalent at a depth of 10.00 mm in soft tissue, Hp(10) (deep dose), as a best estimate for the effective dose, E. Dosimeters designed to measure the dose to the skin and to the eye lens should measure personal dose equivalent at a depth of 3.00 mm and 0.07 mm respectively, Hp(3) (shallow dose) and Hp(0.07) (lens dose) (NCRP-116, 1993), (ISO-14146, 1999), (ISO-12794, 2000) and (ISO-4037, 1994)). The main requirement of a personal dosimeter for the monitoring of gamma radiation doses is the capability of measuring the ICRU (ICRU-46, 1992) quantity of Hp (10) with satisfactory accuracy, independently of the radiation incident angle and the gamma radiation energy.

Processors of personal dosemeters used for record of personal dose in Brazil are required by federal regulation to be accredited by the SMIE (Serviço de Monitoração Individual Externa), which have been approved by the Nuclear Energy National Commission (CNEN – Comissão Nacional de Energia Nuclear) trough the Institute of Radioprotection and Dosimetry (IRD – Instituto de Radioproteção e Dosimetria). In Brazil laboratories are accredited to perform personal external monitoring service for photographic films and thermoluminescent dosimetry systems. The criteria used for the Brazilian accreditation programs ((IRD-RT001, 1995), (IRD-RT002, 1995), (IRD-RT004, 1995) and (IRD-RT003, 1995)) are based on international standards and recommendations ((ISO4037-1, 1994), (DOE/EH-0026, 1986), (ISO-5/1, 1984), (IEC-1066, 1991), (ICRU-39, 1988), (ICRU-47, 1992) and (ICRP-60, 1990)).

The terms "accreditation" and "certification" are sometimes used interchangeably, however, they are not synonymous. Certification is used for verifying that personnel have adequate credentials to practice certain disciplines, as well as for verifying that products meet certain requirements. An accreditation program is a system for accrediting laboratories found competent to perform specific tests or calibrations or types of tests or calibrations. So, the accreditation program is not a certifier of test data, a certifier of products, or an operator of a certification program.

In the following sections, we discuss the requirements for an accreditation program for personal dosimetry using Optically Stimulated Luminescence (OSL). Our purpose uses the Brazilian conformance tests for TLD and photographic films ((IRD-RT002, 1995), (IRD-RT003, 1995)) as a guideline.

1. OPTICALLY STIMULATED LUMINESCENCE – THEORY

The application of OSL in personal and environmental dosimetry is becoming larger and larger with the years due to the high sensitivity of the material Al_2O_3:C to ionizing radiation and the easy and fast readout, when compared to the most common used techniques, like TL (thermoluminescence) and photographic films. In the frame of the ALARA concept (as low reasonably achievable), optically stimulated luminescence (OSL) has been investigated for different radiation, like gamma, beta and UV [(Gronchi & Caldas, 2009), (McKeever, Akselrod, & Markey, 1996) and (Göksu, Bulur, & Wahl, 1999)].

Pure α-alumina crystals are grown in a low pressure in the presence of Carbon atoms that generates a great number of punctual defects (oxygen vacancies, called F centers) which are the luminescent centers. When the material is exposed to ionizing radiation free electrons and free holes are excited trough Compton or photoelectric effect (depending on radiation energy and type) and in sequence electrons and holes are trapped in the punctual defects, becoming F^+ centers (Figure 1).

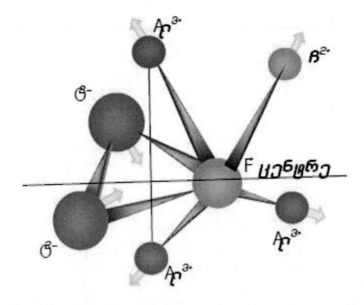

Figure 1. Al_2O_3:C crystaline structure with the F^+ centre (Akselrod, Botter-Jensen, & McKeever, 2006).

Conducting Band

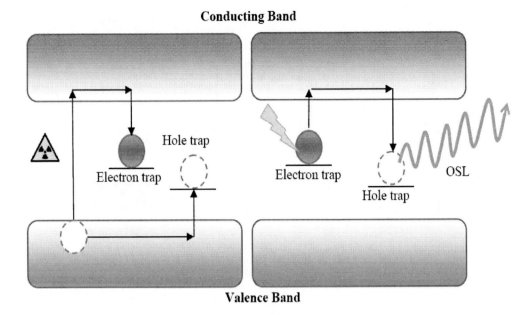

Valence Band

Figure 2. Al_2O_3:C Valence and conduction band and the OSL signal generation.

The traps can be emptied by exciting the trapped electrons with a mono energetic wavelength (usually from green LEDs or lasers, 450 nm) and the recombination of electron-holes releases light (optically stimulated light). The intensity of the luminescence released due the recombination of electrons-holes is proportional to the amount of radiation the material was exposed to, and subsequently, the amount of dose that a person carrying a dosimeter with the Al_2O_3:C material [(Bøtter-Jensen, McKeever, & Wintle, 2003)]. The process is show in the figure 2.

The excitation of the trapped electrons can be performed in different ways. Commonly pulsed, continuous or ramped stimulation are used [(McKeever, Akselrod, & Markey, 1996), (Whitley & McKeever, 2002) and (Edmund, Andersen, Marckmann, Aznar, Akselrod, & Bøtter-Jensen, 2006)]. When the traps are emptied by a constant wavelength stimulation with stationary intensity, the resulted luminescence is called CW-OSL (CW stands for Continuous Wavelength). Al_2O_3:C CW-OSL stimulation and decay in function of time is show in Figure 3a and 3b, the intensity decays exponentially until it reaches a lower limit, meaning that all the traps were emptied. The dose is calculated using integrated or the peak signal.

1.1. Dosimetry System

The OSL dosimetry system (InLight[TM]) used for the tests is manufactured by Landauer Inc. The InLight dosimeter is composed of a detector, a case and a holder. The detector is built from a Al_2O_3:C crystalline powder grain layer, that is compressed by two layers of polystyrene to protect it from external agents (InLight Landauer Systems, 2010). The detectors have an energy range from 5 keV to 20 MeV for gamma and X-ray qualities, being linear from 10 mSv (1 mrem) to in excess of 10 Sv (1000 mrem) as given by the manufacturer.

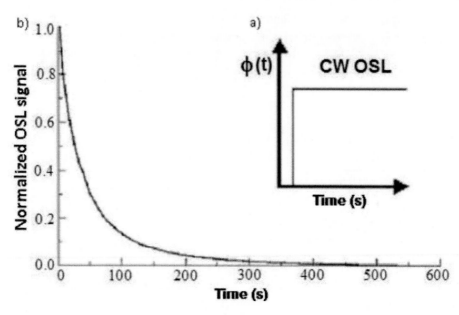

Figure 3. a) CW stimulation and b) OSL generated signal.

The detector is inserted on a case made of plastic with four open windows; two windows are covered by two different metals (for instance, Cu and Al), one is covered by plastic and the latter has no filter. The filters allow the software to determine the quality of the radiation that the dosimeter was exposed to. The detector and case are protected against light and external agents by a Panasonic plastic holder (InLight Landauer Systems, 2010).

The calibration of the equipment is performed by using a batch of pre-irradiated dosimeters with different nominal doses and the same sensitivity (given by the manufacturer). The calibration dosimeters (CD) have no filter. Two calibration factors are calculated after a sequence of measurements with the CD batch, one for high and one for low doses. During ordinary measurements, the reader chooses if the readout will be done with a strong beam, using all the LEDs (for dosimeters with low dose) or a weak beam, with half of the LEDs (for dosimeters with high dose). The choice is made by considering to the intensity of the OSL signal (either low or high). Following this, the calculation of the dose is performed using the appropriate calibration factor.

The quality control of the reader is performed by observing the response of the PMT tube, the weak and strong beams, and the dark current; this is done by the reader's software automatically before a sequence of measurements. The number of measurements taken before a new check is made is chosen by the user (by default, one check for every ten measurements). The dark current quality control measures the minimal signal that can be detected by the PMT, i.e. the noise or background signal (the maximum signal permitted is 20 counts). Quality control of the PMT sensitivity is obtained by irradiating the PMT tube with a ^{14}C beta source (the ^{14}C source is fixed inside the reader), where the maximum deviation accepted is 10%. For the weak and strong beams the goal is to check the response of the LEDs; for both cases the maximum deviation accepted is 10%. The limits and acceptance of the quality control are given by the manufacturer [(InLight Landauer Systems, 2010)].

The InLight^{TM} dosimetry system has an algorithm which calculates the deep dose, shallow dose, lens dose and the presence of beta particles, as well as the quality of the radiation. It uses the total counts (sum of counts for each window), the sensitivity of each detector, and the calibration factor. The result of the measurement and the dose calculation following the algorithm allow passing the NVLAP or DOELAP accreditation program, which are respectively the National Voluntary Laboratory Accreditation Program and the Department of Energy Laboratory Accreditation Program, both from United States ((National Institute of Standards and Technology (NIST), 2010), (DOELAP, 2010)). The system has menu-driven software which runs in an external personal computer and provides control over the setup, analysis and data recording.

2. THE ACCREDITATION PROGRAM FOR PERSONAL DOSIMETRY USING OSL

The requirements for a personal dosimetry certification document are based on an extensive standard regarding the following aspects: (1) general organization; (2) human resources; (3) facilities; (4) quality assurance (QA); (5) detector holder; (6) detector; (7) dosimeter evaluation; and (8) equipment evaluation ((IRD-RT001, 1995), (IRD-RT002, 1995) and (IRD-RT004, 1995)). The first four items are technology independent; they depend only on organizational and facility control aspects. The items from 5 to 8, however, have to be standardized according to the dosimetric technique in use, in this case optically stimulated dosimetry.

2.1. Organizational and Facility Control Aspects

Every country has its own legal requirements and regulations for personal dosimetry. In general the laboratory performing the personal dosimetry service must be certified according to the safety regulations; these include:

Staff: the laboratory must have one or more technical and QA responsible. The staff must present the minimum technical and scientific competence and the number of employees should be so the services can be performed continuously and with quality.

Location: the laboratory installations must fulfill environmental and architectural requirements. A floorplan should be attached to the certification process. Environmental conditions outside the laboratory should not adversely interfere in its operation. The environmental conditions inside the laboratory must be adequate for the operation of the instruments. Environmental parameters, including radiological, should be monitored, especially in the storage area of the dosimeters, in order to ensure the right conditions.

Facilities: hydraulic and electrical conditions of the location must match the necessities of a SMIE

Authorization for radioactive sources: a series of safety requirements must be fulfilled and the laboratory must have the appropriate authorization to manage radiation sources.

Safety and hygiene at work: staff must be assured against accidents, and the facilities environment has to offer the minimal safety and hygienic conditions according to the municipality, state and federal legislations.

Training programs: each new employee must be trained (theoretically and experimentally) to carry out the tasks assigned to it. The competence of the staff should be assessed and documented at least every three years. In addition, all employees must be retrained when procedures or equipment are changed or when the employee is appointed to exercise new responsibilities.

Equipment: the SMIE should have the necessary and suitable equipment for processing dosimetric data.

2.2. Dosimetric Technique

During the accreditation a performance testing laboratory evaluates the technical performance of dosimetry systems and an onsite assessment studies the quality assurance, documentation, and technical adequacy of such systems.

An accreditation program needs both performance criteria for personnel dosimetry and a testing program to determine the criteria have been met.

The procedures and documentation for detectors include: handling and storage of detector; periodic verification of the detectors in routine use; identification of the detectors; repair or replacement of damaged sensors or brackets.

Similar documented procedures with operational conditions must exist for any equipment used to read/anneal/bleach/treat the signal/data from the detector in routine use. For testing and calibration the system of individual monitoring, it is recommended that the SMIE have radiation sources that are in accordance with specific legislation. The instruments used for the measurement of radiation fields, for purposes of calibration, must have a calibration certificate issued by an organization duly authorized for this purpose. If the SMIE doesn't have these sources or equipment necessary for the calibration it must access them in some other institution.

The operational conditions of the dosimetric system also involves precaution on planning measurements, storage and test conditions. The performance test has to cover all the physical and operational aspects of interest to assure that the detectors behave as expected under normal occupational work conditions, in a way the measured quantity from the detectors can correctly represent the absorbed dose a person was subject to.

2.3. Performance Test

Dosimetric performance requirements for the routine dose assessment of external radiation must be based on: general radiation protection requirements, which derive from basic radiation protection principles and include recommended limits of exposure and overall uncertainties (ICRP); workplace conditions prevailing during (routine) work, comprising dosimetric conditions such as energy and angle distribution of the radiation, and non-dosimetric conditions such as air temperature, humidity and electromagnetic fields and; technical requirements for measuring instruments, which are intended to limit the error of measurement or the uncertainty due to variations of the influence quantities within their rated ranges of use (based on ISO and IEC standards (IEC-61525, 1996), (ISO-14146, 1999) and (ISO4037-1, 1994)).

Verification of these requirements is based on periodic performance tests; the Brazilian government has approved accreditation programs with performance tests for photographic films and thermoluminescent dosimetry. A good start on developing a new set of performance tests for a new dosimetry technology is to base it on the existing and accepted ones. In this sense the tests would be adequate to the technology and new tests, when necessary, can be proposed.

2.2.1. Test Conditions

All detectors and dosimeters in test must be identified. The detectors and dosimeters used as control and those being tested must belong to the same manufacturing lot. Depending on the type of testing into account, the irradiation is performed with the dosimeters complete or only with the detectors.

The performance criteria and the different tests are generally presented in terms of the conventional true value of C and the acquired value A. It is considered that the uncertainty in the determination of C may be neglected.

All tests are conducted under standard test conditions (Table 1 and 2), except when noted otherwise. Systems, detectors and readers are tested in the same way as is expected to be used in routine personal work. For example, the detectors must be subjected to cleaning and handling recommended by the manufacturer or by the international literature of recognized merit.

Table 1. Standard test conditions

Quantity	Referemce conditions	Standard test conditions
Reference radiations with photons	According to ISO DIS 4037-1	from 20 to 1250 keV
Ambient temperature	20 ≫C	from 18 ≫C to 25 ≫C
Atmospheric pressure	101,3 kPa	from 86 kPa to 106 kPa
Humidity	65%	from 50% to 65%
Background gamma radiation	0,20 μGy.h^{-1}	< 0,20 μGy.h^{-1}
Radioative contamination	Negletible	Negletible
Light Intensity	50 W.m^{-2}	⟨ 1000W.m^{-2}

Table 2. Radionuclide sources, energies and mean life

Radionuclide sources		
Radionuclide	Gamma energy (keV)	Mean life (days)
^{241}Am	59,54	157788
^{137}Cs	661,6	11050
^{60}Co	1173,3 and 1332,5	1925,5

Radiation sources used for calibration of dosimeters should be calibrated against standards traceable to primary or secondary standard laboratories.

The performance tests for the proposal were evaluated at Sapra Landauer facilities in São Carlos, Brazil. During the tests a device for the detector bleaching was used. This is built using two fluorescent light bulbs of 40W with a glass support for the detectors. The testing room was submitted to climatic treatment 24 h before the measurements, in order to obtain a stable environment (temperature and humidity). The badges were exposed to a ^{60}Co source in air. The nominal exposures (C) were 2 and 10 mGy and the number of dosimeters used per test followed specifications from accreditation documents (IRD-RT002, 1995). The reader was re-calibrated every week and reference tests were performed before every sequence of ten measurements.

2.2.2. Student T Statistics

The statistical analysis of the data is performed using the Student's t-distribution, which is the appropriate probability to use to estimate the mean of a normally distributed population when the number of samples is small [(Gosset, 1908)].

The confidence interval (l) indicates the reliability of an estimate and is used to estimate the population parameter of the distribution. Equations 1.a and 1.b show the confidence interval for the sample mean ($\bar{x}$) and the respective standard deviation (σ). The quantities l_i and l_σ are defined respectively as the half width confidence interval of $\bar{x}$ and σ_i (i corresponds to different sets of measurements).

$$(\bar{x} - l_i, \bar{x} + l_i) \tag{1.a}$$

$$(\sigma - l_\sigma, \sigma + l_\sigma) \tag{1.b}$$

The l_i upper limit with 95% confidence is given by equation 2.a, where the confidence interval for $\bar{x}$ is calculated for n_i measurements. The parameter t_{n_i} is defined as the tabulated t-Student value for n_i measurements ((Abramowitz & Stegun, 1972)). The l_σ upper limit confidence interval for σ calculated for n_σ measurements, with 95% confidence, is given by another formula (eqn. 2.b).

$$l_i(n_i) = \frac{t_{n_i} . \sigma}{\sqrt{n_i}} \tag{2.a}$$

$$l_\sigma(n_\sigma) = t_{n_\sigma} . \sigma . \sqrt{\frac{0.5}{n_\sigma - 1}} \tag{2.b}$$

The half width confidence interval is given by equation 3.b, where the statistical quantity $\bar{x}_i$ (eqn. 3.a) is calculated with k mean values and l_i is the half width confidence for each $\bar{x}_i$ mean value.

$$l = \sqrt{\sum_{i=1}^{k} [\frac{\partial f(\bar{x}_1, \bar{x}_2, \bar{x}_3, ..., \bar{x}_k)}{\partial x}]^2 . l_i^2} \tag{3.a}$$

$$\bar{x} = f(\bar{x}_1, \bar{x}_2, \bar{x}_3, ..., \bar{x}_k) \tag{3.b}$$

2.2.3. Performance Requirements for OSL Dosimetric System

The performance tests are divided into categories concerning the dosimetric system and its individual parts, i.e. the reader, the holder and the detector. For each category a list of performance tests is designed.

2.2.3.1. Reader

The selected performance tests for the OSL reader are the same for TL readers (Table 3).

The reference light reproducibility quality test is performed by the reader every time the user wishes to verify that the PMT, dark current, weak beam and strong beam are working properly; all four measurements are performed simultaneously. The result from this test is verified using the variation coefficient V (eqn. 4).

$$V = \frac{\sigma}{\bar{x}} = \frac{1}{\bar{x}} \sqrt{\frac{1}{n-1} \sum_{i=1}^{n} (x_i - \bar{x})^2} \tag{4}$$

The light influence test has special importance. Only the excitation light from the green LEDs can coexist with the OSL signal during the measurements, which means that the reader has to guarantee the absence of other sources of light. The variation coefficient V (eqn. X) is also used in this test, where $V^{ref} = V^{normal} / V^{light}$, being V^{light} the result under light influence and V^{normal} the result under normal conditions.

Table 3. The reader performance tests reported for photographic film and thermoluminescence (TL) personal dosimetry, and the proposed tests for optically stimulated luminescence (OSL)

Film	TL	OSL
	Reader	
1. **Optic densitometer homogeneity**	1. Reference light reproducibility	1. Reference light reproducibility
	2. Reader stability	2. Reader stability
	3. Climate conditions effect	3. Climate conditions effect
	4. Light exposure effect	4. Light exposure effect

2.2.3.2. Holder

For the holder, we take the resistance to physical impacts from the photographic film's test document and include the light exposure effect test (Table 4). The detector has to be maintained in a dark environment while in use, such that no external light will deplete trapped electrons before the reading.

2.2.3.3. Detector

InLight^{TM} detectors are distributed coupled with the case and the holders, consequently few tests can be performed without considering the entire dosimetric system (Table 5). For InLight^{TM} dosimeters the sensitivity for each detector is given by the manufacturer. The sensitivity test for OSL InLight^{TM} detectors can be evaluated as for TL, but using a batch with equal sensitivity. The test related to the light exposure effect has a different meaning when compared with TL and photographic films. The unprotected detector will be affected by light, since the luminescence stimulation is light dependent. Nevertheless, it is important to observe the effect of ambient light on the detector, by analyzing the manner in which dosimeters with different sensitivities respond to the same light conditions. This test should be considered as a performance test only for trap depleting purposes, i.e. bleaching of the detector.

Since the OSL detector can be annealed or bleached, two performance tests related to the effect of light and temperature could be proposed. However due to the damage that temperature can cause in the layers of polystyrene, the annealing test cannot be performed on InLight^{TM} detectors.

Table 4. The holder conformance tests reported for photographic film and thermoluminescence (TL) personal dosimetry, and the proposed tests for optically stimulated luminescence (OSL)

	Film	TL	OSL
		Holder	
1.	**Filter homogeneity**	No reported	1. Resistance to physical
2.	**Self irradiation**	tests	impacts
3.	**Resistance to physical Impacts**		2. Light exposure effect

Table 5. The detector conformance tests reported for photographic film and thermoluminescence (TL) personal dosimetry, and the proposed tests for optically stimulated luminescence (OSL)

Film	TL	OSL
	Detector	
1. **Emulsion optical density's homogeneity**	8. Batch homogeneity	13. Batch homogeneity
2. **Latent image stability**	9. Light exposure effect	14. Light exposure effect
3. **Ageing remittance**	10. Detector opacity	15. (bleaching)
4. **Artificial ageing**	11. Detector resistance	16. Detector resistance
5. **Natural ageing**	12. to H_2O vapor	17. to H_2O vapor
6. **Envelope opacity**		
7. **Detector resistance to H_2O vapor**		

2.2.3.4. Dosimetric System

In the dosimetric system tests (Table 6), the OSL characteristics are further investigated by analyzing the energy dependence and the limits of dose.

The energy dependence tests obey the same requirements from TL dosimetry, since the Al_2O_3:C luminescent centers are both TL and OSL ((McKeever, Moscovich, & Townsend, Thermoluminescent Dosimetry Materials: Properties and Uses, 1995), (Botter-Jensen & McKeever, 1996) and (G., W., S., E., & S., 2004)).

Table 6. Dosimetric system performance tests accredited for photographic film and thermoluminescence (TL) personal dosimetry and the suggested tests for optically stimulated luminescence dosimetry (OSL)

Film	TL	OSL
Dosimetric system		
1.Inferior detection limit	1. Batch homogeneity	1. Batch homogeneity
2.Reproducibility	2. Reproducibility	2. Reproducibility
3.Linearity	3. Linearity	3. Linearity
4.Energetic dependence	4. Inferior detection limit	4. Inferior detection limit
5.Angular dependence	5. Dosimeter stability	5. Climate conditions effect
6.Influence in the presence	6. Residual signal	6. Fading
7.of a phantom	7. Light exposure effect	7. Residual signal
8.Influence of the	8. Energetic dependence	8. Light exposure effect
9.posterior-anterior irradiation	9. Angular dependence	9. Energy dependence
	10. Influence in the presence of a phantom	10. Angular dependence
	11. Influence of the posterior-anterior irradiation	11. Influence in the presence of a phantom
	12. Resistance to physical impacts	12. Influence of the posterior-anterior irradiation
		13. Resistance to physical impacts
		14. Reproducibility of re-reading

The energy ranges used in the test are 20-25 keV, 30-40 keV, 80-100 keV, for X-ray; and ^{137}Cs or ^{60}Co for irradiations of 10 mGy with gamma radiation. In the linearity tests five dosimeters per nominal irradiation were used, with twenty equally spaced points in the interval from 0.2 to 1000 mGy, as is specified for TL tests. A ^{137}Cs or ^{60}Co source is used to irradiate the dosimeters. The homogeneity test is applied to all dosimeters from the same batch, and the nominal irradiation is 2 and 10 mGy in ^{137}Cs or ^{60}Co sources.

The fading test is important to demonstrate that the cumulated dose stored in the dosemeters do not decay over time, which means that there is no spontaneous recombination of the metastable states prior to light stimulation (reading) and consequently no loss of information. During the dosimeter test for fading a set of dosimeters are irradiated in the same conditions using ^{137}Cs or ^{60}Co sources and the set are divided into groups that are read in different intervals: 0 (no waiting time), 1, 7, 30 and 90 days after irradiation. When performing reproducibility tests a set of ten dosimeters are irradiated, read and annealed in cycles of ten tests. The nominal irradiations for both tests are 10 mGy in ^{137}Cs or ^{60}Co sources.

For angular dependence measurements four groups of dosimeters are positioned in different angles with respect to the normal incidental beam ($0°$, $20°$, $40°$ and $60°$). They are irradiated on each of the four quadrants with a nominal dose of 10 mGy in an energy spectrum of about 60 keV. For both phantom and posterior-anterior influence tests a tissue equivalent phantom is used to simulate a human body. In this test we use the same expectation limits for TL and film tests.

For the inferior detection limit test the dosemeters are read without previous irradiation. A selection of 10 dosemeters are bleached, or annealed, and read. The average detected signal over all dosemeters is the inferior detection limit.

The dosimetric system should not present significant changes due to climate effects, so a test is done with the system under different temperatures and humidity.

After a sequence of irradiation-reading the signal of the dosemeter posterior to annealing should not change. This is an indication that no residual signal is left in the detector. Residual signals affect the true dose, once the final measurement will be a combination of the irradiation dose with the residual signal dose.

The influence in the presence of a phantom test is of importance once in this case the human body is simulated. The dosemeters will be used by workers occupationally exposed to ionizing radiation, and so the dosemeters are expected to be used close to these workers body. During this test the goal is to observe if there is any change when the dosemeter is irradiated in the presence of a phantom and free in the air. The main concern is due to scattering effects.

Another test using a phantom is the posterior-anterior irradiation test, where the dosemeter is irradiated in the phantom with the dosemeter facing the beam and giving the back for it (rotated 180).

In this case two information can be observed, the influence of the filters in the front part of the dosemeter and the total dose in each window without the filter (for the case when the dosemeter is rotated).

In the reproducibility test a selection of 10 dosemeters are irradiated with the same nominal dose of 10 mGy and read at the same time. In sequence the dosemeters are annealed or bleached and irradiated/read in the same conditions as mentioned before. This procedure has to be repeated 10 times to test the reproducibility of the dosemeters under the same irradiation conditions. For each set of measurements of each dosimeter, the test is passed if the tolerance criterion (T) is satisfied (eqn. 5)

Notice that σ_i is defined as the standard deviation of $\overline{A}_i$, and l_i is the half width confidence interval of σ_i (see eqn. 3.a).

$$T = \frac{\sigma_i + l_i}{\overline{\overline{A}}_i} \leq 0.075 \tag{5}$$

Inlight[TM] dosemeters do not have their trapped electrons completely depopulated when they are read, actually only a small fraction of the traps are emptied. This is done in a way the dosemeters can be re-read without losing the information on the total absorbed dose. In this way a new test is suggested, one that was not previously used for the thermoluminescent and photographic film accreditation programs, the reproducibility re-reading test. In this case the dosemeters are irradiated only once and the 10 readings are performed in sequence, without annealing. In this test the tolerance criterion (T) is also used.

2.2.3.5. Performance Tests Expected Results

Once selected all the suitable tests for the whole dosimetric system and each component the expected behavior under each test is desirable. Using the T-student statistic and acceptable results according to the standard documentation table 7 and 8 presents the expected result for one and each of the tests.

Table 7. Summary for performance tests expected results suggested to InLight[TM] dosimeters. a) The reader, b) the holder and, c) the detector

Test		Expected
		a) Reader
1.	Reference light reproducibility	V is equal or below 0.01 for the PMT sensitivity; 0.20 for high and low dose beam current; and for the dark current the test is passed if no measurement above 20 counts is detected.
2.	Reader stability	The quality control performed with 0, 24 and 186 hours of difference cannot differ more than 5 and 10%, respectively
3.	Climate conditions effect	The quality control measurements under different climate conditions cannot differ more than 20%
4.	Light exposure effect	The quality control measurements with and without light (V^{rel}) for PMT, weak and strong beam cannot differ more than 20%. For dark current no measured count can be higher than 20 counts.
		b) holder
1.	Resistance to physical impacts	The holder must support impacts of 1.5 m from the floor with no damages
2.	Light exposure effect	There is no expected result applicable to OSL dosimeters
		c) detector
1.	Batch homogeneity	In a batch the read values cannot differ more than 30% for irradiations of 10 and 2 mSv
2.	Light exposure effect (bleaching)	There is no expected result applicable to OSL dosimeters
3.	Detector resistance to H_2O vapor	The detector must not be affected by the vapor

Table 8. Summary for performance tests expected results suggested to InLight™ OSL dosimetric system

Test	Expected
	Dosimetric System
1. Batch homogeneity	In a batch the read values cannot differ more than 30 %
2. Reproducibility	The calculated T (eqn. 5) value must be lower than 0.075
3. Linearity	On an interval from 0.2 mGy to 1 Gy the measured values cannot differ more than 10%
4. Inferior detection limit	The inferior limit must be equal or lower than 0.2 mGy
5. Climate condition effect	The measured values from dosimeters kept in climate special conditions must not differ from dosimeters kept in normal conditions more than: o 10 % for 30 days of storage under normal conditions o 15% for 90 days of storage under normal conditions o 20% for 7 days of storage under normal humidity conditions and temperature of 122° F o 20% for 30 days of storage under normal temperature conditions and 90 % relative humidity
6. Fading	Three groups of dosimeters are read with 0 (group1), 24 (group 2) and 168 (group3) hours of difference. Group 2 and group 1 ($G_{1,2}$) cannot differ more than 5% Group 3 and group 1 ($G_{1,3}$) cannot differ more than 10%
7. Residual signal	After receiving a dose of 100 mSv and then annealed the residual signal cannot change by more than 10%.
8. Light exposure effect	The system under normal conditions and under light cannot differ more than 10%.
9. Energetic dependence	Four groups are irradiated with 10 mSv in the energy intervals: o G_1 = 20-25 keV o G_2 = 30-40 keV o G_3 = 80-100 keV o G_4 = ^{137}Cs or ^{60}Co No measured value can differ more than 30% from group 4.
10. Angular dependence	Four groups are irradiated with 10 mSv in different orientations: o G_1 = 0 (normal incidence) o G_2 = 20° o G_3 = 40° o G_4 = 60° No measured value can differ more than 15% from group 1.
11. Influence in the presence of a phantom	The measured dose cannot differ the expected value more than 30%
12. Influence of the posterior-anterior irradiation	The measured values cannot differ from each other more than 10%
13. Resistance to physical impacts	The holder must support impacts of 1.5 m from the floor with no damages
14. Reproducibility of re-reading	The calculated T (eqn. 5) value must be lower than 0.075

3. ACCREDITATION PROGRAM IMPLEMENTATION AND FINAL CONSIDERATIONS

Accreditation programs are used to verify that laboratories have an appropriate quality management system and can properly perform certain test methods and calibration parameters according to their scopes of accreditation.

An accreditation program has to cover both the management system of a laboratory and the technical capabilities of a laboratory. The assessment of laboratories must be performed to check compliance with the requirements (e.g. (ISO, 2007)). Upon satisfactory assessment and successful completion of proficiency testing (where applicable), the laboratory is issued a Certificate of Accreditation along with a Scope of Accreditation listing the test methods or calibration parameters that the laboratory is accredited to perform. Usually the accreditation period is one year. To renew its accreditation, a laboratory must demonstrate that it continues to satisfy all requirements for accreditation.

Users of test data should be concerned with both the potential for performing a quality job (quality system) and technical competence (ability to achieve a technical result). The best available method of achieving these two objectives is through laboratory accreditation bodies, operating themselves to best international practice, requiring laboratories to adopt best practices and by engaging assessors who are expert in the specific tests in which the customer is interested.

To achieve the quality system and the technical competence the tests should answer the following questions:

- Are they the most appropriate test procedures to use in the circumstances?
- Will they produce accurate results?
- How have you validated the procedures to ensure their accuracy?
- Do you have effective quality control procedures to ensure ongoing accuracy?
- Do you understand the science behind the test procedures?
- Do you know the limitations of the procedures?
- Can you foresee and cope with any technical problems that may arise while using the procedures?
- Do you have all the correct equipment, consumables and other resources necessary to perform these procedures?

Accreditation programs request an extensive work. In our proposal some technical changes are suggested to adequate existing tests of the physical characteristics of OSL, but in general we adopted the same statistical analysis suggested in ISO 4037-1 ((ISO4037-1, 1994)) and applied to accredited performance tests for personal dosimetry in Brazil. In order to demonstrate the adequacy and applicability of our proposal, a set of tests was performed from 08/2005 to 05/2007 [(Nascimento & Hornos, 2010)] and the data was subjected to statistical analysis. All the tests presented results within the acceptable limits, suggesting that OSL is a good candidate for personal dosimetry under criteria used for both TL and photographic film.

BIBLIOGRAPHY

Abramowitz, M., and Stegun, I. A. (1972). Handbook of Mathematical Functions with Formulas, Graphs, and Mathematical Tables. New York: Dove.

Akselrod, M., Botter-Jensen, L., and McKeever, S. W. (2006). Optically stimulated luminescence and its use in medical dosimetry. *Radiation Measurements 41* .

Akselrod, M., Kortov, V., Kravestsky, D., and Gotlib, V. (1990). Highly sensitive thermoluminescence anion-defect a-Al2O3:C single crystal detectors. *Radiat. Prot. Dosim 33* , 119–122.

Ambrosi, P., Buchholz, G., Marshall, T., Roberts, P., and Thompson, I. (1992). International intercomparisons and accreditation programmes for personal radiation protection dosimetry within the European Community. *Radiat. Prot. Dosim 40* , 17–26.

Botter-Jensen, L., and McKeever, S. W. (1996). Optically Stimulated Luminescence Using Natural and Synthetic Matherials. *Radiation Protection Dosimetry* , 273-280.

Bøtter-Jensen, McKeever, S., and Wintle, A. (2003). *Optically Stimulated Luminescence Dosimetry*. Amsterdam: Elsevier.

DOE/EH-0026. (1986). *Handbook for the Department of Energy Laboratory Accreditation Program for Personnel Dosimetry System*. U. S. Department of Energy.

DOELAP. (2010). Retrieved 2010, from Office of Corporate Safety Programs : http://hss.energy.gov/CSA/CSP/doelap/

Edmund, J. M., Andersen, C. E., Marckmann, C. J., Aznar, M. C., Akselrod, M. S., and Bøtter-Jensen, L. (2006). CW-OSL measurement protocols using optical fibre Al2O3:C dosemeters. *Radiat Prot Dosimetry* , 368-374.

G., Y. E., W., W. V., S., M. S., E., A. A., and S., A. M. (2004). Effect of high dose irradiation on the optically stimulated luminescence of Al2O3:C. *Radiation Measurements* , 317-330.

Göksu, H., Bulur, E., and Wahl, W. (1999). Beta Dosimetry Using Thin Layer a-Al2O3:C TL Detectors. *Radiat Prot Dosimetry 84 (1-4)* , 451-455.

Gosset, W. (1908). The probable error of a mean. *Biometrika 6(1)* , 1-25.

Gronchi, C. C., and Caldas, L. V. (2009). OSL RESPONSE OF Al2O3:C INLIGHT DOT DETECTORS. *2009 International Nuclear Atlantic Conference - INAC* , 1-4.

ICRP-60. (1990). *Recommendation of the International Comission on Radiological Protection*. ICRP Publications.

ICRU-39. (1988). *Determination of the Dose Equivalent REsulting from External Radiation Sources*. Bethesda: International Commision on Radiation Units and Measurements.

ICRU-46. (1992). *Photon, electron, proton and neutron interaction data for body tissues*. Bethesda: International Commision on Radiation Units and Measurements.

ICRU-46. (1992). *Photon, electron, proton and neutron interaction data for body tissues*. Bethesda: International Commission on Radiation Units and Measurements.

ICRU-47. (1992). *Measurements of Dose Equivalents from External Photon and Electron Radiations*. Bethesda: International Commision on Radiation Units and Measurements.

IEC-1066. (1991). *Thermoluminescence Dosimetry System for Personal and Enviromental Monitoring*.

IEC-61525. (1996). *Radiation Protection Instrumentation - X, gamma, high energy beta and neutron radiations: direct reading personal dose equivalent and/or dose equivalent rate monitors.*

InLight Landauer Systems. (2010). Retrieved 2010, from Landauer Inc: http://www.osldosimetry.com/inlight/

IRD-RT001. (1995). *Criterios gerais para certificação de um serviço de Monitoração Individual Externa.* Rio de Janeiro: CASMIE.

IRD-RT002. (1995). *Desempenho de Sistema de Monitoração Individual - Critérios e Condições.* Rio de Janeiro: CASMIE.

IRD-RT003. (1995). *Desempenho de Sistemas de Monitoração Individual: testes no LNMRI.* Rio de Janeiro: CASMIE.

IRD-RT004. (1995). *Processo de Auditoria para a Certificação de um Serviço de Monitoração Individual Externa.* Rio de Janeiro: CASMIE.

ISO. (2007). *ISO/IEC NBR 17799/2007 - 27002.* Retrieved 2010, from http://www.iso.org/iso/

ISO-12794. (2000). *Radiation protection - Individual thermoluminescence dosemeters for extremities and eyes.* Geneva: Draft International Standard.

ISO-14146. (1999). *Radiation Protection - criteria and performance limits for the periodic evaluation of processors of personal dosemeters for X and gamma radiation.* Geneva: Draft International Standard.

ISO-4037. (1994). *4037-1, ISO DIS. X and Gamma reference radiations for calibrating dosemeters and doserate meters for determining their response as a function of photon energy, International Organization for Standardization.* Geneva: Draft International Standard.

ISO4037-1. (1994). *X and Gamma reference radiations for calibrating dosemeters and doserate meters for determining their response as a function of photon energy, International Organization for Standardization.* Geneva: Draft International Standard.

ISO-5/1. (1984). *Photography - Density measurements.* Geneva: ISO.

McKeever, S. W., and Moscovitch, M. (2003). On the advantage and disadvantage of optically stimulated luminescence dosimetry and thermoluminescence dosimetry. *Radiat, Prot. Dosim 104(3)* , 263–270.

McKeever, S. W., Moscovich, M., and Townsend, P. D. (1995). Thermoluminescent Dosimetry Materials: Properties and Uses. *Nuclear Technology* .

McKeever, S., Akselrod, M., and Markey, B. (1996). Pulsed Optically Stimulated Luminescence Dosimetry Using Alpha-Al2O3:C . *Radiation Protection Dosimetry, 65 (1-4)* , 267-272 .

Nascimento, L. F., and Hornos, Y. M. (2010). Proposal of a Brazilian Accreditaton Program for Personal Dosimetry Using OSL. *Radiation Measurements 45* , 51-59.

National Institute of Standards and Technology (NIST). (2010). Retrieved 2010, from National Voluntary Laboratory Accreditation Program: http://ts.nist.gov/standards/ accreditation/index.cfm

NCRP-116. (1993). *Limitation of exposure to ionizing radiation.* Bethesda, Maryland: National Council on Radiation Protection and Measurements.

Whitley, V. H., and McKeever, S. W. (2002). Linear Modulation Optically Stimulated Luminescence and Thermoluminescence Techiniques from Al2O3:C. *Radiation Protection Dosimetry Vol. 100, Nos 1–4* , 61–66.

In: Progress in Education. Volume 26
Editor: Robert V. Nata, pp. 133-145

Chapter 7

"It's not just Dealing with the Bullying Student; Rather It's also their Parents": Teachers' Perceptions of Self-Efficacy in Dealing with Parents of Bullying Students and Victims

Revital Sela-Shayovitz[*]
David Yellin Academic College and
Hebrew University of Jerusalem

Abstract

School is one of the main arenas of violence among children and youths. Findings indicate that home-school cooperation is a key component for the success of combating school violence. Using qualitative interview data, this paper analyzes 48 teachers and school staff's perceptions of self-efficacy in dealing with parents concerning school violence. Three indicators were used to examine teachers' self-efficacy: personal teaching efficacy (PTE), teachers' efficacy in school as an organization (TESO), and teachers' outcome efficacy (TOE). Findings revealed that PTE was found to be high and complicated: most teachers' believe in their capabilities to collaborate with parents, but have low expectations from this cooperation. The majority of teachers described TESO as high: the interpersonal relationships among the team are supportive in dealing with parents. Likewise, teachers' experience and gender is considerably correlated with TOE.

Keywords: School violence, teachers' self-efficacy, parent-teacher cooperation.

[*] Correspondence to: Revital Sela-Shayovitz, Mevo Tidhar 14 st. Mevasert Zion, 90805, Israel. Tel: 972-2-533-4538. E-mail: ron15r@netvision.net.il.

INTRODUCTION

School violence is widely held to have become a major concern over the last decades in many western countries. School principals and teachers are troubled about violence problems and ask for guidance in acquiring skills for intervention (Mallet and Paty, 1999; Price and Everett, 1997). Scholars underline that the success of prevention programmes for combating school violence is enhanced by home-school cooperation (Sheldon and Epstein, 2002; Spriggs, 2007). However, despite the abundance of literature on violence prevention programmes, only a few studies have dealt specifically with teachers' self-efficacy in dealing with violence (Kandakai and King, 2002; Sela-Shayovitz, 2008). Moreover, there is a dearth of research that illuminates how teachers cooperate with parents in treating violent events. This paper attempts to address this important aspect by examining the perceived self-efficacy of teachers in dealing with parents on violence issues. By way of introduction, and in order to elucidate the theoretical and methodological frameworks underlying this research, I will begin by presenting brief descriptions from the literature on teachers' self-efficacy, school violence and school-based violence prevention strategies.

The methodology used in this study will then be presented. This study uses the qualitative approaches of in-depth semi-structured interviews with teachers in three types of schools: elementary schools, junior high schools and high schools.

Finally, the findings will be presented and discussed in light of school violence and teachers' self-efficacy, and further directions for study will be suggested.

THEORETICAL BACKGROUND

Teachers' Self-Efficacy

Following Bandura's (1986) social cognitive theory, the concept of self-efficacy has been well established and the term has entered the lexicon of the general public as well as the literature concerning teachers' ability and function. Bandura (1997;3) conceptualized self-efficacy as "beliefs in one's capabilities to organize and execute the courses of action required to produce given attainments". Self-efficacy is the individual's belief about the level of competence that s/he will display in a given situation. Self-efficacy is a central mechanism affecting the self-image, and mediates between personal knowledge, skills and beliefs on the one hand, and the individual's activities on the other. Self-efficacy influences thought patterns and emotions that enable actions, in which people expend substantial effort in search of goals, persist in the face of difficulty and exercise some control over events that affect their lives (Bandura, 1986, 1997). Social cognitive theory suggests a further kind of expectation - the outcome expectancy, which is dissimilar from efficacy expectations. An efficacy expectation is the individual's conviction that s/he can orchestrate the essential actions to perform a given task, while outcome expectancy is the individual's appraisal of the consequences of carrying out that task at the expected level of competence (Bandura, 1986, 1993). Thus, people with similar competencies can attain different outcomes owing to differences in their self-perceived ability and skills to handle the situation (self-efficacy expectation) and their self-assessment of capacity to perform the mission at the expected level (self-outcome expectancy).

Based on Bandura's (1986) concept, teachers' self-efficacy reflects their belief in advancing their students' achievements, the evaluations of their ability to organize knowledge and skills, and their capability to execute required actions to attain certain goals (Lev and Rich, 1999). Scholars argue that teachers' self-efficacy includes the components of their general self-efficacy and self-efficacy in teaching (Ross, 1995; Soodak and Podell, 1996; Tschannen-Moran, Woolfolk-Hoy, and Hoy, 1998). In this context, Gibson and Dembo (1984) developed a scale measure for teachers' self-efficacy that includes two dimensions: personal efficacy and general teaching efficacy. Personal efficacy refers to teachers' belief in their ability to promote their students' achievements, whereas general teaching efficacy relates to their general belief in the teaching profession as a means of promoting achievement among students, regardless of the personal competencies of a given teacher. A broader perspective for *teachers' efficacy* was proposed by Cherniss (1993), and related three components: task performance, interpersonal relations and interpersonal relationships in the school organization. In a similar vein, Friedman and Wax (2000) also suggested to expand the definition of teachers' self-efficacy to the element of school organization, namely how teachers perceive the relationships and the support they receive from the school administration and team.

Studies on teachers' self-efficacy primarily focused on students' achievements. Findings revealed that teachers' self-efficacy has a significant impact on students' achievements (Allinder, 1994; DaCosta and Riordan, 1996; Milner and Woolfolk, 2003; Ross and Cousins, 1993). More recently, findings suggest a reciprocal influence between teachers' self efficacy beliefs and students' academic achievement. This means that students' previous academic achievement predicted subsequent achievement as well as teachers' self-efficacy beliefs, which, in turn, contributed significantly to students' achievement (Caprara et al., 2006). These findings are in line with social-cognitive theory that points to experience and previous attainments as the most important sources of self-efficacy beliefs (Bandura, 1997). Another aspect is related to the link between teachers' efficacy and their satisfaction with their choice of profession. Teachers' job satisfaction influences the assessment of their ability to effectively handle teachers' tasks and affects their professional role in furthering students' academic achievements (Caprara et al., 2006). Yet, scholars emphasize that teachers' efficacy is primarily affected by the atmosphere within the school organization and by the extent of support that they receive from their colleagues (Tschannen-Moran and Woolfok, 2002). Schools that provided a low level of support for their teaching staff were associated with low levels of teachers' self-efficacy, and these teachers were less willing to cope with their students' problems (Goddard and Goddard, 2001).

School Violence

Since the 1980s, the problem of dealing with school violence has received considerable public and research attention, and a great deal of work has been done to promote prevention programs. However, notwithstanding the development of school-based violence prevention, teachers have often reported that they are unsure of how to deal with violent events. This uncertainty can have a tremendous impact on attempts to maintain safe school environments, and highlights the necessity of training teachers to improve their self-efficacy in coping with violence (Kandakai and King, 2002; Mallet and Paty, 1999; Poland, 1994; Price and Everett, 1997; Thornton et al., 2000). Furthermore, despite the importance of training teachers to acquire skills for intervention in violent events, this theme is not an integral part of the teacher training curriculum. The majority of pre-service teachers did not receive any form of violence prevention training in the general teacher training curriculum (Kandakai and King, 2002; Sela-Shayovitz, 2008).

Findings indicate that most pre-service teachers report that they had less confidence in their ability to deal with bullying and were in favor of teacher training courses regarding ways of combating school violence (Nicolaides, Toda and Smith, 2002). A program of training teachers in bully prevention strategies shows that teachers' self-efficacy in coping with bullying behaviors effectively improved following the course. Teachers who participated in bully prevention programs gained intervention skills for dealing with bullying students and victims. Moreover, teachers' beliefs in their skills and ability to influence their students regarding bullying behaviors significantly increased (Newman-Carlson, 2004). An examination of perceived self-efficacy among pre-service teachers enrolled in violence prevention courses revealed that as a result of the training, female pre-service teachers felt more confident than males about teaching violence prevention.

In addition, pre-service teachers in secondary education received consistently lower efficacy expectation scores than those in kindergartens and elementary schools (Kandakai and King, 2002). Analysis shows that training teachers in violence prevention programs had a significant positive effect on teachers' self-efficacy: teachers who participated in a violence prevention program reported higher levels of self-efficacy than those who did not receive training. Furthermore, teachers who received support and cooperation from school administration reported higher levels of self-efficacy (Sela-Shayovitz, 2008).

These findings indicate the importance of developing cooperation and teamwork-related skills as an integral part of pre-service and in-service training of teachers in dealing with violence.

The literature stresses that the success of violence prevention programs improves by combining multiple domains (Gottfredson, 2001; Howard, Flora and Griffin, 1997). Prevention program success improves by integrating several emphases, i.e., targeting students, school staff training, and home-school cooperation (Espelage and Swearer, 2003; Swearer et al., 2001). Indeed, parent- teacher communication and parent involvement in school was found to be a key indicator for the success of reducing school violence (Blum, Ireland, and Blum, 2003; Resnick et al., 1997). Parent-teacher cooperation increases students' feeling of connection to their schools, and in turn can interact to buffer students from the effects of exposure to violence. Specifically, findings indicate that when students perceived high levels of connectedness to schools, they engaged in fewer types of violent behavior (Brookmeyer et al, 2006).

Furthermore, getting support and conferring with parents were found to have protective effects for adolescents in dealing with violence (Ozer, 2005). These findings underline the important role of parents in dealing with violence and the necessity of parent-teacher cooperation. However, collaboration between parents and teachers seems to be complicated, and some of the teachers are afraid to cooperate with the parents of the bully students (Rigby and Griffiths, 2010).

The Present Study

From the foregoing reviews, it may be summarized that teachers are troubled about students' violence and ask for guidance in acquiring skills for intervention. Self-efficacy has mainly been examined in terms of teachers' contribution to promoting their students' achievements, while only a few studies have dealt with teachers' efficacy in coping with violence. Moreover, although the success of violence prevention programs improves by combining parent-teacher collaboration, there is a dearth of research that elucidates how teachers cooperate with parents on this topic. This study aims to contribute to the existing research knowledge by examining teachers' self-efficacy in dealing with the parents on violence problems.

The following research questions were examined:

- Is teachers' self-efficacy in cooperation with parents affected by the level of the school (e.g., elementary, junior high schools and high school)?
- Is teachers' self-efficacy in dealing with violence affected by socio-demographic variables (such as, teacher's age, teaching experience, and academic background)?
- Are there differences in teachers' self-efficacy in cooperation with parents of bullying students and parents of victim students?

METHOD

This study used qualitative in-depth, semi-structured interviews with 45 teachers from eight different schools. Three further interviews were conducted with other key informants: one school principal and two educational counselors. The interviews were conducted by the researcher during 2010 and lasted approximately 1.5 hours each. The sampling strategy was designed to recruit comparable groups of teachers for each level of school (elementary, junior high and high schools), in order to examine whether there were differences in teachers' self-efficacy in cooperation with parents. The original goal was to sample equal numbers of men and women in order to examine gender differences. However, male teachers proved very difficult to recruit, especially at the elementary school level. Consequently, in the final sample the efforts yielded 16 interviews with male teachers. The structure as well as the strategy of the interviews was designed to make sure that all interviews followed the same principles and guidelines. Furthermore, the primary strategy adopted in this study was to not disclose or mention any identifying details of the participants or their schools. Maintaining anonymity addresses the ethics of qualitative approach of keeping the participants' privacy and confidentiality (Seidman, 2006). Accordingly, all participants are referred to by the number of their interview. Four demographic variables were used in the coding process to classify categories of informants and thereby to facilitate comparison across groups: level of school, gender, experience in teaching, and academic background.

Sample - The sample was stratified according to the type of school where the teachers worked, as follows: 33.3% of the interviewees were teachers in three elementary schools, 33.3% were teachers in two junior high schools, and 33.3% were teachers in three high schools. The age range of the respondents is between 26 and 56 years (*M*=37.7, *SD*=7.2). The academic background of most of them (55%) is a first degree (B.A. or B.Ed), while the others (45%) have a master's degree (M.A.). The participants' experience in teaching ranges from 2 to 36 years (M=11.2, SD=7.7. Based on the literature of teachers' self-efficacy three components were examined as follows:

- Personal teaching efficacy (PTE) – teachers' attitudes and beliefs in cooperating with parents of students in treating school violence.
- Teachers' efficacy in the school as an organization (TESO) – teachers' perceptions of the extent to which they received support from the school organization in dealing with parents of students in treating school violence.
- Teachers' outcome efficacy (TOE) – teachers' perceptions of self-efficacy in the actual dealing with parents of bullying students and victim students.

The presentation of the findings was divided into three broad categories according to the three aforementioned self-efficacy components .

RESULTS

Personal teaching efficacy (PTE) – Findings indicate that personal teaching efficacy in dealing with parents about violence is high but complicated. The majority of teachers perceive parent-teacher cooperation when dealing with violence as important and essential for reducing violence (66.6%), as exemplified in the following teacher's response:

> "Cooperation between the parents and school when dealing with violence is significant and decisive in supplying conflict-solving tools. The educational system and the family framework must back each other up" (R-1).

Furthermore, most of the teachers' believe in their ability to collaborate with parents in handling violent events (62.2%). However, about third of them think that the parents don't really want to work together in order to prevent violence problems (35.5%), and some even perceive the communication with parents as not effective (4.4%). However, almost half of the participants (48.8%) believe that the parents who are willing to cooperate are the parents of non-violent students, while bully students' parents are not ready to collaborate. The following citations demonstrate these points of views:

> "I think that some of the parents want to cooperate. These are the parents of the children who are not violent, but the parents of violent children usually don't come to school and don't cooperate" (R-35).
> "The parents respond, but I don't know if they have power or influence over their children. The feeling often is that we have to handle it, in all aspects, not just violence. The parents are not active" (R-37).

Furthermore, the majority of the teachers (77.7%) believe that the main obstacle to cooperate with bullying students' parents results from their tendency to lay all responsibility on the school staff rather than seeing their child's problems and taking responsibility:

"The parents of violent children very rarely take responsibility. Usually parents don't like to hear criticism of their children. It's hard to confront parents; they immediately respond by criticizing the school" (R-34).

In a similar vein, most of the participants (73.3%) think that victim students' parents also lay all responsibility on the school staff, but more willing to cooperate with the school:

"Look, parents of victims blame the school too, but they understand that we have to deal with the problem together. They listen and they will internalize that something has to be done. My child is a victim, let's see, why did he choose to be a victim? These parents tend to some soul searching and take responsibility" (R-24).

No considerable differences were found for demographic variables (e.g., gender, academic background and years of teaching experience) in personal teaching efficacy.

Teachers' efficacy in the school as an organization (TESO) –Most of the teachers (68.9%) report high levels of teachers' efficacy within school as an organization. In other words, teachers perceive the interpersonal relationships within the school organization and among the team as good and supportive about dealing with parents on violence, as exemplified in the following citation:

"I feel that the school atmosphere is very supportive and it helps me deal with violence. I think it is projected from the administration: whether they believe that it is important to cooperate with the teachers and help them deal with problems. If the administration is uninterested, the problem will be ignored, the teachers will get no support and will find it difficult to deal with violence" (R-37).

A further aspect is related to teachers' perception of the way the school administration deals with parents on violence. Findings indicate that only 29% of the teachers perceive the administration as independent and assertive in dealing with the parents:

"The principal is really not afraid of the parents. She isn't afraid to deal with events, and when necessary she reports to the police. In one case the parents tried to incite and claimed that she was harassing their son, but it made no difference and she dealt with the event" (R-33).

However, more than half of the participants (57.7%) report that the administration is sometimes apprehensive about the parents' reaction regarding the punishment and eight of them (13.3%) perceived the management as highly concerned about the parents. This is illustrated in the following example:

"When dealing with violence, the principal is sometimes afraid. The problem is that the parents are within the system in our community school, and they can interfere with what happens at school. The sense is that they have to be placated... The community school removed our authority, and gave the children the feeling that their parents control the teachers. There is no backup for the system" (R-24).

Teachers' outcome efficacy (TOE) – Findings show that most of the teachers report low level teachers' self-efficacy in actually dealing with parents on violence (57.7%). Furthermore, many of them (62.2%) report that in some of the cases, the parents were aggressive toward them or to other school staff. Moreover, in some of the cases, the school management had to apply for a restraining order to keep violent parents away (11%). Findings show that the educational level of the school correlates with dealing with aggressive parents: the highest frequency of dealing with aggressive parents was found at elementary schools (50%), in comparison to junior high schools (39.2%) and high schools (10.8%). Likewise, most of the teachers (55.5%) report being sometimes concerned about the possibility that parents might harm their prestige (e.g., complain to the supervision of education or cause disreputability by means of the media), while only one third of them (33.8%) report feeling confident in dealing with parents.

Another interesting aspect is related to teachers' outcome efficacy to communicate with parents from different socio-economic levels. Most of the teachers (55.4%) report that there are no differences in their efficacy to communicate with parents from different socio-economic levels on violence. However, about one third of them (31.3%) say that they feel more comfortable cooperating with upper-middle-class parents because those parents tend to be more communicative than parents of the low socio-economic level:

> "Obviously lower-class, less educated parents with economic difficulties, there is more violence there. Parents with better educations and better economic status show more understanding of violent situations. These parents are less verbally abusive, their language is of a higher standard, and they have more understanding of the situation their child is in. Parents with less education, you sometimes feel their frustration, which is expressed in violent language towards the staff" (R-6).

In contrast, around one eighth of the participants (13.3%) state that it is more difficult to cooperate with upper-middle-class parents because they tend to be more protective of their child and criticize school policy. This is illustrated in the following example:

> "It is harder to communicate with upper-middle-class parents. These parents are usually not at home, their children are not under control, and this is expressed in the classroom. These parents think they know and understand everything. They are patronizing and think they are smarter than the teachers" (R-34).

Another noteworthy aspect is related to the differences in teachers' outcome efficacy to cooperate with parents of bully students and parents of victims. Approximately half of the participants (49%) report having the same difficulties to cooperate with both types of parents (e.g. of bullies and victims). However, substantial gender differences were found: more female than male teachers report feeling more comfortable to deal with parents of victims (28.8% vs. 8.8%). While, more male teachers than females respond that it's easier to cooperate with parents of bully students (27% vs. 4.4%). The following citations demonstrate these points:

> "I communicate better with parents of violent children. I feel uncomfortable and under qualified to help children who were victims" (R-48, male teacher).

"Parents of victims, unequivocally… They come from an emotionally difficult place and are more open to accept help. Parents of violent children are violent themselves, and it's harder to communicate with them" (R-24, female teacher).

Furthermore, substantial differences were found between young and senior teachers in cooperating with parents: higher level of difficulties were related to new teachers with less than three years experience (52.6%), in comparison to older teachers who had 3-10 years experience (31.3%) and senior teachers (16.1%). Thus, the longer the teaching experience, the teachers' outcome efficacy in dealing with parents improves.

DISCUSSION

This paper presents the findings of an exploratory study on perceived teachers' self-efficacy in cooperating with parents on handling school violence. To date, there is a dearth of research that illuminates how teachers cooperate with parents on school violence. This study attempts to contribute to the existing corpus of knowledge by extending the focus to teachers' efficacy in collaboration with parents during the course of treating violence. Several findings were particularly noteworthy.

First, findings indicate that personal teachers' efficacy (PTE) to cooperate with parents is high but complicated and has several meanings. On the one hand, most of the teachers believe in their capabilities to collaborate with parents and perceive the cooperation with parents as essential for reducing violence. However, on the other hand, they have low expectations from this cooperation and believe that parents of bully students do not really want to cooperate and hence lay responsibility on the school. These findings have important implications for the success of cooperation with parents on handling school violence. Based on the social-cognitive theory (Bandura, 1986, 1993), one may suggest that there is a reciprocal influence between teachers' beliefs and parents' involvement in dealing with violence. This means that parents' previous attitude to school violence predicted subsequent teacher's self-efficacy beliefs and expectations, which, in turn, contributed to the low level of cooperation in dealing with violence.

Second, findings indicate that teachers' efficacy in school as an organization (TESO) is high: most of the teachers describe the interpersonal relationships among the team as good and supportive. In this context, prior studies have found that teachers' efficacy is primarily affected by the support they receive from their colleagues (Goddard and Goddard, 2001; Tschannen-Moran and Woolfok, 2002).

Thus, it can be assumed that the atmosphere within the school organization and the support that they receive from the team is a key factor for teachers' efficacy in dealing with parents. Yet, it is important to note that most of the teachers don't perceive the school's management as assertive in dealing with parents. They report that the management is sometimes concerned about the parents' reaction and refrains from severe punishment. Thus, even though teachers have good and supportive relationships among the team, the management's concern about the parents' reaction may weaken teachers' efficacy to cooperate with parents.

Third, the analysis shows that most of the teachers describe low teachers' outcome efficacy (TOE) in dealing with parents on violence. The main difficulty related to parents' tendency to lay all responsibility on the school. Furthermore, in some of the cases, parents were aggressive toward teachers and school staff during the treating of violence problems. Likewise, most of them report being sometimes concerned that the parents might harm their prestige (e.g., by complaining to the supervision of education or being defamed through the media). Thus, even though teachers have good and supportive relationships among the team, they have to struggle with various difficulties when cooperating with parents on violence.

Another noteworthy finding is related to teachers' outcome efficacy to communicate with parents from varied socio-economic levels. Most of the teachers report that they have the same ability to communicate with parents from different socio-economic statuses. However, about one third of them prefer to cooperate with upper and middle class parents and argue that those parents tend to be more cooperative and communicative than the lower socioeconomic level. It can be suggested that teachers may be biased and stereotyping in their perception of the cooperation with the parents. Thus, teachers with a middle class frame of reference may lower their expectations for cooperation with parents who come from different value systems, which in turn may contribute to the low level of collaboration with these parents on violence. The current findings show that the educational level of the school is considerably correlated with teachers' outcome efficacy: teachers in high schools have less difficulties to deal with parents than teachers at elementary or junior high schools. It can be assumed, that parents of high school students tend to be less protective toward their child in comparison to parents in elementary schools. As one of the teachers said, "Those parents (e.g., in high school) start to realize that after so many years with violence problems, they can't always blame others for their child's behavior" (R-43). Moreover, it is possible that parents of high school students are more willing to cooperate because they are concerned that the violent event might prevent their child from graduating.

The results demonstrated gender differences in teachers' outcome efficacy: female teachers feel more comfortable to communicate with the parents of victims than male teachers, whereas male teachers found it easier to cooperate with the bully students' parents than female teachers. It can be assumed, that these differences ensue from gender differences in the socialization processes: females are educated to be more empathetic, sensitive and supportive of others in distress, while men are taught to be more assertive and tough. Thus, female teachers may feel more confident to communicate with victims' parents, due to the fact that they learned the skills to be empathetic and supportive. Whereas, male teachers feel more free to be assertive and rigid when treating violence problems.

The analysis shows that teachers' experience is considerably correlated with teachers' outcome efficacy (TOE): teachers with more teaching experience reported higher levels of TOE than those with less experience in dealing with parents on violence. These findings are consistent with prior findings that show that teachers with more teaching experience reported higher levels of TOE in dealing with violent events than those with less experience (Sela-Shayovitz, 2008). It can be assumed that teachers with less experience might have felt more threatened and less confident to deal with parents. Moreover, it is possible that these teachers are more concerned about their professional image at school and afraid that parents could harm their prestige.

The current findings have important practical implications for the process of training teachers in dealing with parents on violence, by training teachers to cooperate with parents and specifically enhancing their skills to deal with parents' defiance and resistance in the course of the cooperation. Furthermore, it would be beneficial to have courses in school violence that include parents and teachers training together to improve their communication. Moreover, it would be most effective to include treatment that obligates the cooperation with bully students' parents rather than just punishing these students.

Although the findings of this study expand our knowledge by providing important insights regarding teachers' self-efficacy in dealing with parents on violence, the relatively small sample makes it difficult to arrive at generalizations. In addition, the present study did not examine the contribution of variables such as the teacher's position at the school and the effect of dealing with different types of violence on teachers' self-efficacy in dealing with parents. It can be assumed that teachers' self-efficacy in coping with physical violence is different than when confronting other types of violence such as vandalism or indirect aggression. These limitations highlight the need for further research on this topic in order to increase our understanding of teachers' self-efficacy in dealing with violence.

REFERENCES

Allinder, R. M. (1994). The relationship between efficacy and instructional practices of special education teachers and consultants. *Teachers Education and Special Education, 17*, 86-95.

Bandura, A. (1986). *Social foundations of thought and action: A social cognitive theory*. Englewood Cliffs, NJ: Prentice-Hall.

Bandura, A. (1993). Perceived self-efficacy in cognitive development and functioning. *Educational Psychologist, 28*, 117-148.

Bandura, A. (1997). Self-efficacy: Toward a unifying theory of behavioral change. Psychological Review, 84, 191–215.

Blum, J., Ireland, M., and Blum, R. W. (2003). Gender differences in juvenile violence: A report from Add Health. *Journal of Adolescent Health, 32,* 234–240.

Brookmeyer, K. A., Henrich, C. C., and Schwab-Stone, M. (2005). Adolescents whowitness community violence: Can parent support and prosocial cognitions protect them from committing violence? *Child Development, 76,* 917–929.

Caprara, G. V., Barbaranelli, C., Steca, P. and Malone, P.S. (2006). Teachers' self-Efficacy beliefs as determinants of job satisfaction and students' academic achievement: A study at the school level. *Journal of School Psychology, 44*, 473–490.

Cherniss, C. (1993). The role of professional self-efficacy in the etiology of burnout. In W. B. Schaufeli, C. Maslach, and T. Marek (eds.), *Professional burnout: Recent developments in theory and research* (pp. 135-149). Washington, DC: Hemisphere.

Da Costa, J. L., and Riordan, G. (1996). Teacher efficacy and field placements. Paper presented at the Annual Meeting of the Mid-South Educational Research Association, Biloxi, Missouri.

Espelage, D. L., and Swearer, S. M. (2003). Research on school bullying and victimization: What have we learned and where do we go from here? *School Psychology Review, 32*, 365-384.

Friedman, Y., and Wax, A. (2000). *Teachers' perceptions of self-efficacy: The concept and its measurement*. Jerusalem: Henrietta Szold Institute (Hebrew).

Gibson, S., and Dembo, M. H. (1984). Teacher efficacy: A construct validation. *Journal of Educational Psychology, 76*, 569-582.

Goddard, R. D., and Goddard, Y. (2001). A multilevel of analysis of the relationship between teacher and collective efficacy in urban schools. *Teaching and Teachers Education, 17*, 807-818.

Goldstein, A. (1994). *The ecology of aggression.* New York: Plenum Press.

Gottfredson, D. (1997). *School-based crime prevention.* In L. Sherman, D.Gottfredson, D. Mackenzie, J. Eck, P. Reuter, and S. Bushway (eds.), *Preventing crime: What works, what doesn't, what's promising – A report to the United States Congress.* Washington, DC: US Department of Justice.

Gottfredson, G. D., and Gottfredson, D. C. (2001). What schools do to prevent problem behavior and promote safe environments. *Journal of Educational and Psychological Consultation, 12*, 313-344.

Howard, K. A., Flora, J., and Griffin, M. (1997). School-prevention programs in schools: State of the science anD impl)cations for future research. *Applied and Preventive Psychology, 8*, 197-215.

Kandak!i T. L., and King, K. A. (2002). Preservice teachers' perceived confidence in teaching school violence prevention. *American Journal of Health Education, 26*, 342-353.

Kingrery, P. M., Doggeshall, M. B., and Alford A. A. (1998). Violence at schools: RecEnt evidence from four national surveys. Pacific Instit5te for Research and Evaluation. Rockville.

Lev, S., and Rich, Y. (1999). Teachers' self-efficacy: Its meaning and measurement, and the contribution of counselors to its enhancement. *Iyunim Behinukh, 4 (new series)*, 87-117 (Hebrew).

Mallet P., and Paty, B. (1999). How French counselors treat school violence: An adult-centered approach. *International Journal for the Advancement of Counseling, 21*, 279-300.

Milner, H. R., and Woolfolk H. A. (2003). A case study of an African American teacher's self-efficacy, stereotype threat, and persistence. *Teaching and Teacher Education, 19*, 263-273.

Newman-Carlson, D. (2004). Bully busters: A psychoeducational intervention for reducing bullying behavior in middle school students. *Journal of Counseling and Development, 82*, 259-267.

Nicolaides S., Toda Y., and Smith P. K. (2002). Knowledge and attitudes about school bullying in trainee teachers. *British Journal of Educational Psychology, 72*, 105-118.

Ozer, E. J. (2005). The impact of violence on urban adolescents: Longitudinal effects of perceived school connection and family support. *Journal of Adolescent Research*, 20, 2, 167-192.

Poland, S. (1994). The role of school crisis intervention teams to prevent and reduce school violence and trauma. *School Psychology Review, 23*, 175-189.

Price, C. M., and Everett, S. A. (1997). Teachers' perceptions of violence in the public schools: The MetLife survey. *American Journal of Health Behavior, 21*, 178-186.

Resnick, M. D., Bearman, P. S., Blum, R. W., Bauman, K. E., Harris, K. M., Jones, J., (1997). Protecting adolescents from harm: Findings from the National Longitudinal Study on Adolescent Health. *JAMA: Journal of the American Medical Association, 278*(10), 823-832.

Rigby, K. and Griffiths, C. (2010) Applying the method of shared concern in Australian schools: an evaluative study. Cyberbullinginforum.org http://cyberbullyingforum.org/wp-content/uploads/2010/01.

Ross, J. A. (1995). Strategies for enhancing teachers' belief in their effectiveness: Research on a school improvement hypothesis. *Teacher College Record, 97*, 227-251.

Ross, J. A., and Cousins, J. B. (1993). Enhancing secondary school students' acquisition of correlation reasoning skills. *Research in Science and Technological Education, 11*, 191-206.

Seidman, I. (2006). *Interviewing as qualitative research: A guide for researchers in education.* Teachers college Columbia University.

Sela-Shayovitz, R. (2009). Dealing with School Violence: The Effect of Training for Prevention of School Violence on Teachers' Perceived Self-Efficacy in Dealing with Violent Events. *Teaching and TeacherEducation, 25, 1061- 1066.*

Soodak, L. C., and Podell, D. M. (1996). Teacher efficiency: Toward the understanding of a multi-faceted construct. *Educational and Psychological Measurement, 52*, 951-960.

Spriggs, A. L. (2007). Adolescent bullying involvement and perceived family, peer and school relations: commonalities and differences across race/ethnicity. *Journal of adolescence Health, 41*, 3, 283-293.

Sullivan, K. (2000). *The anti-bullying handbook.* New York: Oxford University Press. Sheldon, S. B. and Epstein, J. L. (2002). Improving Student Behavior and School Discipline with Family and Community Involvement. *Education and Urban Society* 2002; 35; 4, 4-26.

Swearer, S., Song, S., Cary, P.T., Eagle, J.W., and Mickelson, W.T. (2001). Psychosocial correlates in bullying and victimization: The relationship between depression, anxiety, and bully/victim status. In R.A. Geffner and M. Loring (eds.) *Bullying behavior: Current issues, research, and interventions.* Binghamton, NY: Haworth Maltreatment and Trauma Press/The Haworth Press.

Thornton, T. N., Craft, C. A., and Dahlberg, L. L. (2000). *Best practice of youth violence prevention: A sourcebook for community action.* Atlanta, GA: Center for Disease Control and Prevention, National Center for Injury Prevention and Control.

Tschannen-Moran, M., Woolfolk-Hoy, A., and Hoy, W. K. (1998). Teacher efficacy: Its meaning and measure. *Review of Educational Research, 68*, 202-248.

Tschannen-Moran, M. and Woolfolk-Hoy, A. (2002). The influence of resources and support on teachers' efficacy beliefs. *Paper presented at the Annual Meeting of the American Educational Research*, April 2, 2002, New Orleans, LA.

In: Progress in Education. Volume 26
Editor: Robert V. Nata, pp. 147-161

Chapter 8

GLOBALIZED CLASSROOM, EMANCIPATORY COMPETENCE, AND CRITICAL PEDAGOGY: A PARADIGM SHIFT

Mohammad Ali Salmani Nodoushan[1] and Parisa Daftarifard[2]
[1]Iran Encyclopedia Compiling Foundation
[2]Islamic Azad University, Science and Research Branch, Iran

INTRODUCTION

Since the advent of Audiolingual method as the first scientific, psychometric-based method (Richards and Rodgers, 2003) till the emergence of Communicative Language Teaching Approaches in 1970s, the language teaching pendulum has been swinging from one perspective to another (from empiricist to rationalist), appreciating one method over another (Task-based approaches over functional notional method) and accepting one method at the expense of rejecting another.

With the advent of communicative approaches to language teaching, the history of language teaching has witnessed many changes in quality of methods till the emergence of new paradigm to appropriate the teaching practice to meet the students' attainment prosperity.

Although all methods to date have changed to ameliorate previous methods, we have reached no panacea to solve methodology problem (Richards, 1990; Bell, 2003). This results in a diversion in perspective from prescriptive stance towards teachers' autonomy.

The original questions regarding teacher's and learners' role, methodology, theory of language and learning, learning-centeredness, learner-centeredness, and language centeredness, have been replaced with whether or not teachers should be involved in presenting materials (Richards, 1990).

Universality concept of method has been replaced with more locally oriented concept of methodology within classroom with more focusing on teachers' autonomous power (Kumaravadivelu, 1994, 1995, 2001, 2003a, 2003b). The shift in view occurs from static perspective towards method to a more dynamic, domain-specific vantage point (Richards, 1990), from method to beyond method (Richards, 1990) and from beyond method to post method (Kumaravadivelu, 1994, 1995, 2001, 2003a, 2003b); they all indicate the important role of teacher instead of method in moving learners in the direction of success.

The famous pendulum of language teaching has not stopped and will not; it is still swinging from one method to another and across different values systems: once behavioral, then cognitive, then constructive and not politically-based allied perspective. According to Reagan and Osborn (2002), foreign language education has been engaged "in on-going self-examination and reflection the result of which is dissatisfaction" (p.1).

What is believed nowadays is that success in classroom cannot be attributed to any particular method or "methodology" (Kumaravadivelu, 2006), but to social, political, cultural, historical, and economic contexts in which education is practiced (Reagan and Osborn, 2002). This in Martell's (2000) sense, has resulted in a situation where, "Curriculum is set in a vertical position from up to down instead of horizontal collaborative frames" (cited in Reagan and Osborn, 2000, p. 71).

This leads scholars to back Paulo Freire (1970) to question the aim of pedagogy as Freire explicated in his famous book *Pedagogy of the Oppressed* which highlights the important issue of unequal power-related relationship between teacher and students--which later constructs the society structure. Paulo Freire (1970) criticized this situation in the sense that "schooling transmits hidden biases about language, social class, power, equity that underlie language use" (cited in Reagan and Osborn, 2002, p. 30).

Elsewhere, Wong and Grant (2007) attributed the academic underachievement of minority students varying in race, linguistic, and cultural background to "the history of public education in the United States" (p. 681)

According to Freire (1970), the failure in educational context is due to the oppressed nature of the classroom and he sees the solution in critical pedagogy. In this respect, Van Lier (2004) suggests that the aim of critical education should be to develop students who are able to "develop their own way of thinking based on their own developing positions . . . or their own socially situated authoritative voice in the target language . . . through self reflexive stance or questioning one's own assumption" (p. 188).

This article aims at depicting critical pedagogy and claims that critical pedagogy is the new paradigm that has emerged out of sociopolitical aspects of language teaching.

CRITICAL PEDAGOGY (DEFINITION)

The central problem in any humanization movement is humankind (Freire, 1970); this concern sometimes brings about the recognition of dehumanization. Paulo Freire (1970) proposes the idea of critical pedagogy in his book *The Pedagogy of the Oppressed* on several grounds. Morgan (2007) attributes this negligence on the centrality of human beings to positivists and structuralists. He believes that positivistic view and structuralism are responsible for "anonymising of the learner" and "creating a decontextualized and ahistorical system of language" (p. 1034).

Different Perspectives on Critical Pedagogy

Akbari (2008) believes that Critical Pedagogy (CP) is a kind of teaching practice and "an attitude to language teaching" (p. 276) through which educational setting expanded to the realm of "social, cultural, and political dynamics of language use" (p. 277).

Wang and Grant (2007) refer to CP as "Dialogic pedagogy" as well as "critical literacy" (p. 686) or as 'participatory education' or 'curriculum development' (Auerbach, 1991, cited in Wang and Grant, 2007). Freire criticized banking system model of education in favor of problem posing one.

Accordingly, in banking system knowledge is deposited in students' mind as passive receivers. Dialogic pedagogy has four main features (Wang and Grant, 2007):

1. it is a teacher-student relationship with mutual respect and sharing community;
2. learning in classroom has problem-posing orientations;
3. it stresses learning through action and doing; and
4. in dialogic pedagogy, learners ask questions about different whos.

This way dialogic pedagogy serves for the whole society than an individual.

Historical Origins

According to Kanpol (1999), critical pedagogy is rooted in Western Marxist philosophy. According to Marxist interpretation, students' failure is attributed to their "lower socioeconomic status" (p. 28) while Neo-Marxism related such failures to cultural components like authority, power, and control issues. Schools produce different cultures so culture is the hidden curriculum of schooling.

Critical pedagogy is based on post-structuralism. In this respect, Giroux and Simon (1984, as cited in Peirce, 1989, p. 402) refers to teaching English as a pedagogy not in terms of material advancement but in terms of the way it perceives itself (self perception) and opens up possibilities for students and teachers. To Peirce (1989), language is a socially constructed phenomenon in human life. To Canagarajah (2005), language teaching as a political practice is within the construct of post-everything as (1) Poststructuralism, (2) postmodernism, (3) post Marxism, (4) post colonialism. Peirce (1989) asserts that CP is based on poststructuralist theory of language to "challenge the hegemony of communicative competence as an adequate formulation of principles on which to base the teaching of English internationally" (p. 401).

PRINCIPLES OF CRITICAL PEDAGOGY

Critical Pedagogy has certain characteristics from which the nine most important ones are explicated. Here it is tried to depict the same features in conventional teaching situation.

Dichotomous Classification is the Sign of Oppressed Society

The first characteristic of critical pedagogy is that the relationship between oppressors and oppressed is prescriptive; this means that there is no sense of freedom on what to do and not to do. In teaching and the history of methodology, we always face with prescription too. Therefore, the conventional teaching situation oppressed teachers as Freire criticized. To Freire (1970, p. 9 chap. 1), metaphors as "those people," "foreigners," "natives," "barbaric," subversive" are indicators of oppressed context. Dichotomous Metaphors defining language competence as grammatical / ungrammatical, acceptable / unacceptable, or appropriate / inappropriate indicate the prescriptive world we live in. Although these dichotomous world is created for the purpose of setting commensurability among its dwellers, they oppressed and limit human beings as either/or creature. The current models of communicative competence are mostly indicating static (Johnson, 1999) or apolitical and geographical reality (Canagarajah, 2005, 1993a, 1993b) orientation to look at language. What is proposed originally by Dell Hymes as communicative competence (1972) which encompasses possibility, feasibility, appropriateness, and attestedness and later developed by Canale and Swain (1980) into grammatical competence, sociolinguistic competence, and strategic competence and later elaborated more by Canale (1983) into grammatical competence, sociolinguistic competence, strategic competence and discourse competence are all indicating the static view towards communicative competence in the sense that they predict variability in the fixed defined and well structured framework. This gives the authors the power to prescribe what is dynamic by nature.

Even in testing situation, the same static view to language can be seen in different models proposed to explicate language competence, like the one proposed by Bachman (1990) and Bachman and Palmer (1996, 2010). These models, with a slight difference, explicate language ability in a dichotomized architecture. In these models, communicative language ability was classified into two distinct parts of (1) organizational competence (grammatical, vocabulary, morph, cohesion, syntax, phono and textual (cohesion, rhetoric organization) and (2) pragmatic competence which includes illocutionary competence such as ideational, manipulative, heuristic, and imaginative and sociolinguistic competence which includes sensitivity to dialect, register, naturalness, cultural reference and figures of speech instead of competence they used knowledge.

Another instances of dichotomous metaphor in educational research is related to either being objectivist or subjectivist when approaching research. In critical pedagogy both objectivism and subjectivism are wrong. They should be in a constant dialectical relationship. Subjectivism referred to denial of objectivity in analysis of action while objectivism is the denial of subjectivity when analyzing an action. Elsewhere, Apple (1996 as cited in Reagan and Osborn, 2002) defined objectifying as the criteria against which we measure the improvement of schooling. This way, objectifying leads to social cohesion.

Raising Critical Awareness of Oppressed through Paraxis

Raising critical awareness of oppressed through paraxis is the second feature of critical pedagogy. Paraxis means action/reflection which equals to word and work. Oppression is domesticating and is localizing everything to a specific situation, context, and culture. In language teaching and language testing we have domesticated English to its natives, native speaker norms (Cook, 1991, 1996, 1999 on multi-competence). Klein (1998) criticized SLAR which sets its criterion on native speaker as a norm and foreign language as a deviation from norm. Also, in studying the nature of interlanguage, Nemser's (1971 as cited in Sharwood Smith, 1994) called it as approximate system. This is also true in the concept of fossilization. As Selinker (1996) stated fossilization is only discussed in second language. To Wong and Grant (2007) the term limited English proficiency (LEP) both stigmatizes students and makes them as different from and inferior to the majority.

Criticizing such domestication, Kachru's (1992) proposes the term world Englishes to explain that English is not limited to native speakers but can be expanded from inner circle to include speakers in both outer and expanding circles. However, Peirce (1989) used People's English instead of African English or special Englishes and criticized Kachru of being neutralized and not considering the political and ideological aspect of language.

To nullify the domestication, Reagan and Osborn (2002) suggest the use of the concept of language legitimacy instead of native speaker to touch on the issues of "social class, ethnicity, and culture and is embedded in relations of dominance and power" (p. 34). However, Norton and Toohey (2002) state that legitimate and illegitimate dichotomy is the sign of inequalities. In critical pedagogy, mind is not in the form of either/or in Canagarajah's (2005) sense, mind is not dogma.

Reflection is Essential to Action

Critical reflection is a must in critical pedagogy. It entails the questioning of moral, ethical, and other types of normative criteria related directly and indirectly to the classroom (see Irwin, 1996 as cited in Reagan and Osborn, 2002, p. 23). However, reflection is not a linear process starting with one point and end with a result at the other end; it is a cyclical process which includes in action (in the midst of practice), on action (task takes place after action), and for action (desired outcome of both previous types of reflection) thinking and reflection.

Self-Depreciation

Self-depreciation is another characteristic of the oppressed society or pedagogy. Metaphors like terrible accent, good accent, near native like speech and the like are the signs of oppressed mind. Freire states that " they call themselves ignorant and say the "professor" is the one who has knowledge" (p. 14, chap. 1). The concept of authority is defined either as a source of knowledge, or in the form of replication of the real world; in the case of validity, authority determines how the criteria set outside (of test taker) and set for native speaker should match, or produces a fixed rubrics. In this sense, authority refers to the elites, biggies in the world of testing, teaching, linguistics, and so on.

The Peasant is a Dependent: The Opposite of Autonomy

In critical pedagogy, the concept of autonomy is meaningless; the peasant is a dependent. In critical pedagogy, Teacher as a model has the authority to produce knowledge. He or she chooses, and students enforce his choice.

Education is Suffering for Narration Sickness

Paulo Freire distinguishes between banking system and problem posing questions system. Transformation of knowledge happens from full to empty heads. Knowledge in critical pedagogy should emerge through invention and re-invention. Banking system refers to the knowledge that is disseminated vertically from higher to lower but the problem posing system is when learners try to question and construct knowledge idiosyncratically. In critical pedagogy, we have new terminology of student teacher and teacher student. As Freire (1970) mentions "educators re-form his reflections in the reflection of the students" (p. 8, chap. 2).

Dialogue is a Human Phenomenon

Dialogue is a human phenomenon. The essence of dialogue is word which has two dimensions of reflection and action. The words changed into "Verbalism when we have sacrifice [give up] of action" and "the words changed into Activism when it sacrifices of reflection" (p.1). Freire believes that dialogue exist deep in the hearth of love for the world and people.

Critical Pedagogy is a New Paradigm in EFL

Any paradigm has three pillars: ontology, epistemology and methodology (Kuhn, 1970). Ontology refers to the concept of reality, epistemology refers to the way we approach reality and methodology is the instrument we approach. Paradigm shift happens when current epistemology and methodology collapsed and new one is found. Critical Pedagogy seems to be a new paradigm in the realm of language teaching with the methododlogy of critical ethnography, epistemology of Glocolized concept of language teaching and with seeing language as an emancipatory competence, each of which is explicated below.

Methodology

In Critical pedagogy, the methodology used is critical ethnography. The method as Canagarajah (1993a) states is "an ideologically sensitive orientation to the study of culture that can penetrate the noncommittal objectivity and scientism encouraged by the positivistic empirical attitude behind descriptive ethnography and can demystify the interests" (p. 605).

Comparing descriptive research (normal research) with critical ethnography indicates that critical ethnography does not follow the conventional report in published papers. Descriptive research starts with introduction, then method, results and discussion. Critical ethnography, on the other hand, follows with method, the course, the class, contextualizing classroom life, pre-course determination, midcourse resistance, post-course contradiction, and contextualizing student opposition.

- Method
- The course
- The class
- Contextualizing classroom life
  - Precourse determination
  - Midcourse resistance

- o   Postcourse contradiction
- Contextualizing student opposition

Epistemology: Glocolized Classroom and Paradox of Glocalization

In critical pedagogy, we have both globalization and localization. Roberston (1995 cited in Shin, 2007) introduces the notion of glocalization saying that

> I have tried to transcend [go beyond] the tendency globalization in tension with the idea of localization. Instead maintained that globalization …has involved …the creation and the incorporation of locality, processes which themselves largely shape, in turn, the compression of the world as a whole. (p. 76)

In critical pedagogy, we need to take a pragmatic approach to globalization and localization. As Shin (2007) states with the advent of internet world organization and increase of "transnational corporation" are signs of globalized world (p. 75). On the other hand, some researchers emphasize the importance of localized voices individuals need to develop. Reagan and Osborn (2002), for example, believe that language pedagogy is interdisciplinary in the sense that it connects foreign language with content in other subject matters. They believe that critical pedagogy "values idiosyncratic voices [while] it suggests explicit articulation of multiple perspectives within home culture" (p. 79). Elsewhere, Kaufman and Brooks (1996) believe that curriculum planners who consider the interdisciplinary nature of education, they strengthen educational experiences for students by "helping them break down some artificial disciplinary barriers imposed by educational practice" (p. 80). Elsewhere, Shin (2007) states that domesticating means both localization and globalization: "when we talk about domesticating we talk about localizing and localization in critical pedagogy we have the motion of glocalization a paradoxical terminology" (p. 76).

Some scholars criticized the notion of globalization. Shin (2007) questions globalization on several grounds. (1) Is it possible to have a global textbook? (2) Globalization is a killing agent and schools are everyday committing linguistic genocide (360). De Lissovoy (2008) states that globalization has two different meanings. The first one is related to capitalism and neoliberalism like the global disciplining of workers, poors, and developing societies. The second meaning is related to widening the nation state system. He refers to the second term as "globality" (p. 158).

The argument is that on the one hand we have smaller world through web (globalization) and on the other hand we are dealing with plurality of language (Canagarajah, 1993b) in the sense of world Englishes (Kachru, 1992). As was mentioned earlier, Kachru's (1992) proposes the term world Englishes to explain that English is not limited to native speakers but can be expanded from inner circle to include speakers in both outer and expanding circles. However, Peirce (1989) used People's English instead of African English or special Englishes and criticized Kachru of being neutralized and not considering the political and ideological aspect of language. Therefore, it seems that within the concept of globalization we have the concept of localization. In this sense we believe that in approaching reality of pedagogy we move within glocalizaiton. Glocalization, in this sense, means that while there is plurality in every single phenomena, let's say language, the intention is to move towards similarity to reach fairness. The concepts of fairness and ethics have the same problem. Fairness means to make everything available for everyone (globalization); at the same time fairness can mean to observe the differences and move as required (localization). Therefore, in the critical pedagogy we are facing the paradox of glocalization.

*On*tology: Emancipatory Competence

Ontology means the theory of reality. Once, language was seen as linguistic competence, later it was broadened to encompass more variables in a static nature to form communicative competence. In a sociocultural perspective towards language, language is more glocolized. What does it mean to learn a language? Is it a neutralized system or a system of voice in Bakhtin sense or Paraxis in Freire's meaning? The globalization is the social aspect of language and localization is what Bakhtin refers to as voice. As Lantolf (2007) states human mental activity is always mediated through language which is the internalization of socially constructed activity.

We choose emancipatory competence from critical pedagogy to refer to multivocality nature of language instead of homogeneity and nativized one, and to triadic and dynamic nature of sign and meaning relation instead of dyadic type of relation.

Input as Triadic System

Van Lier (2004) claims that reviewing literature on input one can summarize and encapsulate SLA explanation on input processing into two distinct paradigms of Dyadic versus Dynamic nature of input-related theories. Input is studied in either Saussurian Dyadic or Peircian triadic based semiotics. In Sausurian value system, sign is static, and gains value only in relation to other sign in the system of language. But in Peirce's semiotics, input is dynamic, open, dyn, always changing and always developing into other sings. In the latter, input processing is a never-ending process of semiosis or meaning making. This means that it continually evolves in various directions, growing into other signs, through interpretative process. While Sausurian semiotics has a dyadic nature, i.e. there is a one to one relationship between object and sign or sign and meaning, Peircian semiotics is triadic because it consists of the dynamic interaction between "representamen and the referent or object and interpretant, the meaning or outcome of the sign" (Van Lier, 2004, p. 61).

As Van Lier (2004) states, the triadic sign may have three parts of Firstness, secondness, and thirdness in Aristotelian notion. Firstness is just what is (quality; related to feeling and possibility) with no reference to anything else. Secondness is reaction, relation, change, experience. And finally thirdness is mediation, habit, interpretation, communication, symbolism.

While all models and theories of input processing to date will fall into the first category, i.e. Sausarian dyadic sign, except for Van Lier's (2004) ecological view towards input, i.e., affordance. This paper aims at studying these two extremes view with respect to the three questions raised above as (a) the amount of input that is necessary for language acquisition; (b) various attributes of input and how they may facilitate or hinder acquisition; and (c) instructional method that may enhance input.

Therefore, there are two views on Competence: static forms and models of competence and dynamic forms of competence, each of which is explicated here.

COMMUNICATIVE COMPETENCE
(UNIVERSAL COMPETENCY MODEL)

The term communicative was used by Hymes for the first time in 1972 in reaction to Chomsky's view on linguistic competence (Johnson, 2004). According to Hymes, the followings are the components of communicative competence: (1) Whether (and to what degree) something is formally possible, (2) Whether (and to what degree) something is feasible in virtue of the means of implementation available, (3) Whether (and to what degree) something is appropriate (adequate, happy successful) in relation to a context in which it is used and evaluated (4) Whether (and to what degree) something is in fact done, actually performed, and what its doing entails.

Therefore, there are some differences between the two views. To Hymes, language community is heterogeneous, but to Chomsky, it is homogeneous. Also, to Hymes, language is functional but to Chomsky it is structural. The following table summarizes the differences between the two views.

Table 1. Taken from Johnson (2004, p.88)

Structural or formalist	Functional
Structure of language (code) seen as grammar	Structure of speech (act, event) seen as ways of speaking
Analysis of language code precedes analysis of use	Analysis of use precedes analysis of language code
Referential function is the norm	Gamut of social function is the norm
Single homogeneous code and community	Heterogeneous speech and community

Later the concept of communicative competence was elaborated and expanded to some extent that includes the internal and external factors of interlanguage. In 1980, Canale and Swain first classified communicative competence into a three component based model consisted of three components of grammatical, sociolinguistic and strategic and in 1983 Canale added discourse competence to their original model (Johnson, 2004)

They defined communicative competence in terms of four components: (1) grammatical competence: words and rules, (2) Sociolinguistic competence: appropriateness, (3) discourse competence: cohesion and coherence, (4) strategic competence: appropriate use of communication strategies. In contrast to Hymes, Canale and Swain placed ability for use within communicative performance, which they defined as "the realization of these competencies and their interaction in the actual production and comprehension of utterances

Social Model of Interactional Competence

Johnson (2004) points out that all interactional competence proposed by different scholars all have rooted in Vygotsky's (1978) sociocultural theory. To understand the notion of interactional competence, one should study Vygotsky's thought in detail. However, for the purpose of this article, the authors list the key points of his idea blow.

Collective Scaffolding

Under the notion of the zone of proximal development (ZPD), collective scaffolding is buried. By scaffolding, Vygotsky meant collectively constructed support provided by a cognizant. Donato in (1998 cited in Johnson, 2004) addressed the role of collective scaffolding in the acquisition of French. Accordingly, the main goal of the previous models proposed by Long in 1985 and Swain in 1985 was to send and receive the linguistic input successfully, however, in current perspectives social interaction provided the learner with the linguistic input and this is the learner "who developed second language on the basis of his or her mental processing mechanism" (Johnson, 2004, P. 130).

Emancipatory Competence

We suggest that language is formed as an emancipatory competence in which social and strategic aspects of language would not be dichotomized. This way, native speakers might fail to understand the dialogic messages which are the result of triadic interaction among environment, perceptions, and inention (see Figure 1 for affordance). Bourdieu (1999) states

> Linguistic exchange is also an economic exchange which is established within a particular symbolic relation of power between a producer, endowed with a certain linguistic capital, and a consumer, and which is capable of procuring [obtaining] a certain material or symbolic profit. (p. 502)

To him utterances are (1) signs to be understood; (2) signs of wealth intended to be evaluated and appreciated; and (3) signs of authority, intended to be believed and obeyed.

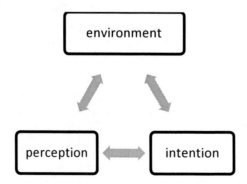

Figure 1. Affordance.

Emancipatory competence emphasizes the importance of interweaving of political, social, multi-voices linguistic competence. This brings about a non dogmatic legitimized speaker. Legitimized speaker is not someone who knows the norms native to one language but someone who has the tolerance of ambiguity and depicting the situational construct and appropriate his or her language to meet the context of interaction. Joseph (2006) believes that study of language and politics is interwoven in the sense that "the study of language and politics is aimed at understanding the role of linguistic communication in the functioning of social units and how this role shapes language itself" (p. 347).

Emancipatory competence is both globalized and localized. It is globalilzed in that people are able to appropriate their speech to the unknown context through picking up the clues. Therefore, the negative concept of linguistic imperialism as Philipson (1992 as cited in Joseph, 2006) proposed, is not meaningful. Linguistic imperialism holds the idea that dominance of English "is asserted and maintained by the establishment and continuous reconstitution of structural and cultural inequalities between English and other languages. (p. 360). However, from emancipatory competence perspective, any language that one acquires can help to reshape learners' competencies both globally (widening the vision) and locally (compounding the internal voice). We are not claiming we have emancipatory grammar but emancipatory competence instead of sociolinguistic competence. Appropriacy should not be limited to target societal norms and narratives. To Berns (2006), "the notion communicative competence has proven indispensable to world Englishes (WE) studies because of its attention to the issue of appropriateness in language use" (p. 718). He states that the questions of whose communicative competence? Innercircle, outer or expanding, the concepts of Fossilization, Lack of intelligibility, homogeneous and monolithic and uniform terms are signs of this inequality. The hidden assumption of communicative competence with inner circle as norm: (1) everyone learning English does so in order to interact with native speakers; (2) the communicative competence learners need to develop is the native speaker's; and (3) learning English means dealing with the sociocultural realities of England or the US, that is, British or American ways of doing, thinking, and being. Even native speakers might be incompetence as far as emancipatory competence is concerned. Norton and Toohey (2002) state

> Language learning engages the identities of learners because language itself is not only linguistic system of sings and symbols but is also a complex social practice in which the value and meaning ascribed to an utterance are determined. (p.115)

CONCLUSION

Critical Pedagogy is not an attitude or a single theory but a new paradigm with a new epistemology, methodology and ontology. Epistemologically speaking, Critical Pedagogy views classroom not only in terms of globalization (Kachru, 1992) but also in terms of localization (Philipson, 1992 as cited in Joseph 2006). Methodologically speaking, it is critical ethnography: an ideologically sensitive orientation to the study of culture that can penetrate the noncommittal objectivity and scientism encouraged by the positivistic empirical attitude behind descriptive ethnography and can demystify the interests (Canagarajah, 2005, p. 605). Ontologically speaking, to us it should take emancipatory competence instead of dynamic competence (Johnson 2004) because dynamic competence and static competence are neutral terminology. It is emancipatory because it meets all the tenants of CP proposed by scholars and mainly by Freire. In this sense, even native speakers might be miscompetent as far as critical ability is concerned.

CP has its own terminologies as Johnson (1999) states.

1. Emancipatory knowledge
2. Narrativism
3. Subjectivism
4. Activism
5. Dialogic pedagogy

Within this new paradigm Freire has set all previous terminologies has got a new value. Appropriate use of language is not dichotomized anymore: Native speakers might fail in saving the face of others because of their lack of recipriocal and emancipatory competence which is the result of cooperativism instead of dogmatism. Social justice needs to be reverberated: Justice is defined in terms of homogenizing classroom, access, test while language is highly multivoiced and multidimension when the context of situation is concerned (Bakhtin, 1999). Language is a tool and mediator in Vygotsky's terms and mediated in Bakhtins's terms therefore it is multi voiced. As Bakhtin stated each utterance is a voice. Therefore, communicative language competence should be an emancipatory communicative competence, another component so that we can add or insert the ideological political aspects of language competence or knowledge.

REFERENCES

Akbari, R. (2008). Transforming lives: Introducing critical pedagogy into ELT classrooms. *ELT Journal, 62*(3), 276-283.

Apple, M. W. (1996). *Cultural politics and education.* New York: Teachers College Press.

Auerbach, E. R. (1991). Politics, pedagogy, and professionalism: Challenging marginalization in ESL. *College ESL, 1*(1), 1-9.

Bachman, L. F. (1990). *Fundamental considerations in language testing.* New York: OUP

Bachman, L. F., & Palmer, A. S. (1996). Language testing in practice. Oxford: OUP.

Bachman, L, F., Palmer, A. (2010). Language assessment in practice. Oxford: OUP.

Bakhtin, M. M. (1999). The problem of speech genres. In A. Jaworski and N. Coupland (Eds.), *The discourse reader* (pp.121-132). NY: Routledge.

Bell, D. M. (2003). Method and postmethod: Are they really so incompatible? *TESOL Quarterly, 37*(2), 325-336.

Berns, M. (2006). World Englishes and communicative competence. In B. B. Kachru, Y. Kachru, and C. L. Nelson (Eds.), *The handbook of world Englishes* (pp. 718-730). MA: Blackwell Publishing.

Bourdieu, P. (1999). Language and symbolic power. In A. Jaworski and N. Coupland (Eds.), *The discourse reader* (pp.502-513). NY: Routledge.

Canagarajah, A. S. (1993a). Critical ethnography of a Sri Lankan classroom: Ambiguities in student opposition to reproduction through ESOL. *TESOL Quarterly*, 27(2), 601-626.

Canagarajah, A. S. (1993b). Up the garden path: Second language writing approaches, local knowledge, and pluralism. *TESOL Quarterly, 27*(2), 301-306.

Canagarajah, S. (2005). Critical pedagogy in L2 learning and teaching. In E. Hinkel (Ed.), *Handbook of research in second language teaching and learning* (pp.931-950). New Jersey: LEA.

Canale, M. (1983). From communicative competence to communicative language pedagogy. In J. C. Richards and R. W. Schmidt, eds. Language and Communication. New York: Longman.

Canale, M., & Swain, M. (1980). Theoretical bases of communicative approaches to second language teaching and testing. Applied Linguistics, 1 (1): 1-47.

Cook, G. (2003). *Applied linguistics*. Oxford: OUP.

Cook, V. J. (1991). The poverty-of-the-stimulus argument and multicompetence. *Second Language Research, 7,* 103-117.

Cook, V. J. (1996). Competence and multi-competence. In G. Brown, K. Malmkjar, and J. Williams (Eds.), *Performance and competence in second language acquisition* (pp. 57-69). Cambridge: CUP.

Cook, V. (1999). Going beyond the native speaker in language teaching. *TESOL Quarterly, 33*(2), 185-209.

De Lissovoy, N. (2008). *Power, crisis, and education for liberation: Rethinking critical pedagogy*. NY: Palgrave Macmillan.

Donato, R. (1998). Assessing the foreign language abilities of the early language learner. In M. Met (Ed.), *Critical issues in early second language learning* (pp. 169-197). Glenview, Illinois: Scott Foresman- Addison Wesley.

Freire, P. (1970). Pedagogy of the oppressed (chaps. 1,2,3). Retrieved November 1, 2009, from http://marxists.anu.edu.au/subject/education/freire/pedagogy/

Freire, P. (1973). Pedagogy of the oppressed. New York: Seabury Press.

Fulcher, G., and Davidson, F. (2007). *Language testing and assessment: An advanced resource book.* NY: Rutledge Applied Linguistics.

Giroux, H., & Simon, R. (1984). Curriculum Study and Cultural Politics. *Journal of Education, 166*(3) 226-238.

Hymes, D. H. (1972). On communicative competence. In J.B. Pride and J. Holmes, eds. Sociolinguistics. Harmondsworth, England: Penguin Books. Richards, J. C. (1990). *The language teaching matrix*. Cambridge: CUP.

Irwin, J. W. (1996). *Empowering ourselves and transforming schools: Educators making a difference*. Albany, NY: State University of New York Press.

Johnson, B. (1999). Putting critical pedagogy in its place: A personal account. *TESOL Quarterly, 33*(3), 557-656.

Johnson, J. (2004). *A philosophy of second language acquisition*. New Haven: Yale University Press.

Joseph, J. E. (2006). Language and politics. In A. Davies and C. Elder (Eds.), *The handbook of applied linguistics* (pp. 347-366). Oxford: Blackwell Publishing Ltd.

Kachru, B. (1992). Teaching world Englishes. In B. Kachru (Ed.), *The other tongue* (2nd ed., pp. 355-365). Chicago: University of Illinois Press.

Kanpol , B. (1999). *Critical pedagogy an introduction (2nd ed.)*. London: Bergin and Gravy.

Kaufman, D., and Grennon Brooks, J. (1996). Interdisciplinary collaboration in teacher education: A constructivist approach. *TESOL Quarterly, 30*(2), 231-251.

Klein, W. (1998). The contribution of second language acquisition research. *Language Learning. 48*, 527-550.

Kuhn, Th. (1970). *The structure of scientific revolution.* Chicago: Chicago University Press.

Kumaravadivelu, B. (1994). The postmethod condition: Emerging strategies for second/foreign language teaching. *TESOL Quarterly, 28*(1), 27–48.

Kumaravadivelu, B. (1995). The author responds. *TESOL Quarterly, 29*, 177-180.

Kumaravadivelu, B. (2001). Toward a postmethod pedagogy. *TESOL Quarterly, 35*(4), 537-560.

Kumaravadivelu, B. (2003a). A postmethod perspective on English language teaching, *World Englishes, 22*(4), 539-550.

Kumaravadivelu, B. (2003b). *Beyond method: Macrostrategies for language teaching.* New Haven, CT: Yale University Press.

Kumaravadivelu, B. (2006). *Understanding language teaching: From method to postmethod.* New Jersey: Lawrence Erlbaum Associates, Publishers.

Lantolf, J. P. (2007). Sociocultural theory: A unified approach to L2 learning and teaching. In J. Cummins and Ch. Davidson (Eds.), *International handbook of English language teaching* (pp.693-700). NY: Springer.

Martell, C. (2000). The age of information, the age of foolishness. *College & Research Libraries, (January)*, 10-27.

Morgan, B. (2007). Poststructuralism and applied linguistics: Complementary approaches to identity and culture in ELT. In J. Cummins and Ch. Davidson (Eds.), *International handbook of English language teaching* (pp.1033-1052). NY: Springer.

Nemser, W. (1971). Approximate systems for foreign language learners. *IRAL, 9*, 115-123.

Norton, B., and Toohey, K. (2002). Identity and language learning. In R. B. Kaplan (Ed.), *The handbook of applied linguistics* (pp. 15-123). Oxford: OUP.

Peirce, B. N. (1989). Toward a pedagogy of possibility in the teaching of English internationally: People's English in South Africa. *TESOL Quarterly, 23*(3), 401-420.

Phillipson, R. (1992). *Linguistic imperialism.* Oxford: Oxford University Press.

Reagan, R. G., and Osborn, T. A. (2002). *The foreign language educator in society: Toward a critical pedagogy.* London: LEA.

Richards, J. C. (1990). *The language teaching matrix.* Cambridge: CUP.

Richards, J. C., & Rodgers, Th., S. (2003). *Approaches and methods in language teaching* (2nd ed.). Cambridge: Cambridge University Press.

Robertson, J.P. (1995). Screenplay Pedagogy and the Interpretation of Unexamined Knowledge in Pre-Service Primary Teaching. *Taboo: The Journal of Culture and Education*, 25-60.

Selinker, L. (1996). On the notion 'IL competence' in early SLA research: An aid to understanding some baffling current issues. In G. Brown, K. Malmkjar, and J. Williams (Eds.), *Performance and competence in second language acquisition* (pp. 89-113). Cambridge: CUP.

Sharwood Smith, M. (1994). *Second language learning: Theoretical foundations.* London: Longman.

Shin, H. (2007). English language teaching in Korea: Toward globalization or glocalization? In J. Cummins and Ch. Davidson (Eds.), *International handbook of English language teaching* (pp.75-86). NY: Springer.

Van Lier, L. (2004). *The ecology and semiotics of language learning: A sociocultural perspective*. Massachusetts: Kluwer Academic Publishers.

Vygotsky, L.S. (1978). *Mind in Society*. Cambridge, MA: Harvard University Press.

Wong, Sh., and Grant, R. (2007). Academic achievement and social identity among bilingual students in the U.S. In J. Cummins and Ch. Davidson (Eds.), *International handbook of English language teaching* (pp.681-691). NY: Springer.

In: Progress in Education. Volume 26
Editor: Robert V. Nata, pp. 163-172

ISBN 978-1-61324-321-3

Chapter 9

EGOMORPHISM IN SIMPLE WORDS: DISCURSIVE PEDAGOGICAL ARTIFACT IN/FOR ENVIRONMENTAL EDUCATION

Jayme Bruno de Oliveira,[1] *Reis Giuliano*[2]
and Michael Roth-Wolff[1]

[1]University of Victoria, Victoria British Columbia
[2]University of Ottawa, Ottawa, Canada

ABSTRACT

In this study we introduce the concepts of *egomorphism* to the field of environmental education. Egomorphism determines that humans understand their environment through their own personal experience with the environment, and that the speaker's *self* or *ego* is the focus point for such understanding. Using concepts of discourse analysis and cultural historical activity theory as theoretical framework, we conclude by asserting that in the field of environmental education, egomorphism mediates learning by constructing a hybrid language (scientific and non-scientific) that is appropriate to the environmental education context in which participants may find themselves.

Keywords: Egomorphism, cultural historical activity theory, environmental education, fieldtrips.

INTRODUCTION

In the field of environmental education (EE), teachers use anthropomorphism to explain environmental concepts to their students (Kallery and Psillos, 2004; Zohar and Ginossar, 1998). Anthropomorphism can be defined as the tendency to attribute to non-human beings not only life but also feelings and human characteristics (Piaget, 1929; Wynne, 2007). Instead of anthropomorphism, in this article we expand the concepts of egomorphism to the EE arena and argue that egomorphism is a more appropriate term in the context of environmental activities.

Anthropomorphism attributes characteristics that belong *only* to humans to non-human entities (Asquith, 1997). One example of anthropomorphism is when dog owners attribute feelings and mindedness[1] to their dogs. This attribution of feelings and emotions to animals is a product only of the owners' assumptions (Milton, 2005) and can only ever be a metaphoric device, and never a mechanism for understanding what non-human animals are thought to be really like. If this is the case, egomorphism is an appropriate term, because it is based on the assumption that people's personal experiences rather than human-ness are the primary points of reference for understanding both human and non-human things (Milton, 2005). Egomorphism determines that humans understand their environment through their own personal experience (i.e., this understanding is achieved by *perceiving* human characteristics *in* non-human entities), and that the speaker's *self* or *ego* is the focus point for such understanding (Milton, 2005). In environmental education, egomorphism is associated with teachers using a language to articulate his or her self or ego to understand their object of study (e.g., animals and plants). In so doing, teachers open the opportunity for any participant in an environmental activity to perceive their own selves and egos in their object of study as well. Hence, we claim that egomorphism in an environmental context is an appropriate term to use when humans understand non-human animals through individuals' own personal experience in the sense that we, as human beings, understand our environment (e.g., non human creatures), based on our selves or ego. In other words, the understanding of non-human animals by humans is based on the perception that the animals are "like me", rather than "human like" (Milton, 2005).

STUDY DESIGN

Data Collection and Preparation

Our database emerged from environmental fieldtrips that we videotaped during a six-month period at an elementary school located in an urban area of British Columbia, Canada. We observed 25 grade 5 students and their teacher. We videotaped five day long environmental fieldtrips to local parks and 15 environmental related computer sessions, which corresponded to a total of 25 hours of video. Once the videos had been made, our first step was to create a content list, where, right after the data collection, we made any pertinent annotation and explication of events about the videos. In so doing, our memories were still "fresh" about the events that had happened during the data collection.

Our content list was indexed by the time stamp for each videotape. Each consisted of a heading that gave identifying information, followed by a rough summary listing of events as they occurred on the tape. The content list was useful in providing us with a quick overview

---

[1] Previous studies on human and dog interactions have noted that dogs have a mind. "Mind, in this view, is possessed by individuals and is an indirectly accessible interior place whose physiological home is the brain wherein its reason, intelligence, and personality reside. Mind, then, is taken to be in some way a play of inner representations (symbols, mental images, pictures) looked upon by a dog" (Laurier, Maze, & Lundin, 2006, p. 3). However, when we interact with dogs, and interpret its behavior towards us as loving, caring, we do not necessarily relate the dog's behavior to human behavior in general.

of the data corpus for locating particular sequences and issues, and as a basis for doing full transcripts of particularly interesting segments.

The use of the camcorder for data collection allowed us to play the recorded material on the computer. We used iMovie™ version 3.0.3, a free software package for Apple computers, to watch the video frame-by-frame. The software allows playing videos back and forth as needed. This same software also facilitated playing the movie during transcribing. To avoid fully transcribing all the videos, we designed a coding system (an Excel™ spreadsheet containing the number of the tape, the date on which it was recorded, the name of the research assistant who was responsible to videotape, and a brief description of its contents). This spreadsheet helped us to find the phenomena we were studying in any one of the videotapes.

To facilitate the data analysis, we produced smaller (one to two minutes) episodes of selected parts from the total hours of recorded material, exporting these episodes into QuickTime™. Then, each QuickTime™ short episode was transcribed verbatim, including pauses and verbal descriptions of nonverbal actions when necessary. The short videos and their respective transcripts were entered into the database, which also contained our fieldnotes. All these materials helped us to better understand the role of egomorphism during environmental fieldtrips.

Theoretical Framework

As we are interested in understanding egomorphism within the cultural, institutional and historical context where such interactions happen, the theoretical framework we used throughout is based on the concepts of the cultural-historical activity theory (CHAT) (Leont'ev, 1981; Engeström, 1987; Roth, 2005). This theory was developed from the founding work of Lev Vygotsky (1978), and its fundamental concept is that human beings do not act directly towards the object of their actions but they rely, amongst other factors, on their language in use, which in the case of this study, egomorphism. For instance, in order to mediate student's understanding about environmental related issues, teacher uses egomorphism, which we further articulate is a hybrid language (scientific and non-scientific) when talking to the students. In CHAT the subject is a person or group of people that acts toward a specific object. For example, during environmental fieldtrip, the fact that the group may be observing the local fauna and flora is the overall object of activity for students and teachers (subjects) in the context of environmental fieldtrips. Their language use mediates the relation between students, teachers and the understanding of their activity. During an environmental fieldtrip, the outcome of their activities is mediated by the verbal communication amongst teacher and students. The units (e.g., subject, object) of an activity are not still entities but can change as the context changes (Nardi, 1996), and this aspect of the cultural-historical approach is evident throughout our research.

We have chosen CHAT as our theoretical framework, because it allows us to take into consideration the context in which language takes place. In this way, CHAT helped us to avoid assumptions about what goes on inside teachers' and students' heads, because language is social and historical constructed and it is situated in the context in which language is performed.

In conjunction with CHAT we used discourse analysis (Edwards and Potter, 1992) as an analytical tool for interpreting the videotaped fieldtrips as well as the videotaped computer sessions. Discourse analysis as an analytical tool (e.g., Roth and Alexander, 1997), help us to understand teacher and students' interactions during their environmental activities. Discourse is indeed a central part of our lives, and what we do with others is always mediated through some kind of communication. Hence, discourse itself is related to social interactions, including different forms of talking. Based on this premise, discourse becomes an important tool that mediates communication amongst teacher and students. Therefore, analyzing discourse that happens during environmental fieldtrips is useful in understanding how teacher and students interact amongst themselves.

The episodes we present in the next sections illustrate egomorphism, which we identify as a hybrid language (scientific and non-scientific language), mediating teacher-students interactions when they act towards their object of study. Such hybrid language mediates students' understanding of environmental concepts during environmental related activities.

Findings

Extending the concept of egomorphism to EE, we present two examples of egomorphism happening during two different environmental fieldtrips. Both episodes were extracted from our database. In the first example we articulate one aspect of egomorphism, which is concerned with how people understand non-human animals based on the assumption that the animals are "like me." In this sense, the speaker articulates his or her self or ego, characterizing egomorphism, rather than what anthropomorphism implies, that animals are human-like. In this first example, the instructor, using a hybrid language (e.g., egomorphism), introduces the students to concepts of conservationism towards animals.

Egomorphism Mediating Discussion about Marine Environment Conservation

Here, Kelly, a public school educator is giving an introductory speech to grade 5 students. During this talk, students are getting ready for an environmental fieldtrip where they would have contact with the local marine environment. In the following, Kelly refers to the marine animals:

01 They are other living creatures just like you and I are
02 living creatures so you wanna treat them like you would
03 somebody else who's your friend

In this episode, Kelly introduces students, concepts of conservationism towards animals by asking the student to treat the marine animals as they would treat one of their friends. Kelly explains that those animals should be handled gently and treated with the same respect as any other living creature—whether it is human or otherwise. At a first glance, the teacher's language might be considered an example of anthropomorphism because by saying "they are other living creatures just like you and I" (turn 01) the instructor compares the marine animals to human beings. Yet, this is not the case of anthropomorphism, because Kelly is indeed comparing the marine animals to humans (living creatures just like you and I [turn 01]).

However, being a living creature obviously is not property or an exclusively human characteristic. Therefore, what Kelly said cannot truly be anthropomorphism, because according to its definition, anthropomorphism is the attribution of human characteristics (that belong only to humans) to non-human animals. Thus, if it is not anthropomorphism, egomorphism is an appropriate theoretical concept to use.

In Kelly's speech, it is noticeable that there are two different "social" groups. Elementary students form the first group and the marine animals form the second group. What Kelly does is to compare these two different groups by putting them all together in the same group. Kelly says that these animals should be treated as the students' friends, which means that if before the animals that were once a part of only the marine animals' group, now these same animals are part of the group of students. Since marine animals and elementary students are part of the same social group, it opens the possibility for students to understand these animals as they understand their classmates or their friends (turn 03). In other words, students understand marine animals as someone like themselves that belong to the same group. In this sense the marine animals that Kelly talks about are like human, not "human-like" or human forms. More so, by comparing "living creatures" to "you and I" (turn 01), Kelly creates both the possibilities for learners to see themselves in the animals, and the possibility for students to experience a social relationship with the same animals (since now, they are all parts of the same social group).

Kelly, as an educator, is aware that other animals are not human beings, although she compares them to humans when she says, "living creatures, just *like* you and I" and "somebody else who's your friend." By saying this, Kelly shows that like them (the students and herself), the creatures are also living beings deserving care and respect. In the second and third turns, "you wanna treat them like you would somebody else who's your friend." In summary, Kelly tells students that the marine animals are living beings and like them (students and the teacher), are part of the environment.

Kelly articulates what we might consider students' selves or egos and her own self to describe human understandings of animals. This is exemplified in turn 01 where she uses the pronouns "you" and "I." When Kelly compares animals to humans, using a student's self (e.g., you) and her self (e.g., I) to describe to the students how fragile marine animals can be, and how gently they should be handled, she clearly separates *her* self from her *students'* selves. Instead of saying: they are other living creatures just like *us,* Kelly says: "they are other living creatures just like *you and I.*" We cannot ever know *why* she says it in this way, but in separating her *self* from her students, she creates the possibility for the students to explore their own *selves* in their object of study (e.g. marine animals). For the present purposes and consistent with CHAT and discourse analysis, we am interested in the function that Kelly's expressions have in the particular context in which she speaks. Furthermore the students' *selves* are projected into animals (by Kelly). In this way, the possibility is created for the students to understand animals as they understand *themselves* or *their own* friends on the basis of their own perception that they (marine animals) are "like them" (students themselves) rather than human-like. This illustrates the concepts of egomorphism.

In this episode, Kelly employs egomorphism, which we identify as a hybrid language that relates the students to their object of study (e.g., the marine animals). In EE, such hybrid language mediates teachers' interaction with their students, whose primary language is that of the everyday world rather than the one used in scientific publications. In Kelly's example, this language underscores the fact that the animals can be harmed if not handled carefully, being not immune to actions performed by others.

In the following section, we present a second example of egomorphism as it has occurred during a science lesson within the school setting. In this study we have identified the occurrence of egomorphism not just in animal related discussion but also in plant related discussion.

Egomorphism Mediating Discussion about Plant Physiology

Back at the school, the same group of students who were engaged in a previous fieldtrip is now gathered around their computers in the computer laboratory. As part of their environmental fieldtrip, they were required to videotape the fieldtrip and to further produce a short video with the highlights of their outdoor experience using software for movie edition. Before they start working on their video, their teacher recounts with them what they saw during their fieldtrip:

1	Mr.MacBeth	*You remind* standing at the river, what kind of plants were
2		all around us? Yes. *((one student rises up his hands to answer*
3		*teacher's question))*
4	Mark	Trees.
5	Mr.MacBeth	Lots of big high trees. And *you* know what kind of trees?
6		(0.1) Yes Sarah?
7	Sarah	Um, ceda-, evergreen trees.
8	Mr.MacBeth	Evergreen trees, yep, and? There is another kind of tree too.
9		
10	Sarah	Oh!
11	Paul	Garry Oaks?
12	Mr.MacBeth	*I don't think* that was oaks right down by the water,
13		because we were right by the edge of the river (0.1).
14		And the edge of the river
→ 16		Garry-oaks *don't like* to have their *toes* in the river.

In this episode, as Mr. MacBeth (pseudonymous) is talking to a group of students, he uses a personal pronoun (you) to refer to the whole group when he affirms: "*you* remind standing at the river" (turn 01). This pronoun uttered by the teacher can have two different meanings: (a) *you* can refer to every student as an individual or (b) *you* can refer to the group as a whole. In other words, the same pronoun can be singular or plural, depending on the context. However in this example it relates to the plurality of students. Singular or plural pronoun, when the teacher says "you" he opens the opportunity for each student in the classroom to consider their own selves in the teacher's speech. Second the teacher opens up the opportunity to anyone as an individual to answer the question he is about to ask.

When the teacher utters the word *remind*—although the use of this word is not grammatically correct in this sentence—he creates the possibility for the student to give him feedback about the fieldtrip (e.g., through remembering the time they were standing by the river during the fieldtrip). As the teacher had previously used the pronoun *you*, giving students the chance to consider their own selves, and now, in uttering the word "remind," the students have the possibility to articulate their own experience in whatever the teacher is about to say. Hence, the words *you remind* are related to the individual's self experience even though the teacher talks to a group of students. In addition, the question the teacher is anticipating in uttering, "remind," refers to something that happened in the past, therefore the students have to recall that event in particular.

In advance, Mr. MacBeth formulates for students that a question is going to be asked, and the way he accomplished that is through cueing the students with "standing at the river" (turn 01). In so saying, the teacher refers to some event that happened in the past when they were *standing at the river*, and the specific event the teacher is asking the students to recall (to remind). Hence, from that moment on, the discussion they have is concerned with some event that happened in the past. When the teacher utters "you remind standing by the river," Mr. MacBeth mediates students' feedback, because in so saying, he gives the students the opportunity to remember on the excursion and go back to that specific site and time. In doing so, the teacher also constrains students' answers or actions because he is putting a previous experience in context, that is, he asks the students to remember a specific event that happened in a specific time.

Right after the teacher's anticipation of his inquiry, he asks the students what kinds of plants were around them (turns 01 and 02). After Mr. MacBeth asked this question, one of the students, Mark, immediately rises up his hand to answer the teacher's question. Mr. MacBeth then says, "yes," giving Mark the opportunity to complete the question–answer adjacency turn. Mark takes this opportunity by saying that trees were the kind of plants they saw when they were by the river (turn 04). The teacher confirms the student's answer saying that they did indeed see lots of "big high trees" there, then the teacher asks, "And *you* know what kind of trees?" (turn 05). At this point of their interaction, Mr. MacBeth once again uses the personal pronoun (you) when he refers to the student, giving Mark, the opportunity to consider his own self about his experience. In other words, the teacher could have said "and *yourself* (Mark) or *yourselves* (if he was talking to the group of students as a whole), know what kind of trees?"

After a short pause the teacher says, "yes Sarah" thereby giving the named student the opportunity to answer the question (turn 06). Sarah starts articulating that the big trees by the river were "ceda-." Noticeably, she did not finish saying the type of the tree she saw by the river, instead she immediately changes her answer to evergreen trees (turn 07). After Sarah's answer, Mr. MacBeth confirmed it, saying that evergreen trees were indeed a kind of tree that they saw when they were standing by the river. Although that was not yet the answer the teacher was "waiting for." The teacher kept instigating the students on the same subject, allowing us to hear that he wanted a specific answer. In a correct or an incorrect manner, the question was already answered. If the student had given the teacher the wrong answer, he could have said that that was wrong answer and said what the right answer was and finally changed the subject. The fact that the teacher was waiting for the right answer is also articulated in his use of the conjunction followed by the word "and?" meaning that what Sarah had said was a right answer but not a complete one. Then, he said that there was another kind of tree (turn 08 and 09).

In response to the teacher, Sarah utters an interjection "oh!" (turn 10). After that, another student, Paul, hesitatingly answers the teacher with a question: "Garry oaks?" (turn 11). Mr.

MacBeth answers Paul's question saying that *he does not think* that the oaks are kind of trees that they could find by the water, because since they were right on the edge of the river, and the Garry oaks, according to Mr. MacBeth are a kind of trees that does not like to have their *toes* in the river (turns 12, 13 and 14). Here, the teacher compares the roots of the trees to toes.

The fact that the teacher perceives a human characteristic (e.g., toes) in the plant could be seen as anthropomorphism, in which however, anthropomorphism is the attribution of (only) human characteristics to non-human things. Since having toes is a characteristic that does not belong only to humans, for example, there are in the nature, other animals (e.g., dogs, chimpanzees, chickens) that also have toes, this example cannot be treated as anthropomorphism. We therefore suggest that egomorphism is an appropriate term, because here, the teacher is not just using characteristics that are not exclusive to humans in the plants, but he is also sharing with the students his own perception of what toes are, and what they represent for the plant. Although we could never know what the teacher's feeling are, in uttering that the Garry oaks do not like to have their toes into the water, this could be the teacher's personal experience be reproduced onto that plant. If this is the case, egomorphism is an appropriate term to use. This is noticeable right before his usage of the word toes, when he says "I don't think" (turn 12). In uttering, "I don't think" he gives the opportunity for his listeners to expect that what he is going to utter next is referred to his own opinion of the subject. In other words, the teacher is articulating what that specific subject means for him. Otherwise, the teacher would be only using a metaphoric device and not opening opportunities for students to understand what those plants are thought to be really like.

In the last excerpt, Mr. MacBeth uses a hybrid language, which we identify as egomorphism. It is a hybrid language in the sense that the teacher articulates scientific concepts through a non-scientific language. More specifically, Mr. MacBeth explains plant physiology and the water requirements of different trees. For instance, there are some kinds of plants, such as the Garry-oaks, that do not need as much water to survive, thus they are not frequently found next to rivers, or any other water sources. In other words, in this final example, the teacher substitutes the word roots for the word toes to mediate students' understanding about a natural phenomenon.

CONCLUSION

Building upon previous studies on egomorphism (Milton, 2005), in this article we provided the reader with a background of egomorphism, expending its concept to EE. Egomorphism was first claimed by Milton (2005), which so far has solely been used in the field of anthropology. Egomorphism is concerned with how a speaker articulates his/her own self or ego towards the understanding of non-human beings. In the educational arena, egomorphism mediates teachers' and students' interactions during science lessons. More specifically, egomorphism mediates the canonical science and everyday language and experiences during environmental fieldtrips. Additionally, we point out that egomorphism in EE is indeed a hybrid language (i.e., non-scientific and scientific) that teachers employ when they articulate environmental concepts with their students in a way that it is accessible to everyone in class. If this is the case, we conclude that egomorphism is an appropriate term to use since teachers may use their *selves* to articulate science concepts to students.

We used genuine examples extracted from our database to illustrate our findings in which egomorphism is employed by environmental educators when they articulate different topics with their students during environmental fieldtrips. The first episode presented illustrates a teacher employing egomorphism to articulate concepts of conservationism towards marine animals with her students. Here, the environmental educator puts students and animals at the same social group (humans). In so doing, the educator gave the students the chance to understand those animals in the sense that they (animals) are like humans, not human-like. In the second episode, the teacher used human characteristics that do not belong only to humans, to give students the chance to understand what the roots of the plants are really like.

Without doubt, students bring to the school their own way of understanding the world surrounding them (e.g., natural phenomena) and sometimes they attempt to describe it using their own everyday life-world language. Children bring to the classroom their own way (language) of seeing and explaining their surroundings based on the context they are embedded. In this scenario, environmental educators have the challenge of bringing to the students scientific knowledge in a manner that it is intelligible to everyone in the class. In other words, teachers during their lessons use scientific and non-scientific language to communicate with their students.

When this non-scientific language meets the scientific language a hybrid language is created. One form this hybrid language may take is *egomorphism*, a language that is appropriate to environmental contexts. Literature has often ignored teacher's contribution to the occurrence of such events. After all, their discourses must be intelligible to their students—this would be different if they were talking to other environmental educators or adults. In this way, instructors deploy this hybrid language as a strategy to make their object of study familiar to their students.

During an informal conversation with the teacher (Mr. MacBeth) , he affirms that he uses a more expedient vocabulary, which is "more appropriate to the age of students" and having learned this from a fieldtrip specialist. In reviewing my episodes and based on the teacher's conversation with me, we learn that there is a hybrid language (*egomorphism)* that has been transferred from the fieldtrip settings to the classroom settings. This hybrid language in the educational arena may have been produced during science fieldtrips and reproduced onto students in the classroom setting. *Egomorphism* is indeed a new concept in science education and there may be benefits to investigate the phenomenon at a deeper level.

REFERENCES

Asquith, P. J. (1997). Why anthropomorphism not metaphor: Crossing concepts and cultures in animal Behavior studies. In R. W. Mitchel, N. S. Thompson, and H. L. Miles (Eds.), *Anthropomorphism, anecdotes and animals* (pp. 22–34). New York: State University of New York Press.

Edwards, D., and Potter, J. (1992). *Discursive psychology*. London: Sage.

Engeström, Y. (1987). *Learning by expanding: An activity-theoretical approach to developmental research*. Helsinki, Finland: Orienta-Konsultit.

Kallery, M., and Psillos, D. (2004). Anthropomorphism and animism in early years science: Why teachers use them, how they conceptualize them, and what are their views on their use. *Research in Science Education, 34*, 291–311.

Kinchin, I. M. (1999). Investigating secondary-school girls' preferences for animals or plants: A simple 'head-to-head' comparison using two unfamiliar organisms. *Journal of Biological Education, 33*, 95–99.

Laurier, M., Maze, R., and Lundin, J. (2006). Putting the dog back in the park: Animal and human mind-in-action. *Mind, Culture, and Activity, 13*, 2–24.

Leont'ev, A. N. (1981). The problem of activity in psychology. In J. V. Wertsch (Ed.), *The concept of activity in Soviet psychology* (pp. 37–71). Armonk, NY: Sharpe.

Milton, K. (2005). Anthropomorphism or egomorphism? The perceptions of non-human persons by human ones. In J. Knight (Ed.), *Animals in person: Cultural perspectives on human-animal intimacies* (pp. 255–271). Oxford, England: Berg.

Nardi, B. A. (1996). Studying context: A comparison of activity theory, situated action models, and distributed cognition. In B. A. Nardi (Ed.), *Context and consciousness: Activity theory and human-computer interaction* (pp. 69–102). Cambridge, MA: MIT Press.

Piaget, J. (1929). *The child's conception of the world*. New York: Harcourt Brace.

Roth, W.-M. (2005). *Doing qualitative research praxis of method*. Rotterdam: Sense Publishers.

Roth, W.-M. and Alexander, T. (1997). The interaction of student's scientific and religious discourses: Two case studies. *International Journal of Science Education, 19*, 125–146.

Vygotsky, L. S. (1978). *Mind in society: The development of higher psychological processes*. Cambridge, MA: Harvard University Press.

Wandersee, J. H., and Schussler, E. E. (2001). Toward a theory of plant blindness. *Plant Science Bulletin, 17*, 2–9.

Ward, P. I., Mosberger, N., Kistler, C., and Fischer, O. (1998). The relationship between popularity and body size in zoo animals. *Conservation Biology, 12*, 1408–1411.

Wynne, C. D. L. (2007). What are animals? Why anthropomorphism is still a not a scientific approach to behaviour. *Comparative Cognition and Behaviour Reviews, 2*, 125–135.

Zohar, A., and Ginossar, S. (1998). Lifting the taboo regarding teleology and anthropomorphism in biology education—heretical suggestions. *Science Education, 82*, 679–697.

In: Progress in Education. Volume 26
Editor: Robert V. Nata, pp. 173-182

ISBN 978-1-61324-321-3
© 2011 Nova Science Publishers, Inc.

Chapter 10

EFFECT OF PERFORMANCE AND GENDER ON MOTIVATION AND CLASSROOM PSYCHOSOCIAL

Nor Balkish Zakaria
MARA University of Technology, Malaysia

1. INTRODUCTION

A classroom conditions is essential to meet the students' educational needs. These conditions include cordial classroom atmospheres where the lecturers and the students openly discuss instructional matter and explore learning activity. It is often argued that students whose learning environment is perceived to be conclusive for studies unfold the tendency to achieve more then those with fundamental requisites of instruction such as physical facilities and equipment, among others are inadequately provided.

According to Kyriaccou (1991), the kind of classroom ambience maintained by the instructors can have the significant influence on students' motivation and attitude towards learning. Classroom supposes to be purposeful, task oriented, relaxed, warm, supportive, and has a sense of order. Such learning environment would maintain students' positive attitudes and motivation towards the lesson. It is thus apparent that assessment of the association between classroom climate and achievement motivation can be undertaken.

Slavin (1994) posits that in a classroom, students desire to interact effectively in their world through two dimensions: their learning and their relationships. He added that classroom which support students' needs for competence and control in their learning and in their relationships will lively tap into and enhance motivation. This theory rest on the conjecture that educators could create a situation that is so powerful, building upon whatever personal motivation of students already exists. Slavin explicitly identifies the factors which educators can manipulate to enhance achievement motivation; competence, control, active involvement, curiosity, challenges, honour voices, belonging and plays.

Conceptually, it can be said that the student's motivation to perform better in school related endeavor would be ameliorated once they feel that their learning environment is stimulating, invigorating and inspiring (Figueroa,(1992) . William (1993) concludes that when the learning environment supports the learners' psychological need for self-determination, the students develop greater competence. These belief and competence could be observed as students develop and manifest their achieving tendencies. Universities authorities should therefore measure the expected positive outcomes among the students.

Gender differences have previously been found on perceived ability in favor of males (Catsambis, 1995, Weinberg, 1995). However, researchers do not know whether the gender differences are moderated by classroom pyschosocial or achievement level. It seems plausible that gender differences may narrow or disappear among students who are high achievers or who are unhappy with the classroom atmoshphere. Given the impact of students' motivation and classroom pyshosocial, one should understand how factors such as performance and gender could have an effect.

This paper is aiming to ascertain the motivation level of the undergraduate's student in one of the Public Higher Learning Institute in Malaysia. Furthermore the paper is determining the students' perception of their classroom environment study how the students' achievement motivation level and perception of the classroom environment significantly related to their performance (measures by Cummulative Grade Point Average or CGPA) and gender.

The findings of this study hope to serve as baseline information for administration of the institute regarding certain aspects of classroom teaching-learning environment that need to be focused to which has a significant influence on student's achievement motivation. It could provide useful information on how to organize classroom in order to improve students' academic achievement and how to establish alternative models or preventive models of education. The findings of this study suggest that educational administrator may benefit from an increased awareness of the importance of the psychosocial classroom environment hence to improve students' motivation.

The remaining parts of the paper are organized as follows. Section 2 reviewed some of the prior studies regarding the motivation level and psychosocial relationship in a classroom. Section 3 shows the hypotheses developed and discuss the instruments and the statistical method used. Results of the study are being discussed in section 4 and finally section 5 concludes the study.

2. PRIOR STUDY OF STUDENTS' ACHIEVEMENT MOTIVATION AND STUDIES ON CLASSROOM PHYCHOSOCIAL

Empirical analysis of peer effects on student achievement has been open to question because of the difficulties of separating peer effects from other confounding influences. Each student could influence his/her classmates not only through knowledge spillovers and how teachers respond to his/her, but also in how s/he affects classroom standards. A less disciplined student is more likely to disrupt her classmates, forcing the teacher to devote more time in class to disciplining rather than transmitting knowledge (Weili and Steven, 2007). Therefore, a student's performance in school may be influenced by the characteristics and behaviour of her peers. If these peer group effects are substantial, government policy may exploit them by optimally grouping students in different classrooms to achieve desired socioeconomic outcomes.

While most econometric attention has been directed at issues of simultaneous determination of peer interactions, Hanushek, Kain, Markman and Rivkin (2003) indicate that peer achievement has a positive effect on achievement growth. Moreover, students throughout the school test score distribution appear to benefit from higher achieving schoolmates.

Based on China setting, Weili and Steven (2007) find strong evidence that peer effects exist and operate in a positive and nonlinear manner; reducing the variation of peer performance increases achievement; and our semiparametric estimates clarify the trade-offs facing policymakers in exploiting positive peer effects to increase future achievement.

According to Smith (1997), students become more motivated to learn when the teacher is able to arouse curiosity from what is being said or demonstrated. Described as intrinsic motivation, the teacher must be able to explain to the students what the learning task itself is all about so that they will have the drive to learn for learning's sake. Students could also simply being motivated to reach certain level of target. Abu Zahari and Reynaldo (1998) recommended other perspective for students' achievement motivation is by setting the minimum grade point average (GPA) every semester, perhaps "D" to enable student proceed their respective program. In other word, setting minimum standards of performance is a reason for students to achieve, thus up grading their achievement motivation level.

Literature shows that teacher's behavior can influence climate that prevails in the classroom. Specifically, authorities along this area have noted the teacher's role in strengthening and maintaining a positive classroom climate. For instance according to Sun Geun Baek and Hye Jeong Choi (2002), it was claimed that classroom environment was a good predictor of students' academic achievement. Good and Brophy (1984) said, teachers can foster positive classroom climate by establishing rules clearly where rules are needed, allowing the students assume independent responsibility; minimizing disruption and delays and carrying out independent activities as well as organised lessons.

With regard to students' gender, Woessmann (2004) in his study found that girls perform statistically significantly worse than boys in Maths as conmpared to boys in Switzerland, Belgium, French and Denmark[1] Ross, Bondy and Kyle (1993) advocate caring and respectful communication in promoting classroom climate. They assert that: when students feel valued, they are likely to believe the classroom is a safe place. In such environment they may feel free to question to wonder, to step into uncertain territory. Barrow's (1984) discusses direct and indirect teacher influence on classroom climate. Direct influence consists of stating the teachers' own opinion or ideas, directing the students' action, criticizing his behavior, or justifying the teacher's authority or use of that authority. On the other hand, indirect influence consists of soliciting the opinions or ideas of the students, applying or enlarging on those opinions or ideas of the students, praising or encouraging student's participation, clarifying and accepting their feelings.

Emmons (1993) disclosed that classroom climate has a significant influence on student achievement. Harris (1996) revealed the same finding. Specifically he found that classroom climate was significantly related to academic achievement in reading, mathematics and language. Perez (1995) found that classroom environment was significantly associated with motivation to work with classmates and acceptance of classmates' personalities; teacher and student interaction; and physical lay out of the classroom. The findings of the investigation done by Fujita-Starck (1994) suggested that there can be no substitute for providing

---

[1] The study was conducted in 10 European Countries but not in the United States.

instruction that is well organised and clear, and also identified more suitable components that may be essential ingredients for a satisfying learning experience.

In an investigation made by Bartholomay (1994) the findings indicate that the students and instructors viewed teacher support and organisation and clarity as the two most prevalent dimensions in the classroom environment. Students' preference for an ideal classroom environment indicated a desire for increased attention to involvement, affiliation, and personal goal attainment and student influence but not to task oriented.

In general, the literature showed the significance of a wholesome classroom climate to a number of educational inputs and outcomes when given due consideration in the academic, positive student's achievement may be anticipated.

The students reviewed on student's achievement motivation and classroom climate point out varying conditions that might influence their development and sustainability. The researcher of the present study presuppose that when teacher deliver lectures, give comments and remark to students, as well as relate professionally and socially to them and evaluate their coursework and performances, and conduct teaching-learning activities, among others, they should see to it that students understand what is conveyed to them in a satisfying and gratifying manner and tone of expression. These, most likely, can ensure better learning in wholesome psychological environment

3. RESEARCH METHOD AND INSTRUMENTATION

The data in this study were collected through the use of two questions; University Class Inventory (UCI)[2] and Mehrabian) Achieving Tendency Scale (MATS). In UCI, Fraser (1989) devised the yes-no format and the scoring procedures were retained scales for interpreting scores. Each *'Yes'* answer brings three marks and each *'No'* answer brings one mark. To get a description of all over the classroom climate, the subject scores in each dimension were summered up and the aggregate raw scores were interpreted as 'positives' or favorable classroom climate and 'negative' or unfavorable classroom climate employing the following scale: 66.00 and above, positive classroom climate and below 66.00 is the negative classroom climate.

The other question was known as Mehrabian Achieving Tendency Scale. (MATS)[3] was constructed, validated and standardised by Mehrabian (1994) from University of California, Los Angeles. It provides a broad-scoped assessment of individual characteristic associated with achievement motivation level. It is a copyrighted research instrument, which is devised

---

[2] UCI is used to study the relationship that exists during the classroom teaching - learning situation (cloassroom phychosocial) perceived by the students. UCI is a modified version of Fraser's (1989), My Class Inventory (MCI). Both MCI and UCI were developed by originally to measure elementary pupil's perception of the socio-psychological aspects of classroom environment. It assesses five dimensions of classroom climate; Satisfaction dimension which measures the extent of enjoyment in the class; Friction dimension which measure the amount of tension and quarreling among students; Difficulty dimension which measures the extent to which students find difficulty with the class work; Cohesiveness dimension measures the extent to which the students know, help and are friendly towards each other; Competitiveness dimension, which measures the degree of competition among students.

[3] Mehrabian Achieving Tendency Scale (MATS) described as ' very high', 'high', 'moderate', 'low' and 'very low' as regards desire to pursue success, fear of failure, attribution of success or failure, feedback on personal performance perseverance, enjoyment in the tasks, levels of aspiration and future orientation.

for this current research. A total score is computed for the subjects by algebraically summing their responses to all items.

Means, percentage and standard deviations were utilized for descriptive statistical analysis. The chi-squared was employed in determining the significant differences on the student achievement motivation and their perception of the classroom climate when they are grouped by CGPA and gender.

A one way analysis of variance (ANOVA) was used in determining the significant differences on the subjects' achievement motivation and perception of the classroom climate, when they were categorised by CGPA performance and gender. All statistical analysis was done through the utilisation of SPSS for Windows computer software at 0.05 level of significance. Sample of this study comes from the undergraduate students from various courses in MARA Technology University of Segamat, Malaysia[4] in the year of 2006. A random sampling of 422 students was chosen for the questionnaire and the questionnaire was being answered by them within 15-20 minutes.

3.1. Hypothesis of the Study

H1:   There are significant differences in the achievement motivation level of the students when they are grouped by CGPA
H2:   There are significant differences in the achievement motivation level of the students when they are grouped by gender
H3:   There are significant differences in the classroom climate perception of the students when they are grouped by CGPA
H4:   There are significant differences in the classroom climate perception of the students when they are grouped by gender

4. RESULT AND FINDINGS

According to MATS, the total score of motivation achievement level is computed for the subjects by algebraically summing their responses to all items[5].As shown in table 1, 64 % or 268 out of 422 subjects scored 'high' category while another 91subjects or 22 % had medium level of achievement motivation. Subjects showed a good signal of achievement motivation level by marked only 15% or 63 of them fell in the' low' category of achievement motivation level. The data obtained is very encouraging because as overall, the students are found to have a high level of achievement motivation.

---

[4] MARA Technology University of Malaysia is one of the Public Higher Learning Institute in Malaysia. The classroom is being set according to the student's course without specific criteria eg. Regardless of the students CGPA result and their socio background.

[5] Marks for each item will depend on the scale that the subject chose. Total marks of 19 and above is considered 'high', mark between 6 to 18 is said as 'medium' and between −7 to 5 it is considered as a 'low'.

Table 1. Percentage of achievement motivation level by the subjects

	Achievement Motivation		
Level	Frequency	Percent	Cumulative %
High (> 19)	268	64	64
Medium (6 to 18)	91	22	85
Low (-7 to 5)	63	15	100

As tabulated in table 2; satisfaction (mean = 19.791; SD = 2.71), friction (mean = 10.57; SD = 2.53) and difficulty (mean = 12.66; SD = 3.39) were perceived to be moderate according to the UCI interpretation for each dimension scoring scale. A high level of cohesiveness (mean = 14 .10; SD = 2.28) and competitiveness (mean = 14.14; SD = 2.37) and was noted. The finding outlined the psychosocial relationship in the classroom were wholesome, invigorating and stimulating. The overall mean of all dimensions was 71.25, which indicated that the subjects' perceived a positive classroom climate since it was above 66.00.This is interesting because it highlights the important role of a healthy teaching-learning environment among the subjects.

Table 2. Dimension of classroom climate prevailed by the subjects

Dimension of classroom climate[*]	Mean	Standard deviation
Satisfaction	19.79	2.71
Friction	10.57	2.53
Difficulty	12.66	3.39
Cohesiveness	14.10	2.28
Competitiveness	14.14	2.37
Overall	71.25	2.66

[*] Classroom climate in this research refers to the psychosocial relationship that prevailed in a classroom and being measured by satisfaction, friction, difficulty, cohesiveness and competitiveness dimension.

Table 3. Differences in achievement motivation of the subjects by CGPA and gender

Independent variables	Value	df	Asymp. Sig. (2-sided)
CGPA	59.928[a]	6	0.00
Gender	42.324[a]	4	0.32

[a] 0 cells (0.0%) have expected count less than 5.

In order to determine whether or not significant differences occurred in the mean scores of the subjects, the Chi-Squared test was employed. As shown in the table 3, statistically significant differences occur in the scores of the subjects in performance but not in gender. This indicates that the subjects differed significantly in their achievement motivation when grouped according to performance insignificantly differed when they are grouped according to gender.Hence H1 is accepted where there is significant difference in the achievement motivation level when the sample students are grouped by performance. However, the findings fail to support H2 where there is significant difference in the achievement motivation level of the students when they are grouped by gender. Both of these findings conforms Abu Zahari and Reynaldo (1998). They added that, achievement motivation is more personal rather than social aspects. "If one desire to achieve a goal, achievement of this is more depended on his/her own efforts rather than the prompting of other people around him/her". In this study, no matter how hard a student pushes to accomplish an objective, if he/she does not want to achieve, nothing much can actually be accomplished.

Table 4. Subjects' achievement motivation level according to performance and gender

Independent variables		Achievement Motivation		
		Low	Medium	High
CGPA	3.50 and above	14.3%	20.2%	65.5%
	3.00 – 3.49	11.3%	18.7%	70.0%
	2.30 – 2.99	9.2%	23.9%	66.9%
	2.29 and below	55.6%	27.8%	16.6%
Gender	Girls	66.9%	38.4%	34.7%
	Boys	33.1%	61.6.5%	65.3%

Table 5. Differences in subjects' perception of classroom climate

Independent variables	F	Level of significance
CGPA	2.593	0.050
Gender	0.021	0.523

Table 6. Subjects' perception on classroom climate according to performance and gender

Independent variables		Perception of classroom climate (Mean)
CGPA	3.50 and above	71.4524
	3.00 – 3.49	70.7063
	2.30 – 2.99	72.3662
	2.29 and below	68.7778
Gender	Girls	71.241
	Boys	71.524

Table 4 indicates that subjects' with 'excellent' performance has a high achievement motivation with 65% as compared to 'weak' on which only indicated that 17% scored in the same category. Whereby 56% of the subjects from 'weak' performance have low achievement motivation. The result agrees the study conducted by Abu Zahari and Reynaldo

(1998), they found out that performance would upgrade the students' level of achievement motivation. Based on gender grouping, boys (65%) seem to be part of the factors contributed to the subject's high achievement motivation level. Girls show a low achievement motivation level (67%).This finding also support Levin and Gordon (1989), who disclosed that where boys had significantly more positive affective attitudes toward computers than girls. In looking the perceived ability and stereotyped views of science, Debacker and Nelson (2000) posit that Boys had higher scores than Girls.

In Table 5, the differences in the over all classroom climates were determined. . Results revealed that there were statistically significant differences in the mean score of the subjects performance (F = 2.593; P = .050). The finding accepts H3 that there are significant differences in the perception of the subject of the classroom climate when they are grouped by performance. The result of this finding agrees Sun Geun Baek and Hye Jeong Choi (2002) that classroom environment was a good predictor of students' academic achievement. The finding led to the rejection of the H4 that there are significant differences in the perception of the subjects towards classroom climate when they are classified according to gender since the value of was F = 0.021 and P = 0.523.It means that there are no significant differences when the students are grouped according to gender. This indicates that there are no significant differences on girls or boys perception towards their classroom environment.

In determining the significant differences in the mean score of the subjects, ANOVA was employed. The subject scores in each dimension were summered up and the aggregate raw scores were interpreted as 'positives' or favorable classroom climate and 'negative' or unfavorable classroom climate employing the following scale: 66.00 and above, positive classroom climate and below 66.00 is the negative classroom climate.

Table 6 shows that in all performance categories from 'excellent' to 'weak' subjects showed a positive classroom environment. This was evidenced by the mean scored, which was above 66.00 for all category of pereformance. Girls and Boys perceived the same positive classroom climate perception. The mean scored was averagely at 71.00, which was above 66.00. As a conclusion, the students in this study have positive classroom perception towards their psychosocial relationship.

CONCLUSION

The psychosocial relationships that perceived by the subjects were found favorable. The students reflected moderate satisfaction or sense of enjoyment in class. However moderate level of friction or tension in the class was also perceived. Despite the level of friction, the students still have a high level of cohesiveness or the extent of knowing, helping and being friendly to each other. This discrepancy might be attributed to the moderate level of difficulty with class work the students perceived. However the high level of competition spirit of the students does not jeopardise the sense of enjoyment, satisfaction and helping one to another.

There was a significant difference in the achievement motivation of the students when they are grouped by performance but not significant whenever they are grouped based on gender. The more excellent subjects'performance, the greater their achievement motivation level. In terms of gender, boys show a higher achievement motivation level.

There were significant differences in the subjects' perception of classroom climate when they were categorised by performance but no significant differences shown by the students based on gender grouping. As a conclusion to the issue of classroom climate in this study, it was found that, the students who involved in this study showed a positive perception of classroom environment regardless of performance and gender.

REFERENCES

Abu Zahari and Reynaldo (1998). 'Classroom climate and teacher education students' achievement at University Brunei Darussalam', Research Report Publishing, University Brunei Darussalam.

Barrow, R (1984). 'Giving teacher back to teachers: A article introduction to curriculum theory', Sussex : Wheatsheaf Books.

Bartholomay, A.C (1994). 'Perceptions of classroom social environment held by Virginia Community College students and instructions in development course',Ph D.Dissertation, East Tennessee State University.

Catsambis, S. (1995). Gender, race, ethnicity, and science education in the middle grades. Journal of Research in Science Teaching, 32, 243-257

Debacker, T. and Nelson, M. (2000). 'Motivation to Learn Science: Differences Related to Gender, Class Type, and Ability'. The Journal of Educational Research, Vol. 93, No. 4

Emmons, C.C (1993). 'School development in an Inver city: An analysis of selected program using latent variable structural questions model', Ph. D Dissertation. The University of Connecticut, Dissertation Abstract International.(DAI).

Figuoroa, C. (1992). 'Students ' perception of their intrinsic motivation to learn', Ed. D. Dissertation. West Virginia University, Dissertation Abstract International (DAI).

Fraser, B.J (Ed) (1989) 'Two decoded of research on perceptions', (vol. 1). Oregon Assessment Research.

Fujita-Starck, P.J. (1994). 'The motivation and classroom environment on the satisfaction of noncredit continuing education students', Ed.D.Dissertation, University of Hawaii. Dissertation Abstract International, 55 (06).

Good,T.L and Brophy, J.E (1984). 'Cooking in classroom', 3rd edition, New York:Harper and Row.

Hanushek, Eric A., John F. Kain, Jacob M. Markman, and Steven G. Rivkin, 'Does the Ability of Peers Affect Student Achievement?' Journal of Applied Econometrics 18:5 (2003), 527–544.

Harris, L. (1996). 'The relationship between classrooms climate and academic achievement in reading, mathematics, and language for a group of fourth grade suburban elementary students', Ed D. dissertation. The University of Memphis. DA1,57 (01).

Kyriacou, C. (1991). 'Essential teaching skills', Oxford : Blockwell Education.

Levin, T. and Gordon, C. (1989). 'Effect of Gender and Computer Experience on Attitudes Toward Computers'. Journal of Educational Computing Research, Vol. 5, No. 1.

Mehrabian, A (1994). 'Manual for the revised achieving Tendency Scale', Albert Mehrabian: Monterey, California.

Perez, M (1995) 'Factors effecting English and second language learning for new and returning international college students enrolled at an English language institute in the United States', P.h. D. dissertation, Texas AandM University.

Ross, D., N Bondy, E., and Kyle, D. (1993). 'Reflective teaching for student empowerment', New York: Macmillan.

Smith (1997). 'Research and theory on the role of echo in motivation children and adolescents', in Burns, R.B (Ed) 'prepares children and adolescents for the next millenium', Working Paper of University of Brunei Darussalam.

Slavin, R. (1994). 'Educational psychology. Theory and practice.', Boston :Ally and Bacon.

Sun, G., Baek,,H. and Jeong, C. (2002) 'The relationship between students' perception of classroom environment and their academic achievement in Korea', Asia Pacific Education Review. Vol 3 No. 1.

Weili, D.and Steven, F. (2007) 'Do Peers Affect Student Achievement in China Secondary Schools?' Review of Economics and Statistics, Vol 89, pp300.

Weinberg, M. (1995). Gender differences in student attitudes toward sei ence: A meta-analysis of the literature from 1970 to 1991. Journal of Research in Science Teaching, 32(4), 387-398.

William, G. (1993). 'Internationalization of biopsycho social values by medical students', Ph. D dissertation, University of Rochester.

Woesmann, L. (2004). 'How equal are educational opportunities: Family background and students achievement in Europe ands the US', CESifo Working Paper No 1162

In: Progress in Education. Volume 26
Editor: Robert V. Nata, pp. 183-192

ISBN 978-1-61324-321-3
© 2011 Nova Science Publishers, Inc.

Chapter 11

REFORMS FOR TECHNOLOGY INTEGRATION INTO TURKISH EDUCATION SYSTEM

Ahmet Baytak[*]
Harran University, Şanlıurfa, Turkey

ABSTRACT

This chapter aims to provide current status of technology integration and practical policies for technology integration to reform Turkish educational system (TES). With the new technological developments, it is necessary to embed these new technological devices into the educational system to increase students' achievement. Based on the theoretical framework and previous academic researches, this chapter provides different options of reforms to be done in education systems in order to use technology effectively. The chapter specifically uses TES as a case, describes the current development, and discusses how these new reforms could be effective for students' learning.

Keywords: Reforms in education, technology integration, schooling, Turkish Educational System, Computer-based Instruction.

INTRODUCTION

After the first establishment of Turkish educational system TES by the founder of Turkey, Ataturk, there have been several modification and addition to this educational system. From school structure to assessments, students in different generation experienced different schooling in TES. As a current example, the length of school year was decreased to 5 semesters in 1994 where now it is increased to 8 semesters. More importantly, there have been several changes for university entrance exam (OSS).

---

[*] Ahmet Baytak: Assistant professor of Computer and Education at Harran University, abaytak@harran.edu.tr (Part of this chapter was presented at BilişimTeknolojileri Işığında Eğitim Kurultayı, 2009, Ankara).

More importantly, there have been big shifts in this educational system about teaching and learning philosophy. Consistent with global educational trends, policymakers for Turkish educational system also revised the educational system and school structures. With grow of Behaviorism; educators in Türkiye also suggested new policies to reform TES. Most recently, after the popularity of Constructivism globally, there have been moves toward to this educational philosophy.

Meantime, technology development in the last century has a huge influence on education systems. The electronic devices such as radio and televisions have change the delivery of instruction. After the use of computers in industries and telecommunications, educational institutions also adapted these new technologies into their learning environments. The Internet technologies have promoted this adaptation and now technology becomes as part of education systems.

The developments in technology reshaped educational systems worldwide. School districts in developed countries such as in US made reforms to integrate new technologies in to their educational systems. Starting from 1950, television and radio became part of education. Distance education that was being done with mailing integrated with television for corresponding learning. Penn State World Campus for example (PSU, 2009), is one of the first institutions that start this system. With the development of technologies over years, the policies towards education have changed in US Educational Systems. The following vision established by US Department of Education clearly show that educators in this country are aware of the influence and the power of technology in education and it has to be integrated most possibly.

"The use of educational technologies, including computers in the classroom, can improve student achievement, support professional development, and increase the learning resources available to our students. In this information age, students must be prepared to use computers and other technology in school and beyond." (US Department of Education, 1995)

The development of technologies have influences Turkish Educational System as well. The educational council by ministry of education has 18 official council meetings since 1920. These council meetings are planned to be held every year but it has usually been gathered every five years. The 18th meeting was held in 2010. In these council meetings educators and administrators discussed next five-and ten-year educational plans and policies. Because of less economical development, and therefore less technology development, between 1920s and 1950s, the council meetings in these times were more focused on printed instructional materials. In the next 20 years, the meetings suggested the ministry to physically develop and repair classrooms and materials for instructions (It is important to note that the official status of this council is not more than a suggestion office for the Ministry of Education where most of the time the outcomes and suggestions of these meetings became regulations in Turkish education). In this period, mail-based distance education; visual and audio materials have been developed for some schools. With the more involvement of Anadolu University, the fist and biggest open university of Turkey, in distance education programs, the use of technology in education has been prompted. Radio and television based courses has been delivered everyday for most subject areas from elementary level courses to university level courses. After this involvement, Turkey started to develop its own technology based instructional materials. The center of education with film, radio and television were opened in these years and until now it has served the system with different names. Recently Anadolu University and Government television station TRT came to agreement to start a new TV channel (TRT Okul) just for educational purposes. However, during 70s and 80s, because of lack of teachers, educational council suggested using more technologies in education to fill the educational gap. Some of these technologies were film, radio, television, mail, and computers (MEB, 1972).

Another high level planning department of Turkey, The State Department of Planning, has come to important decisions for the use of technology in education. These decisions were tend to for next 5 year plan but it still has influence in the system but fully. The following list is part of the suggestion the department made to plan the future of Turkey (DPT, 1994).

- The learning environments in Turkish Education System should be contemporary environments where students are able to freely ask question, critics teacher, get involve the process, respect to the individuals, and curious.
- The students' researchers have to be selected from the elementary school and prepared after that.
- The program designed for schools and their curriculum should be based new technology based education policies.
- The main purpose of education should be preparing communities that have interrelation with information and technology.
- It is mostly important for education to prepare students who have sustainable mission to follow new information and technology.
- The culture of information and technology requires a long planning and investment from education.
- It also requires a community that is reconciled with new technologies and able to develop new technologies based on the local needs.

In addition, there have been uses of different technologies during the last few decades. Based on the developments and trends, educational institutions and governments decided to implement these new technologies for purpose of learning. For example, starting in 80s, schools set computers, which functioned, like a TV. In other words, computers were used as a one-way communication tool. In the beginning of 1980, computers were more available for instructions and later in this decade it becomes more productive. With multimedia, in 1990, technology became influenced in education systems (Nonis, 1999).

If technology is appropriately designed for instruction, Earle (2002) believes, there are potentials to produce positive outcomes, social interactions, changes in teaching styles, more effective teaching, increased student motivation, and enhanced student learning. It is also found that technology is part of instructions more than ever and teachers are also encouraging the students to use technology for their lessons (Beers, et al. 2000). Speaker's study (2004) results that most of the students felt that their learning was improved by integrating technology into their lessons.

On the other hand, there are unconvinced views in the literature for the integration. For example, Beaver and Moore (2004) do not accept the current technology use as "true integration", although delivering instruction with technology can be useful. Earle (2002) also brought up an interesting perspective and questioned whether educators are trying to fit curriculum to the computers or fitting computers to curriculum by using technology in classrooms.

TYPES OF REFORMS

Reforms are generally defined as making changes to improvements in order to remove neglect, injustices, or dissatisfactions. Reforms are not limited to a certain area. There could be reform in the economical system or other public services. The reform in this paper focuses on educational systems and specified on technology integration into education. As it was indicated before, Turkish educational system has been reformed several times in order to make the system better. However, with the new technology developments, it is essential to integrate technology into the learning places such schools and universities.

Based on Guba's categorization, policies or reforms are related to three types of process; policy-in-intention, policy-in-action, and policy-in-experience (1984). Policy-in-intention is about the group who think about new policies and reforms for a system. Some of the groups in policy-in-intention are legislators (TBMM), Ministry of National Education (MEB). Policy-in-action is about representatives who apply, teach, control, and monitor these new policies and reforms. For example, faculty of education in universities (eğitim fakülteleri), school administrator (Okul idaresi), local administrator (Milli Eğitim Müdürlükleri) are some of the groups in policy-in-action. Policy-in-experience is the main focus of new policies and reforms. Especially in educational systems teachers, students, and supportive staff are the groups that experience and live the policies or reforms. In other words, these groups of people know how a reform is applicable and feasible for the setting. Later in this paper, the new suggested reforms will be discussed for these types of processes.

However, educators in worldwide had hard time to follow the rapid changes in computing and other technologies. Especially, with the invention of the Internet, educators and researchers started discussing the effect of these new technologies in educational system. Even though most of these scholars are favor of integrating technologies in education, there are also some who strongly criticize this integration. As it was indicated before, this paper does not aim to prove whether technology integration is more effective or not. This paper is built based on the strong statements from the previous research that technology integration can be more effective and efficient in most educational settings. Thus, this paper goes further and suggests new policies and reforms for Turkish educational system to integrate technologies in education more effectively and efficiently.

ZERO REFORM

Since reforms or policy changes usually apply to a wide range of public, there are always disagreements with these changes. Some people in policy-in-intention group can be favor of other educational system and therefore they may not want to suggest any new reforms in order to integrate technologies in schools. A new reform could conflict with the current national legislation and rules. Thus, MEB or TBMM may have fear to suggest new reforms for integrating technology in classroom.

Institution and educational offices that are part of policy-in-action may have different perspectives against technology integration. Universities that are required to prepare new teachers may not be ready for technologies or their teaching philosophies may not include technology integration, therefore they insist to stay with the current educational system. Similar to that, regional school administrators may have a fear of controlling and monitoring students with the new technologies in the classrooms. Thus, some are against reforms for use of technology in classrooms.

As can be expected against other reforms, the researches show that some teachers, the essential members of educational community and policy-in-action, are against to integrating technology into current education system. According to previous researches, the followings are some of the barriers that make teachers opponent to technology integration;

- Fear of technology use
- Lack of support
- New responsibilities
- Changes in teaching attitude
- Lack of equipments
- Unclear directions and instruction for integration
- Lack of training
- Overwhelming in the current system

LIGHT REFORMS

Light reform for technology integration means that there are suggested changes, but these changes are limited to minors. In other words, Researchers suggest that using different types of new multimedia and hypertext have positive influence on students learning. With a light reform, technology does not replace the current educational settings. Students will still go to school, teachers will still use whiteboard, and administrators and educational settings will still test students to measure their achievements in the traditional way or with slight changes. However, the only changes are about the way they access information. After light reforms for technology integration, which is currently happening in some of our schools, teachers may put questions on a 10 slide PowerPoint instead of writing them on the board every time. Students may go to computer lab and do their search for their homework on the Internet in shorter time comparing with traditional way.

Some legislators or policy makers for educational systems are favor of this reform because of the following reasons; other developed countries already integrated technology in their classrooms, there is a demand from public and students to use more of technology in classroom, and there is need for changes in educational system to make it better. For example, there are numerous students getting "0 points" in their university entrance exam and this result pushes educators to look new ways to improve achievements. Some legislators and administrators also have misassumption that when they provide new technologies for schools, the teachers and school community will easily accept these technologies as part of old way teaching styles. However, these misassumptions do not always have happy ends. New technological equipments were kept in locked rooms in several schools without using as part of education.

Some institutions that prepare teacher are favor of technology use in schools because they follow the current research trend and find it necessary for the today's schools. Even though it is low, but still few local school administrators try to integrate technology properly in their schools to gain better achievements from their students. The main barrier that these school administrators have to overcome is about lack of equipments. In other words, local school administrators have a limited budget to spend for their schools and they may not be able to spend that budget for experience new technological equipments. Thus, these local school administrators may contact with national or even international business for grant and support in order to provide new equipments for their schools (i.e. Intel has provided equipments for some schools in Turkey).

Teachers who believe in the power of the technology in education already started to integrate ithat in their lessons. There are several examples that these teachers open websites to provide examples of integration for other teachers and educators. These teachers think that technology attract students and motivate them to learn better. Teachers also find the new technologies helpful to reproduce electronic material to reuse in their classrooms. With the Internet, they are also able to access a wide range of information that they can share with their students.

Students are also excited to have technology in their classrooms. Especially new generation find new technologies such as computers and phones 'cool' and they want to use those in their classrooms as well. With computer applications such as Word processing and Excel, they think schooling become less stressful for them.

However, within this light reform, there are some major problems have been accruing and should be expected. For example, teachers may use computers as a tool to give break for themselves. They may refer students to some unrelated websites and students may not learn anything. Students, indeed, may take advantages of these technologies and use them inappropriately. It was observed in several schools that students been taken to computer labs for research and they ended up spending most of their class time on online chat or games. Thus, it is necessary to establish reforms that teachers and students are prepared for.

RADICAL REFORMS

Radical reforms for technology integration suggest more than simple use of technology in education. It is based on Piaget's constructivism and Papert's Constructionism theories (1993). As it was indicated before, there was shift in TES from behaviorism to constructivism. However, when it comes to use of technology in education, administrators and teachers are still following behaviorist approach. This causes conflict between practice and theory.

In Constructivism and Constructionism, learning is not a simple transformation of information. Students engage in activity or build products to learn about subject. In other words, students learn by building products and interact with their peers for a better production and sharing. Within this learning environment, students' learning is not limited to teachers' knowledge. Teachers' responsibilities in these approaches are facilitation, which mean that teachers create a learning environment, make all necessary resources available for students, and manage the class activities. With new technologies, students' learning becomes meaningful and teachers' facilitation becomes easier.

In this section of the current paper, I will briefly explain what legislators, school administrators, and teachers should do within this reform. First of all, legislators or MEB has to look the case in two directions; in theory and in practice. In theory, within definition of Papert's and application of Kafai and Baytak et. al, technology become part of learning and students think-with-technology (Baytak, Land, and Smith 2009; Kafai, 2006). Based on these approaches, researchers (Overmars, 2004) use learning by design approach where students build products on computers in order to learn about math and science. Thus, legislators may suggest this approach to be implemented in schools.

In practice, this approach seems overwhelming for teachers who experience the reforms. To reduce that, MEB should increase technical support for teachers. Moreover, there should be positions as technology coordinators in every city that could support teacher for how to integrate technology properly into education. These coordinators must work Eğitim Teknolojileri Genel Müdürlüğü for new trends and developments.

Indeed, it may take time for the Radical Reform to take place. Especially current teachers who have been using different teaching philosophy in their classrooms may resist against the changes. It is highly recommended that this reform should start with new teacher candidates who are still taking classes in university therefore these universities have to change their curriculum for teacher preparation.

Before the new teacher start to apply the new reform, the current school curriculum should be modified based on constructivist approach. In addition, local school administrators should also support teacher use of technology in classrooms. These supports should not be limited to technical support. It may include promotion, motivation, and recognition. Individual school may also assign an experienced teacher as technology specialist who can lead technology integration in schools and become liaison between teachers and administrator for technology integration.

Teachers who will experience these changes have to understand the concept of the reform before starting teaching. Besides that, there should be ongoing teacher training for the new trends. Teacher should be aware of the new technologies, which make them confident in classroom in front of the students. These ongoing trainings should cover how to integrate these new technologies in the curriculum properly. It is also important to bring to attention that most of these trainings should be done by teachers who are already doing integration. It was found that teachers feel more feasible when another teacher explain their experience.

Another solution to keep teachers motivated for integration is designing a social network system such as ning.com that teachers can share their experience with other teachers, learn new trends, post questions, and respond peers' questions about integration. This forum type of online social places found useful.

In addition, students who are also part of the group that will experience these reforms should also be engaged in the reforms. Thus, the first step should be arranging student training on use of technology (for that purposes technology education or computer classes could be used). At early ages students may learn how to do certain things such as searching and ethics. For example, students should be taught about how to do search or how to use information from the Internet.

Since the new generation students learn earlier, some teachers may also have fear that their students know more than they do. However, the task should not be 'knowing the tool', it should be 'knowing how to integrate the tool in the lesson plan'. In that case teacher will be more knowledgeable than the students and students learning will be more meaningful.

According to Baslanti, a full integration is above a personal effort of teacher. The whole school communities and institutions should feel responsibility to expect better results. Thus, these expectations required a top-down rearrangement and restructuring of the programs, and school visions (2006). In addition, reforms are tend to be prepared by legislators who sometimes have not any background or information specifically about the education (Williams, Brien, Sprague, Sullivian, 2008). A school wide involvement which includes teachers, students, parents, administrators, and legislators is a key step to successful reform in education.

FATIH: FIRST STEP TO RADICAL REFORMS IN EDUCATION TECHNOLOGY

FATIH project is the most recent change in Turkish Educational Systems, started at the end of 2010, to use more technologies in learning environments. FATIH which stands for Movement for Increasing Opportunities and Enhancing Technology means conqueror in Turkish. The project aims to give more technology to most schools to fill the gap. More broadly, the goal of FATIH project is to give equally opportunities in education to everyone, providing more technologies to all schools in order to increase achievement and understanding the content with various senses. As part of the project, the government is planning to provide laptop computers, projector, smart board, and high-speed internet connection to 620.000 classrooms of pre-schools, elementary, and high schools nationwide (MEB, 2011).

In addition, with this project, it is planned to train teachers about how to use information technologies effectively and efficiently in education. After that, it is expected that instructional programs will be technology based and more electronic learning materials will be developed. There are five main components of the project which are (1) establishing infstructure of hardware and software; (2) providing and managing educational e-content; (3) Using technology effectively in instructional programs; (4) training for teachers; and (5) Providing conscious, secure, manageable, and measurable information technology integrations. Let's explain those components in detail.

1. Establishing infstructure of hardware and software: In this step, the current Turkish government is planning to provide a laptop, and a projector in each classroom (total of 620.000 classrooms). In addition, every school will have a special classroom which will have a multi functional copy machine, smart board, document camera, and a microscope. With the project, each city will have distance conference system for teacher trainings.

2. Providing and managing educational e-content: As a second step, it is planned to design e-content for school that will be based on the curriculum and support students.

This e-content will have visual and audio features. This content will be available to teachers and students through the Internet.

3. Using technology effectively in instructional programs: In order to establishing an effective integration, teacher guidance handbooks will be rewritten based on the new technologies and their use for education.

4. Training for teachers: As a part of FATIH project, around 600.000 teachers will be trained about the technologies installed in classrooms, using e-content, and the teacher guidance handbook. Some of these training will be provided face-to-face where some of them will be done from distance at the one of 110 distance learning centers.

5. Providing conscious, secure, manageable, and measurable information technology integrations: The high-speed internet connection is the key for the project. Thus, as part of the project, network infstructure for each classroom will be ready. More importantly, the project aims to ensure that teachers and students can safely go on online and the necessary software and hardware will be installed in each classroom.

The FATIH project is coordinated under the Ministry of Education and the Ministry of Transformation which provides network on the Internet connection will support the project. The project is planned to be done in three years; in the first year all the high schools in Turkey will implement the project; in the second year all middle schools; and in the third year all elementary schools will have this project running as part of their educational system. As a pilot, the project has been implemented in one of the elementary school in Ankara.

Overall, on paper, the goal of FATIH project seems promising for Turkish Educational System. If the project works as they planned, it may provide more opportunities for students and teachers. However, the project is locked with the teacher centered approach that a teacher with laptop and projector showing already designed content over and over again. Within these project, it is highly possible that most of the students will be passive learner where they just listen the visual content but not able to interact. Thus, the project could be big step to make radical reforms in TES to increase students' achievement. The current project itself is lack of instructionally designed and technology supported framework.

CONCLUSION

As it has been briefly explained, the new developments in technology and the need in educational systems require new policies and reforms that technology can be integrated into education. Even though I do agree with some of the concerns that anti-reformist bring about misuse of technology in education, the benefits are more valuable though. Light reforms have been already implemented in our current educational system but it seems obvious that this only an act of making patch.

In other words, with light reforms, legislators, researchers, educators and teachers are suggesting based on the new technological trends. However, policies and reforms for education should be arranged for next 10 years not the current day. Thus, it is necessary for policy makers to set new educational settings that will be affected by the simple technological changes and could work with new technological equipments. As it was suggested, setting a perspective that Papert suggested, thinking-with-tool should be the main focus (1993).

REFERENCES

Anadolu Üniversitesi anadolu.edu.tr

Baslanti, U., (2006). Challenges in preparing tomorrows teachers to use technology: Lessons to be learned from research. *The Turkish Online Journal of Educational Technology 5(1)* 33-37.

Baytak, A., Land. S. M., and Smith, B. (2008). An exploratory study of kids as educational computer game designers. In M. Simonson (Ed.), *the Association for Educational Communications and Technology. Thirty-First Annual Proceedings, 2008* (39-47). Orlando: AECT.

DPT. (1994). Devlet Planlama Teskilati *Bilim ve Teknoloji, Yedinci Beş Yıllık Kalkınma Plan Özel İhtisas Komisyonu Raporu*, Ankara p.12.

Guba, E.G. (1984). The effects of definition of policy on the nature and outcomes of policy analysis. *Educational Leadership 46*, 63-70.

Kafai, Y. B. (2006). Playing and making games for learning: Instructionist and constructionist perspectives for game studies. *Games and Culture, 1(1)*, 36-40.

MEB. (1972). Milli Eğirim Reformu Stratejisi. *14335 Sayılı Resmi Gazete.*

MEB. (2011) FATİH projesi, http://fatihprojesi.meb.gov.tr/

Nonis. S. A (1999). Understanding teachers' experince of a state mandate to provide technology training; An examination of policy implementation. *Doctoral Thesis.*

Overmars, M. H. (2004). Learning object-oriented design by creating games. *IEEE Potentials,* 23(5), 11-13.

Papert, S. (1993). *The children's machine: Rethinking schools in the age of the computer.* New York: Basic Books.

PSU. (2009)Penn State World Campus worlcampus.psu.edu

Williams, R. Brien, K., Sprague, C., and Sullivan, G. (2008). Professional learning communities: Developing a school-level readiness instrument. *Canadian Journal of Educational Administration and Policy, 74*, 1-17.

In: Progress in Education. Volume 26
Editor: Robert V. Nata, pp. 193-203
ISBN 978-1-61324-321-3
© 2011 Nova Science Publishers, Inc.

Chapter 12

TEACHING HEALTH PROMOTION IN NURSING: PROMOTING ACTIVE LEARNING

Eva Brunner[*] and Olivia Kada

Carinthia University of Applied Sciences, School of Health and Care
Hauptplatz 12, 9560 Feldkirchen
Austria

ABSTRACT

Part-time nursing students who are seeking for academic qualification besides their everyday working life are confronted with manifold strains: Finding a balance between work, study and family commitments, high work load and the "foreignness" of academic demands are often reported to be stressful (Evans, Brown, Timmins, and Nicholl, 2007). In order to ensure a motivating and healthy learning environment universities have to consider the students' needs. Universities have been identified as an important setting for health promotion (Whitehead, 2004). In the case of nurse education health promotion plays a crucial role focussing two perspectives: We have to care for the students' health and health promotion is an integral part of the curricula. Following these considerations a course for health promotion for part-time nursing students at the Carinthia University of Applied Sciences (Austria) was designed. Besides lectures regarding theories and concepts of health promotion different methods for assessing strains and resources were presented. Health circles (Meggeneder, and Sochert, 1999) and a standardized questionnaire for work strains (Prümper, Hartmannsgruber, and Frese, 1995) were not only discussed theoretically. Students actively took part in health circles (2 circles with 8 and 10 participants) which were dedicated to explore strains and resources at the university. They also completed a questionnaire ($N = 17$) which helped to identify stressors at their workplace. Balancing work, study and family, time pressure as well as the organizational structure of the study programme were found to be the major stressors. The students also reported a lack of variety of tasks and task identity in their workplace. The results indicate a need for action in the university, but also at the workplace. A concept integrating "Health Promoting University" and "Health Promoting Workplace" is required. Furthermore, the students had the possibility to become acquainted with health

---

[*] Corresponding author: E-mail: e.brunner@fh-kaernten.at.

promotion from a practical point of view using introspection which promotes active learning.

Keywords: health promotion, active learning, health circles, part-time students.

INTRODUCTION

Nurses who are working in practice and who aim at participating in continuing professional education are facing the challenge to balance work, study and private commitments (Johnson, Batia, and Haun, 2008). Therefore, seeking for academic qualification besides everyday working life is associated with manifold strains: Part-time students report academic tasks such as exams or scientific writing as being stressful (Evans et al., 2007). Inappropriate self-organization, lack of feedback and disorientation within the university setting as well as pressure to perform are major stressors (Brunner, Maier, Gritsch, and Jenull, 2009; Großmaß, and Hofmann, 2007). Furthermore, missing support from the workplace often leads to problems regarding getting time off for studying; as a result poor attendance in lectures can be observed (Rochford, Connolly, and Drennan, 2009). Lacking time for the family is associated with feelings of guilt and an increase of social tensions (Stanley, 2003). Thus, structural, social and time-related strains are shadowing part-time students' life (Giacobbi, Tuccitto, and Frye, 2007).

Working as a nurse is well-known as a demanding profession characterized by strains like time pressure, staff shortages, conflicts within the interprofessional team or confrontation with death and dying (Jenull, Salem, and Brunner, 2009). Public stereotyping and the low social value of nursing have a negative impact on the attractiveness of nursing and the self-image of nurses (Jinks, and Bradely, 2004; Kada, and Brunner, 2010; McAllister and McKinnon, 2009). In Austria, nursing education is still offered on the secondary level (Spitzer, and Perrenoud, 2006) which inhibits the academic development and the improvement of the status of nursing. Therefore, many nurses tend to participate in a part-time study programme not only to ensure the quality of care but also to become more valuable and to achieve better career opportunities. They are often confronted with colleagues who do not appreciate their new skills which can again lead to workplace conflicts (Stanley, 2003).

Whether part-time nursing students are capable of meeting these demands emerging from study, workplace and family environment depends on their individual coping strategies. Theoretical frameworks such as the transactional stress theory (Lazarus, 2007) or the theory of salutogenesis introduced by Antonovsky (1987) can serve as a background. Both approaches assume that we are confronted with stressors in everyday life and that stress occurs if we do not find adaptive ways to cope with various situations. Unsuccessful coping can lead to poor health, psychosomatic symptoms and risky behavior (e.g. smoking, drinking alcohol, self-medication) whereat high prevalence can be found among nurses and (part-time) students (Dodd, Al-Nakeeb, Nevill, and Forshaw, 2010; Jenull et al., 2009; Unger, and Wroblewski, 2007). As a support, health promoting interventions addressing behavioral and structural changes must be designed and implemented. Following the Ottawa Charter (WHO, 1986) health promotion empowers people to enhance their health. The charter states that people have to be addressed by the interventions in their everyday life; "...where they learn, work, play and love" (WHO, 1986, p. 3). Therefore, health promotion is realized in different settings. For part-time nursing students two settings have to be considered, namely the workplace and the university. While the European Network for Workplace Health Promotion (ENWHP, http://www.enwhp.org/) was established in 1996, universities as a potential setting were discovered later on. In 1998, Tsouros, Dowding, Thompson, and Dooris edited a WHO-supported book spotlighting the importance of health promotion in universities and stressing the need for the establishment of a European Network of Health Promoting Universities. To meet the needs of part-time nursing students, an integrative approach taking into account both settings is crucial.

THE PART-TIME STUDY PROGRAMME AT THE CARINTHIA UNIVERSITY OF APPLIED SCIENCES

The Carinthia University of Applied Sciences (CUAS; http://www.fh-kaernten.at/en.html), School of Health and Care, is situated in Austria and offers a part-time bachelor degree programme named healthcare management. The programme addresses predominately health professionals and most of the students are nurses. During the six semester course, lectures targeting among others health law, social policies, health and care economics as well as health and care management are provided. Communication skills, interprofessional collaboration and conflict management are considered as important leadership characteristics and therefore they represent an integral part of the curriculum. Health and care sciences, including health promotion, are also incorporated. The study programme qualifies for jobs in the middle management of the health care system.

Conceptualization of the Courses "Health Promotion I + II"

Health promotion plays a significant role in nurse education in general: First, nurses are legally obligated to offer health promoting interventions to their patients (cf. Austrian Health Care and Nursing Act; Schwamberger, 2006). Secondly, they should reflect on their own health status and on possibilities to promote their own health in the sense of self-care strategies (Kratvis, McAllister-Black, Grant, and Kirk, 2010). Thirdly – in the case of the described part-time study programme – the students as future leaders in the health care system must recognize workplace health promotion as an essential managerial responsibility (Federal Association of Company Health Insurance, 1999).

During the fifth and sixth semester of the study programme, in each case one course is provided: The first one is called "Health Promotion I" and focuses on the origin and the theories of health promotion. Based on these contents the second course "Health Promotion II" highlights the practical implication of health promotion with an emphasis on two settings, namely the workplace and the university. Both courses are designed using blended learning – a combination of elearning and "traditional" face-to-face lectures (Akkoyunlu, and Yılmaz-Soylu, 2008). This leads to manifold benefits: The virtual learning environment offers the opportunity for flexible and self-directed learning (Johnson, Hornik, and Salas, 2008) which is especially unburdening for part-time students who have to balance work, study and family commitments. Furthermore, blended learning helps to promote the students' ICT-skills (Kiteley, and Ormrod, 2009). Both courses are offered by the first author, part I during the winter term and part II during the summer term. In terms of the second course, there is a great emphasis on active learning (Eugéne, 2006). The students should become active participants which promotes the construction of knowledge and the development of skills (Baid, and Lambert, 2010; Vittrup, and Davey, 2010).

METHODS AND AIMS

To guarantee the active involvement of the students during the course "Health Promotion II" the students do not only learn theoretically about the phases of workplace health promotion. They also have the possibility to take part in an employee survey using the "Kurzfragebogen zur Arbeitsanalyse [short questionnaire for work analysis]" (KFZA; Prümper et al., 1995) and they discuss their study conditions in health circles (Meggeneder, and Sochert, 1999). Table 1 illustrates detailed information regarding the applied methods. For the analysis of the quantitative data (KFZA) the software PASW Statistics 17 was used. For the documentation of the health circles' results moderation techniques were applied (e.g. flashlight, brainstorming, prioritization of themes; Lipp, and Will, 2008) and an extensive protocol was prepared and discussed with the participants in the sense of communicative validation (Steinke, 2004). Afterwards, qualitative content analytical techniques (Elo, and Kyngäs, 2007) were chosen to identify the main strains (entitled as categories) and to find inclusion and exclusion criteria for each category (entitled as category definition).

Table 1. Methods

KFZA	Health circle
• quantitative assessment of working conditions	• qualitative exploration of resources and strains
• 26 items, 5-point Likert scale (1 = very little to 5 = very much, or 1 = does not apply at all to 5 = applies completely)	• 6-10 participants (seen as persons concerned or experts)
• 4 dimensions	• voluntary, temporary, and thematically determined work
work contents: variety and task identity	• external or internal moderator
stressors: qualitative / quantitative work strain, interruption of work and environmental strain	• participants from one hierarchical level ("Berlin model") or
resources: scope of action, social support and teamwork	• participants from different hierarchical levels ("Düsseldorf model")
organizational climate: information, co-determination and operational benefits	• participatory development of interventions improving health and eliminating strains
• high values indicate good conditions, except for stressors (high values – high degree of stressors)	• need for prep and wrap-up → documentation is essential
• comparison actual-ideal values	• widely used method in workplace health promotion
Martin, Prümper, and von Harten, 2008; Prümper et al., 1995	Aust and Ducki, 2004; Meggeneder and Hirtenlehner, 2006; Meggeneder and Sochert, 1999
mixed methods quantitative ⇔ qualitative	

In the sense of mixed methods (Plano Clark, and Creswell, 2008) quantitative and qualitative methods were combined to get an entire picture of the students' situation with respect to their working and study conditions.

Employing this approach the following aims should be reached:

- The practical implication of health promotion should become visible.
- The students should actively participate in health promotion.
- The students should reflect on their resources and strains.
- Information for the improvement of the students' study and working conditions should be collected as a basis for intervention planning.

Therefore, the course is not only about health promotion, it even puts health promoting aspects into action.

Course Participants

During the summer term 2009, 18 part-time students participated in the course "Health Promotion II". The students' age averaged 36.41 years (SD = 7.84), the mean working hours per week were 29.03 hours (SD = 8.84). The course participants reported on average 14 years of professional experience (SD = 7.81) and most of them were female (n = 15). All students took part in one of two health circles (health circle 1: n = 8; health circle 2: n = 10) and seventeen answered the KFZA.

RESULTS

Using the KFZA the students reported their actual working conditions in comparison with their desired ones. Figure 1 shows the means for both values (actual and ideal) per dimension. Subsequently conducted significance tests pointed out meaningful differences in the students' rating of all dimensions. Thus, the students wish to have more miscellaneous and holistic working tasks, less stressors (e.g. qualitative and quantitative work strains), more resources (e.g. social support, teamwork) and a better organizational climate (e.g. information, co-determination).

Using the threshold values introduced by Martin et al. (2008) the degree of need for action (low, medium, high) can be identified for each dimension (cf. table 2). Especially in terms of the stressors and the organizational climate a medium or high need for action is indicated for many students.

Table 2. Need for action regarding the KFZA-dimensions

work contents			stressors			resources			organizational climate		
lNfA	mNfA	hNfA	lNfA	mNfA	hNfA	lNfA	mNfA	hNfA	lNfA	mNfA	hNfA
10	4	3	6	11	0	9	6	0	5	10	2

Notes. lNfA = low need for action; mNfA = medium need for action; hNfA = high need for action. The number of respondents per category is provided for each KFZA-dimension.

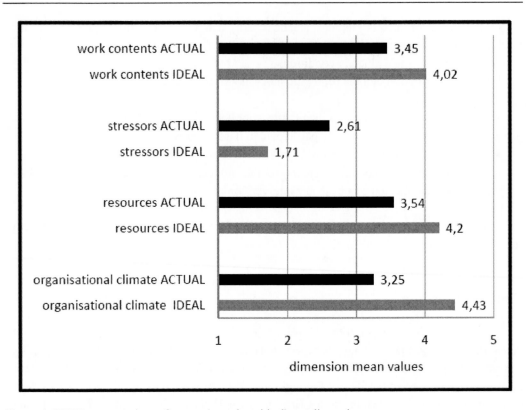

Figure 1. KFZA – comparison of means (actual vs. ideal) per dimension.

In the course of the health circles numerous resources located in the study environment could be found: The students stressed the positive impact of the opportunity for professional and personal development due to studying. Furthermore, they felt well supported by fellow students and by the university staff. The transparent policy and procedures as well as the infrastructure of the university were mentioned as important resources. On the other hand, a broad range of burdening aspects was discussed by the students. Table 3 summarizes the reported strains which were given top priority by the students. Qualitative content analytical procedures were applied (Elo, and Kyngäs, 2007).

Table 3. Health circles – reported strains at the university (given top priority)

Category	Category definition
missing flexibility	compulsory attendance (at least 80 % of the time units in each course)
pressure	time pressure, pressure to perform
organizational issues	(too) long days of lecture, unclear course aims, intransparent exam conditions
work-study-family-imbalance	reduction of social contacts due to manifold commitments
missing self-discipline	inadequate personal time management

The students also proposed various interventions to minimize the perceived strains. Following, some of them are described:

- To overcome the missing flexibility and to promote a balance between work, study and family, they stressed that more blended learning courses should be implemented. Thus, the compulsory attendance on site could decrease and learning would become more flexible.
- To make course aims, contents and exam conditions more transparent a standardized course description should become compulsory for each lecturer. This description should be given to the students at the beginning of the respective course and should be binding.
- To overcome time pressure and missing self-discipline the students wished for specific seminars and counseling offers regarding these issues.
- To prevent missing support from the workplace the students should discuss potential changes due to the engagement in the study programme with colleagues and the employer before starting the study programme. Furthermore an "educational contract" which assures time off for studying should be signed by the employer.
- To become aware of the challenges which are associated with a part-time study programme the Carinthia University of Applied Sciences should nominate experienced students as testimonials. The testimonials can be contacted by prospective students and they can communicate a real image of the challenges. This intervention can help to produce realistic expectancies and it can also minimize the dropout rate during the study programme.

CONCLUSION

The course "Health Promotion II" offers an innovative approach for the promotion of active learning and students' participation (Baid, and Lambert, 2010; Vittrup, and Davies, 2010). The students were actively involved into the process of health promotion using a survey to explore their working conditions and health circles to identify resources and strains in the university setting. Therefore, the course became a health promoting intervention per se. The consequent aspects can be summarized as the lessons learned:

- The students were highly motivated due to the given opportunity of participation. This is reflected in the high attendance rate during the course as a whole.
- In accordance with further studies (Evans et al., 2003; Johnson, Batia, et al., 2008; Rochford et al., 2009) manifold strains experienced by part-time nursing students within the university setting could be identified.
- The quantitative assessment of the workplace conditions highlighted need for action, especially regarding the stressors and the organizational climate.
- The implementation of health circles proved to be useful to give voice to the students. A detailed documentation and structured analysis of the procedures is essential to assure inter-subjective comprehensibility of the results (Steinke, 2004).

- The students proposed various interventions to fight the reported unfavorable conditions. Now their ideas serve as a basis for the improvement of the study conditions of part-time nursing students at the Carinthia University of Applied Sciences, School of Health and Care. Therefore, the course can be interpreted as a "kick off event" for the realization of health promotion within the mentioned university.
- To promote part-time nursing students' health effectively overall interventions addressing both settings – namely workplace and university – are needed. Therefore, it is time for a new comprehensive conceptualization and implementation of health promotion, rethinking the present understanding of the term "setting".

In the next step, courses focusing on health promotion are designed in an integrative way for full-time and part-time students of the bachelor degree programme healthcare management at the University of Applied Sciences, School of Health and Care. Therefore, the first author offered the course "Health Promotion II" during the summer term 2010 for both target groups together. To get an insight into the differentiated strains and resources reported by full-time and part-time students a worldcafé was conducted (The World Café, 2008). This method turned out to be helpful to gather information from many participants (N = 36 students) and to bring together full-time and part-time students. The results are in preparation and serve as a basis for tailored interventions meeting the special needs for both students' groups. A health promoting university has to reflect on the common and specific challenges which are potentially burdening for full-time and part-time students to guarantee a healthy environment for all students.

REFERENCES

Akkoyunlu, B., and Yılmaz-Soylu, M. (2008). Development of a scale on learner's views on blended learning and its implementation process. *Internet and Higher Education*, 11, 26-32.

Antonovsky, A. (1987). *Unravelling the Mystery of Health*. London: Jossey Bass.

Aust, B., and Ducki, A. (2004). Comprehensive health promotion interventions at the workplace. Experiences with health circles in Germany. *Journal of Occupational Health Psychology*, 9, 258-270.

Baid, H., and Lambert, N. (2010). Enjoyable learning: The role of humour, games, and fun activities in nursing and midwifery education. *Nurse Education Today*, 30, 548-552.

Brunner, E., Maier, M., Gritsch, A., and Jenull, B. (2009). Die Universität – ein kohärentes Setting? Messung des studentischen Kohärenzgefühls [The university – a coherent setting? Measurement of the students' sense of coherence]. *Prävention und Gesundheitsförderung*, 4, 66-70.

Dodd, L.J., Al-Nakeeb, Y., Nevill, A., and Forshaw, M.J. (2010). Lifestyle risk factors of students: A cluster analytical approach. *Preventive Medicine*, 51, 73-77.

Elo, S., and Kyngäs, S. (2008). The qualitative content analysis process. *Journal of Advanced Nursing*, 62, 107–115.

Eugéne, C. (2006). How to teach at the university level through an active learning approach? Consequences for teaching basic electrical measurements. *Measurement*, 39, 936-946.

Evans, W., Brown, G., Timmins, F., and Nicholl, H. (2007). An exploratory study identifying the programme related stressors among qualified nurses completing part-time degree courses. *Nurse Education Today*, 27, 731-738.

Federal Association of Company Health Insurance (1999). *Quality Criteria of Workplace Health Promotion.* Online in Internet: http://www.enwhp.org/fileadmin/downloads/ quality_criteria_01.pdf [26.08.2010].

Giacobbi, P.R., Tuccitto, D.E., and Frye, N. (2007). Exercise, affect, and university students' appraisals of academic events prior to the final examination period. *Psychology of Sport and Exercise*, 8, 261-274.

Großmaß, R., and Hofmann, R. (2007). Übergang ins Studium - Entwicklungsaufgabe und Statuspassage im Spiegel von Beratungserfahrungen [Transition to university study – developmental task and status passage considered from a counseling perspective]. *Verhaltenstherapie und Psychosoziale Praxis*, 39, 799-805.

Jenull, B., Salem, I., and Brunner, E. (2009). Is caring for the elderly a health risk? A qualitative study on work experience, coping and health behaviours of nurses. *International Journal of Psychology Research*, 4, 345-369.

Jinks, A.M., and Bradely, E. (2004). Angels, handmaiden, battleaxe or whore? A study which examines changes in newly recruited students nurses' attitudes to gender and nursing stereotypes. *Nurse Education Today*, 24, 121-127.

Johnson, B., Batia, A.S., and Haun, J. (2008). Perceived stress among graduate students: roles, responsibilities, and social support. *VAHPERD* (Spring 2008), 31-35.

Johnson, R.D., Hornik, S., and Salas, E. (2008). An empirical examination of factors contributing to the creation of successful e-learning environments. *International Journal of Human-Computer Studies,* 66, 356-369.

Kada, O., and Brunner, E. (2010). Maskulinität und Femininität in Selbst- und Idealbildern diplomierter Gesundheits- und Krankenschwestern [Masculinity and femininity in self-perceptions and ideals of registered nurses]. *Pflegezeitschrift*, 63, 490-495.

Kiteley, R.J., and Ormrod, G. (2009). Towards a team-based, collaborative approach to embedding e-learning within undergraduate nursing programmes. *Nurse Education Today,* 29, 623-629.

Kratvis, K., McAllister-Black, R., Grant, M., and Kirk, C. (2010). Self-care strategies for nurses: A psycho-educational intervention for stress reduction and the prevention of burnout. *Applied Nursing Research*, 23, 130-138.

Lazarus, R. S. (2007). Stress and emotion: a new synthesis. In A. Monat, R. S. Lazarus, and G. Reevy (eds.), *The Praeger Handbook on Stress and Coping* (pp. 34-51). Westport: Praeger.

Lipp, U., and Will, H. (2008). *Das große Workshop-Buch. Konzeption, Inszenierung und Moderation von Klausuren, Besprechungen und Seminaren* [The big workshop-book. Conceptualization, staging, and moderation of meetings and seminars]. Weinheim: Beltz.

Martin, P., Prümper, J., and von Harten, G. (2008). *Ergonomie-Prüfer zur Beurteilung von Büro- und Bildschirmarbeitsplätzen (ABETO)* [Examination of ergonomics for the evaluation of desk work and screen handling (ABETO)]. Frankfurt am Main: Bund-Verlag.

Meggeneder, O., and Hirtenlehner, H. (Eds.). (2006). *Zehn Jahre betriebliche Gesundheitsförderung in Österreich* [Ten years of workplace health promotion in Austria.]. Frankfurt am Main: Mabuse.

Meggeneder, O., and Sochert, M.R. (1999). WHP interventions and work organisation: the health circle approach. *Promotion and Education*, 6, 14-16.

McAllister, M., and McKinnon, J. (2009). The importance of teaching and learning resilience in the health disciplines: a critical review of the literature. *Nurse Education Today*, 29, 371-379.

Plano Clark, V.L., and Creswell, J.W. (2008). *The mixed methods reader.* Thousand Oaks, CA: Sage.

Prümper, J., Hartmannsgruber, K., and Frese, M. (1995). KFZA. Kurz-Fragebogen zur Arbeitsanalyse. [KFZA. Short questionnaire for work analysis] *Zeitschrift für Arbeits- und Organisationspsychologie*, 39, 125-132.

Rochford, C., Connolly, M., and Drennan, J. (2009). Paid part-time employment and academic performance of undergraduate nursing students. *Nurse Education Today*, 29, 601-606.

Schwamberger, H. (2006) *Bundesgesetz über Gesundheits- und Krankenpflegeberufe (Gesundheits- und Krankenpflegegesetz – GuKG) mit den hierzu erlassenen Verordnungen, Gesetzesmaterialien, weiteren Erläuterungen und Verweisen* [National law about nursing (Austrian Health Care and Nursing Act – GuKG) with the for this enacted regulations, law materials, further comments, and references]. Wien: Verlag Österreich.

Spitzer, A., and Perrenoud, B. (2006). Reforms in nursing education across Western Europe: implementation processes and current status. *Journal of Professional Nursing*, 22, 162-171.

Stanley, H. (2003). The journey to becoming a graduate nurse: a study of the lived experience of part-time post-registration students. *Nurse Education in Practice*, 3, 62-71.

Steinke, I. (2004). Quality criteria in qualitative research. In U. Flick, E v. Kardoff, and I. Steinke (Eds.), *A companion to qualitative research* (pp. 184-190). London: Sage.

Tsouros, A.D., Dowding, G., Thompson, J., and Dooris, M. (Eds.). (1998). *Health Promoting Universities. Concept, experience and framework for action.* Copenhagen: WHO Regional Office for Europe. Online in Internet: http://www.euro.who.int/__data/ assets/pdf_file/0012/101640/E60163.pdf [26.08.2010].

Unger, M., and Wroblewski, A. (2007). *Studierenden-Sozialerhebung 2006. Bericht zur sozialen Lage der Studierenden* [Student social survey 2006. Report of the students' social situation]. Wien: IHS.

Vittrup, A.-C., and Davey, A. (2010). Problem based learning – 'Bringing everything together' – A strategy for graduate nurse programs. *Nurse Education in Practice*, 10, 88-95.

Whitehead, D. (2004). The health promoting university (HPU): the role and function of nursing. *Nurse Education Today*, 24, 466-472.

WHO (1986). *Ottawa Charter for Health Promotion. First International Conference on Health Promotion Ottawa, 21 November 1986 - WHO/HPR/HEP/95.1.* Online in Internet: http://www.who.int/hpr/NPH/docs/ottawa_charter_hp.pdf [26.08.2010].

The World Café (2008). *The World Café presents ... Café to Go! A quick reference for putting conversations to work ...* Online in Internet: http://www.theworldcafe.com/articles/cafetogo.pdf [27.08.2010].

In: Progress in Education. Volume 26
Editor: Robert V. Nata, pp. 205-215

ISBN 978-1-61324-321-3
© 2011 Nova Science Publishers, Inc.

Chapter 13

EDUCATION AND TRAINING OF FUTURE WETLAND SCIENTISTS AND MANAGERS

Douglas A. Wilcox[*]

U.S. Geological Survey–Great Lakes Science Center,
Ann Arbor, Michigan, USA

ABSTRACT

Wetland science emerged as a distinct discipline in the 1980s. In response, courses addressing various aspects of wetland science and management were developed by universities, government agencies, and private firms. Professional certification of wetland scientists began in the mid-1990s to provide confirmation of the quality of education and experience of persons involved in regulatory, management, restoration/construction, and research involving wetland resources. The education requirements for certification and the need for persons with specific wetland training to fill an increasing number of wetland-related positions identified a critical need to develop curriculum guidelines for an undergraduate wetland science and management major for potential accreditation by the Society of Wetland Scientists. That proposed major contains options directed toward either wetland science or management. Both options include required basic courses to meet the general education requirements of many universities, required upper-level specialized courses that address critical aspects of physical and biological sciences applicable to wetlands, and a minimum of four additional upper-level specialized courses that can be used to tailor a degree to students' interests. The program would be administered by an independent review board that would develop guidelines and evaluate university applications for accreditation. Students that complete the required coursework will fulfill the education requirements for professional wetland scientist certification and possess qualifications that make them attractive candidates for graduate school or entry-level positions in wetland science or management. Universities that offer this degree program could gain an advantage in recruiting highly qualified students with an interest in natural resources. Alternative means of educating established wetland scientists are

---

[*] Present address: Department of Environmental Science and Biology, 350 New Campus Drive, SUNY-Brockport, Brockport, New York, USA 14420; Email: dwilcox@usgs.gov.

likewise important, especially to provide specialized knowledge and experience or updates related to new management discoveries, policies, and regulations.

Keywords: accredited wetland science and management major, education, training.

EVOLUTION OF WETLAND EDUCATION AND TRAINING

Wetland Science

Although research in fields of wetland science was evident in the first half of the twentieth century (Mitsch and Gosselink 2007:20), it did not become prominent until the last two decades of the century, when new environmental laws and recognition of the problems associated with loss of wetlands came to the forefront. Formation of the Society of Wetland Scientists (SWS) in 1980 promoted the evolution of "wetland science" as a distinct discipline. The aims of SWS include fostering conservation and understanding of wetlands; advancing public education and enlightenment concerning the World's wetland resources; providing a forum for interchange regarding wetlands; developing and encouraging wetland science as a distinct discipline by supporting student education, curriculum development, and research; encouraging and evaluating educational, scientific, and technological development and advancement of wetland science, and encouraging knowledgeable management of wetland resources. These aims suggest that education is a major driving force within the mission of SWS.

Wetland Education

An informal survey of past and present Associate Editors of *Wetlands* provided insights into wetland training at 25 academic institutions. The survey suggested that the roots of education and training in wetland science were found in wildlife biology courses, especially those focusing on waterfowl management. However, those courses were typically directed at management of species and did not incorporate more complex topics such as interactions between biological and physical sciences. Courses with "wetlands" in the title began to appear in the late 1970s. By 1990, 12 such courses were being offered by those 25 universities. An additional 20 courses were first offered in the next decade, and six more courses were added through 2006. Several of those universities offer more than one wetlands course, and two schools subsequently dropped their course or folded it into a class with a broader focus. These figures are not intended to be comprehensive, but they provide insight into the evolution of academic training in wetland science. Most of the courses were described as popular, and although many universities still offer no specific wetland courses, the number of courses offered is increasing. Potential techniques for teaching wetland ecology in the classroom and field have also been described by practicing professors (e.g., O'Neal 1995, DeSteven 2000, Titus 2000, Baldwin 2001).

Regulatory and management concerns relating to wetlands also generated a need for specific training of environmental professionals. Agency-sponsored training courses appeared in the United States in the mid-1970s. The U.S. Army Corps of Engineers initiated training with the three-week, intensive "Wetland Specialist" course organized and taught by Richard Macomber, a key founder of the Society of Wetland Scientists (C. Newling, pers. comm.). Other courses were added in the early 1980s, including "Wetland Science and Technology," "Wetlands of the U.S.," "Wetland Construction and Restoration," "Wetland Executive," "Wetland Soils and Hydrology," and "Basic Wetland Delineation" (Macomber 1981, C. Newling, pers. comm.). The U.S. Environmental Protection Agency also began to offer wetland training courses in the mid-1980s with assistance from the Corps of Engineers (C. Newling, pers. comm.). Federal agencies now collaborate to offer wetland training courses (e.g., http://www.pwrc.usgs.gov/wli/wettrain.htm, http://www.wli.nrcs.usda.gov/training/, http://el.erdcusace.army.mil/wetlands/wetlands.html), and some state agencies also offer training courses. Private wetland-training firms formed in response to the need for training and now also serve many agencies and individuals. Popular topics include wetland delineation, soils, hydrology, plant identification, construction, restoration, and regulatory policy (e.g., http://www.sws.org/training/, http://www.wetlandtraining.com/, http://www.wetland.org/educ_procourses.htm, http://www.richardchinn.com/).

Professional Certification

Several environmental professional organizations offer professional certification in their disciplines (e.g., Ecological Society of America, The Wildlife Society, Society of American Foresters) as a means of assuring prospective employers or contracting organizations that the certified scientists possess worthy credentials. Several states have wetland delineator certification programs (e.g., http://www.state.va.us/dpor/wet_reg.pdf, http://www.mnwetlands.umn.edu/cert/),http://www.nhes.state.nh.us/elmi/licertoccs/wetlands.htm.

However, a broader need for certification of wetland scientists was identified in the early 1990s.

The Society of Wetland Scientists Professional Certification Program (SWSPCP) was founded in 1994 and now serves as an independent, not-for-profit corporation that meets the needs of professional ecologists, hydrologists, soil scientists, educators, agency professionals, consultants, and other wetland scientists in demonstrating their qualifications to assess and manage wetland resources (http://www.wetlandcert.org). To receive Professional Wetland Scientist (PWS) certification, five years of professional experience specific to wetland science are required, and minimum academic standards at the collegiate level must be met. The required course work includes 15 semester hours each in appropriate biological and physical sciences, six semester hours in quantitative sciences, and 15 semester hours specific to wetlands, which may include equivalent short courses or continuing education credits based on semester credit equivalency (http://www.wetlandcert.org). Wetland Professional In Training (WPIT) designation is possible for scientists with at least a bachelors degree that meet most criteria for PWS but still require additional specific course work or professional experience.

AN ACCREDITED WETLAND SCIENCE AND MANAGEMENT MAJOR

The increasing need for well-trained professionals with strong credentials in wetland science and management suggests that there is also a critical need for an accredited major at the bachelors degree level to ensure that future students can receive the training needed for WPIT or PWS certification or to qualify for employment in government, academia, or the private sector. Other scientific organizations sponsor accreditation or approvals of majors in their specific disciplines (e.g., American Chemical Society, Society of Wood Science and Technology, Society of American Foresters). None, however, meet the needs of wetland science.

In February 2006, the Board of Directors of the Society of Wetland Scientists encouraged development of a draft curriculum that could serve as a foundation for an accredited undergraduate major in wetland science. The draft curriculum was based on the semester system widely used in the United States but with recognition that other equivalent systems could be adopted also. Several modifications were made to the original draft following input from numerous wetland scientists and students. Those modifications addressed issues such as 1) allowing sufficient credits to fulfill the general education requirements (e.g., history, arts, humanities, social science, language) of many universities; 2) changing some of the credit-hour requirements for basic required courses; 3) adding an independent study requirement; 4) adding more optional upper-level specialized courses; and 5) dividing the major into two options – wetland science and wetland management. Both options share many course requirements but diverge in some specialized courses. Both require a rounded education expected of most college graduates, a foundation in basic math and science, and a focus on communications. Other native languages could be substituted for "English" depending on the country in which the curriculum was offered, but technical writing would always be a requirement.

Wetland Science Option

This option (Table 1) is intended to produce graduates with a well-balanced understanding of wetland functional processes and underlying scientific principles. Students that complete this option should be well-prepared to undertake graduate education in many specialized fields of wetland science or to fill technical positions in research, government agencies, non-government organizations (NGOs), or consulting firms. Coupled with basic required courses, the specialized required courses move beyond the typical wildlife biology curriculum to ensure an understanding of both the physical and biological drivers of wetlands. The optional upper-level specialized courses allow students to focus on their personal area of interest. A key element in the curriculum is the required four-credit Wetland Independent Study, which should include in-field, problem-solving experiences. An example of a four-year course schedule that might be selected is shown in Table 2.

Wetland Management Option

Table 1. Proposed curriculum requirements for the Wetland Science option of an accredited major in Wetland Science and Management

Credits	Topic
A. The Basics (all required)	
6	English (including technical writing)
3	Public Speaking
3	Environmental Policy/Management
9	Mathematics (entry + differential and integral calculus)
6	Statistics (intro. and applied biometrics)
12	Chemistry (general and one semester of organic)
4	Physics
4	Geology
11	Biology (general biology or botany/zoology;general ecology)
1	Senior Wetland Seminar
20-22	Electives to meet requirements in history, arts, humanities, social science, language
79-82 total	
B. Upper Level Specialized Courses (all required)	
3	Wetland Ecology
3	Aquatic Plants
3	Wildlife Ecology
3	Aquatic Invertebrates
3	Fisheries Biology or Ichthyology
3	Hydrology
3	Soils
3	Wetland Policy and Management
4	Wetland Independent Study
29-30 total (allowing for some lab credits)	
C. Optional Upper Level Specialized Courses (4 required)*	
3	Population Ecology
3	Community Ecology
3	Conservation Biology
3	Ornithology
3	Mammalogy
3	Herpetology
3	Algal Biology
3	Limnology
3	Freshwater Ecology
3	Marine Ecology
3	Restoration Ecology
3	Landscape Ecology
3	GIS/Remote Sensing
3	Biogeochemistry
3	Genetics
3	Specialized wetland courses (e.g., pocosins, peatlands, BLH, mangroves, salt marshes)
12 total	
120-124 CURRICULUM TOTAL	

*Additional courses could also be considered within the optional category.

This option (Table 3) is also intended to produce graduates with a balanced understanding of wetland processes because effective managers must know how wetlands function. However, students that complete this option would take more course work in policy and management to prepare them for entry or mid-level operational positions in government, NGOs, or private firms.

As with the Wetland Science Option, key components include blending of physical and biological sciences and the required four-credit Wetland Independent Study focusing on in-field problem solving. This option could be attractive to students with skills that extend beyond science and could serve as a strong preparation for developing wetland managers. Again, the optional upper-level specialized courses allow students to focus on their area of interest. An example of a four-year course schedule for this option is shown in Table 4.

Table 2. Example four-year course schedule for Wetland Science Option, with courses likely to cover university minimum general education requirements denoted by*

Semester 1 (17 credit hours)		Semester 5 (16 credit hours)	
3	English (basic technical writing)*	3	Statistics
3	entry math*	3	Soils
4	General Chemistry I*	3	Aquatic Plants
4	General Biology I	3	Wetland Policy and Management
3	American History*	4	Upper Level Optional Course
Semester 2 (17 credit hours)		Semester 6 (16 credit hours)	
3	Differential Calculus	3	Biometrics
4	General Chemistry II	4	Wildlife Ecology
4	General Biology II	3	Hydrology
3	Western Civilization*	3	Upper Level Optional Course
3	social science elective*	3	elective of choice
Semester 3 (17 credit hours)		Semester 7 (16 credit hours)	
3	Integral Calculus	3	English (advanced technical writing)
4	Organic Chemistry I	3	Wetland Ecology
4	Physics	3	Fisheries Biology
3	World Civilizations course*	4	Upper Level Optional Course
3	arts elective*	3	elective of choice
Semester 4 (16 credit hours)		Semester 8 (15 credit hours)	
4	Geology	3	Public Speaking
3	General Ecology	3	Aquatic Invertebrates
3	Env. Policy and Management	4	Upper Level Optional Course
3	humanities elective*	4	Wetland Independent Study
3	elective of choice	1	Senior Wetland Seminar

Table 3. Proposed curriculum requirements for the Wetland Management option of an accredited major in Wetland Science and Management

Credits	Topic
A. The Basics (all required)	
6	English (including technical writing)
3	Public Speaking
3	Environmental Policy/Management
3	Economics
6	Mathematics (entry + intro. to calculus)
3	Statistics
8	Chemistry
4	Physics
4	Geology
11	Biology (general biology or botany/zoology; general ecology)
1	Senior Wetland Seminar
20-22	Electives to meet requirements in history, arts, humanities, social science, language
72-74 total	
B. Upper Level Specialized Courses (all required)	
3	Wetland Ecology
3	Aquatic Plants
3	Wildlife Ecology
3	Aquatic Invertebrates
3	Fisheries Biology or Ichthyology
3	Hydrology
3	Soils
3	Environmental Economics
3	Natural Resource Policy
3	Natural Resource Management
3	Wetland Policy and Management
4	Wetland Independent Study
37-38 total (allowing for some lab credits)	
C. Optional Upper Level Specialized Courses (4 required)[*]	
3	Population Ecology
3	Community Ecology
3	Conservation Biology
3	Freshwater Ecology
3	Marine Ecology
3	Restoration Ecology
3	Landscape Ecology
3	Wildlife Management
3	Fisheries Management
3	Water Resources Management
3	Invasive Species Management
3	Natural Resources Law
3	GIS/Remote Sensing
3	Natural Resources Sociology
3	Outdoor Recreation
12 total	
121-124 CURRICULUM TOTAL	

[*]Additional courses could also be considered within the optional category.

Table 4. Example four-year course schedule for Wetland Management Option, with courses likely to cover university minimum general education requirements denoted by*

Semester 1 (17 credit hours)		Semester 5 (16 credit hours)	
3	English (basic technical writing)*	3	Natural Resource Management
3	entry math*	3	Natural Resource Policy
4	General Chemistry I*	3	Aquatic Plants
4	General Biology I	3	Soils
3	American History*	4	Upper Level Optional Course
Semester 2 (17 credit hours)		**Semester 6 (16 credit hours)**	
3	Intro. To Calculus	3	Wetland Policy and Management
4	General Chemistry II	3	Statistics
4	General Biology II	3	Hydrology
3	Western Civilization*	4	Wildlife Ecology
3	social science elective*	3	Upper Level Optional Course
Semester 3 (16 credit hours)		**Semester 7 (16 credit hours)**	
3	Economics	3	English (advanced technical writing)
3	Env. Policy and Management	3	Wetland Ecology
4	Physics	3	Fisheries Biology
3	World Civilizations course*	4	Upper Level Optional Course
3	arts elective*	3	elective of choice
Semester 4 (16 credit hours)		**Semester 8 (15 credit hours)**	
3	Environmental Economics	3	Public Speaking
4	Geology	3	Aquatic Invertebrates
3	General Ecology	4	Upper Level Optional Course
3	humanities elective*	4	Wetland Independent Study
3	elective of choice	1	Senior Wetland Seminar

Recognition and Incentives

One ultimate goal of either optionwould be recognition by SWSPCP for PWS or WPIT certification. Completion of the required courses in either option should meet the certification requirements (H. Jones, pers. comm.). A second goal would be for local, state, provincial, or federal agencies to recognize that persons with an accredited wetland science and management degree meet their requirements for specific positions that are offered (both wetland and general natural resource positions). A tangential result could be that components of these curricula, especially the inclusion of physical sciences, may also become requirements in traditional wildlife biology and other natural resource majors. Finally, in the tight market in which universities are competing for the best-qualified applicants, a wetland major that spells out the specific course load could catch the interest of high school students with a strong interest in natural resources and thus help meet enrollment goals. As witnessed by the SWS jobs web site (http://www.sws.org/jobs/), there is a constant demand for persons to enter the wetland field. University administrators that recognize this opportunity and take advantage of it in advertising campaigns might attract highly motivated students with an inherent interest in natural resource sciences.

Implementation

Many universities will be unable to offer either the wetland science or wetland management option because their science majors are enveloped in liberal arts programs that require much broader generalized course work and do not allow enough credits to meet the requirements of this or any other accredited science major. I recognized this fact before beginning development of the curriculum. However, many specialized colleges and universities already have similar specialized majors. During the process of seeking input to modify requirements for the major, many participants commented that their university already offered nearly every course required. Even if only a few colleges or universities in a geographic region chose to adopt this program, the goal of producing new, well-qualified wetland scientists and managers could be met. In addition, those schools could become regional magnets for the best-qualified applicants.

Implementation would require approval by SWS and establishment of an accreditation review board that operates as an independent organization to develop guidelines for the program and administer university applications for accreditation. The board would evaluate courses intended to fulfill requirements and use discretionary authority to make allowances for differences in approaches to teaching specific courses. Although universities may already offer many of the required courses, examination of the topics covered in sometimes broad-focused courses such as hydrology would ensure that students are exposed to the elements of the science most critical to wetlands. The board would also administer post-implementation surveys of students, faculty, universities, agencies, and various other employers that could be used to make modifications to the program as needed.

As universities acquire the ability to provide the major, the option of seeking representation and support from the Association of Specialized and Professional Accreditors could be explored, and formal recognition of the accreditation program by the Council for Higher Education Accreditation could be pursued, although this is not a common practice among professional scientific societies (C. Davenport, Association of Specialized and Professional Accreditors, pers. comm.; J. Watkins, Council for Higher Education Accreditation, pers. comm.; Terry Clark, Society of American Foresters, pers. comm.).

ALTERNATIVE EDUCATION OPPORTUNITIES

Classroom education cannot address all components required to produce the scientists that will carry wetland science into the future or the managers to whom we will entrust the resources of the future. Instinct developed by being in the field as a child, teenager, college student, or graduate can play a role in understanding or managing the resource. Therefore, alternative opportunities should also be encouraged. Formal mentoring from well-qualified wetland scientists and managers or formal internship programs could provide recent graduates with practical experience. Agencies that incorporated internships into their programs (with funding) could reap the benefits of both the accredited wetland science and management major and the personal knowledge handed down to future employees by their mentors. Such internships might also be sponsored by granting organizations, such as the National Science Foundation.

If an accredited wetland science and management major becomes a reality and is implemented by enough universities to provide an adequate supply of well-trained candidates for scientific and management positions, the process will likely take at least a decade to meet those needs. Many currently practicing wetland managers lack the rigorous formal training in wetland science that is proposed here, especially process-based physical science, and some have had few opportunities to collaborate with scientists regarding management decisions. Innate capabilities and experiences in the field may have served them well in decision-making (L. Fredrickson, pers. comm.); however, examples abound in which management decisions created environmental problems that might have been avoided with appropriate scientific input (see examples in Smith et al., this issue). A strategy is needed to improve contacts and collaborations among existing wetland managers and wetland scientists and to bridge the gap in time until new managers with a stronger wetland science background become available.

Individual wetland scientists and managers may take personal initiatives to create collaborations, as in the past, but more organized efforts would likely achieve better results. An open invitation to scientists to use managed wetlands as study sites for research that is not specifically related to management could result in interactions that ultimately focus on management questions also. Alternatively, inquiries made by scientists could also identify important management challenges that require research attention. Current managers typically receive training in workshops that address many topics, including supervision and specific management practices. In the U.S., the National Conservation Training Center in Sheperdstown, West Virginia operates to present this specific type of training. Training could be supplemented with a series of agency-sponsored workshops in which wetland scientists provide managers with abbreviated training in relevant aspects of the course work proposed in the wetland science option or on scientific approaches to specific management problems. Efforts could also be made to attract wetland managers to meetings of scientific societies, such as SWS. A regular series of workshops or invited symposia at annual meetings, with a focus on science in managed wetlands, could attract managers from at least the regions in which the meetings are held. Buy-in and encouragement from agency administrators would enhance this opportunity. Wetland scientists could also make greater efforts to attend meetings that are typically attended by managers.

Finally, because scientific knowledge changes with each new discovery and regulatory policies change, continuing education in the form of refresher courses, specialized training, and workshops or specialized symposia at scientific meetings should be on everyone's agenda, including those who complete an accredited major. Continuation of these efforts (including monetary support) and participation in them by new and old wetland practitioners is a necessity to meet the goal of having educated wetland scientists studying and managing the resources and, ultimately, having a positive influence on the quality, functions, and values of the wetlands.

Acknowledgments

Guy Baldassarre, Andrew Baldwin, Thomas Burton, Walter Duffy, Lee Foote, Leigh Fredrickson, Susan Galatowitsch, Carter Johnson, Sammy King, Catherine Owen Koning, and Loren Smith provided comments and suggestions that served to improve the Wetland Science and Wetland Management options presented here.

Many past and present Associate Editors of *Wetlands* provided information on the origins of wetlands courses at their respective universities. Richard Chinn, Leigh Fredrickson, Harold Jones, and Charlie Newling provided insight on agency training programs, PWS certification, and alternative education opportunities. Very useful reviews of the initial draft manuscript were provided by Bryant Browne, Chip Euliss, Leigh Fredrickson, Mary Kentula, and Loren Smith. Two anonymous referees also provided useful comments during review.

Literature Cited

Baldwin, A. H. 2001. Got mud? Field-based learning in wetland ecology. *Journal of College Science Teaching* 31(2):94–100.

DeSteven, D. 2000. Teaching wetland ecology: what if you can't take students into the field? *SWS Bulletin* 17(1):19–21.

Macomber, R. 1981. Federal government wetlands training courses: 1981. *SWS Bulletin* 1(2):10–11.

Mitsch, W. J. and J. G. Gosselink. 2007. *Wetlands, fourth edition*. John Wiley and Sons, Inc., Hoboken, NJ, USA.

O'Neal, L. H. 1995. Using wetlands to teach ecology and environmental awareness in general biology. *American Biology Teacher* 57:135–139.

Smith, L. M., N. H. Euliss, Jr., D. A. Wilcox, and M. M. Brinson. 2008. Wetland management case histories: consequences of a static view and application of a variable geomorphic/time vision. *Wetlands* 28:(this issue).

Titus, D. M. 2000. Teaching wetland ecology: what if students can go into the field? *SWS Bulletin* 17(2):16–19.

INDEX

D

N

O

P

Q